To the Flagstaff City Coconino
Public Library

With best wishes —

Ralph J Crandall

GENEALOGICAL RESEARCH IN NEW ENGLAND

Edited by Ralph J. Crandall

*Director, The New England Historic
Genealogical Society*

Published Under the Direction of
The New England Historic Genealogical Society

Baltimore
GENEALOGICAL PUBLISHING CO., INC.
1984

Originally published in *The New England*
Historical and Genealogical Register, thus:
"New Hampshire Genealogy" 130 (October 1976): 244-258 (© 1976)
"Maine Genealogy" 131 (October 1977): 243-266 (© 1977)
"Vermont Genealogy" 133 (January 1979): 3-19 (© 1979)
"Connecticut Genealogical Research" 134 (January 1980): 3-26 (© 1980)
"Genealogical Research in Massachusetts" 135 (July 1981): 163-198 (© 1981)
"Genealogical Research in Rhode Island" 136 (July 1982): 173-219 (© 1982)

Reprinted with additions and corrections and a new introduction.
Genealogical Publishing Co., Inc. Baltimore, 1984.
Copyright © 1984 by Genealogical Publishing Co., Inc.
Baltimore, Maryland. All Rights Reserved.
Library of Congress Catalogue Card Number 83-82075
International Standard Book Number 0-8063-1050-2
Made in the United States of America

CONTENTS

INTRODUCTION 7
Ralph J. Crandall

MAINE GENEALOGY:
SOME DISTINCTIVE ASPECTS 15
John Eldridge Frost

Additions 39

NEW HAMPSHIRE GENEALOGY:
A PERSPECTIVE 43
David C. Dearborn

VERMONT GENEALOGY:
A STUDY IN MIGRATION...................... 59
Edward W. Hanson

GENEALOGICAL RESEARCH IN
MASSACHUSETTS: A SURVEY AND
BIBLIOGRAPHICAL GUIDE.................... 77
Edward W. Hanson and *Homer Vincent Rutherford*

Additions and Corrections 113

CONNECTICUT GENEALOGICAL RESEARCH:
SOURCES AND SUGGESTIONS 115
Elizabeth Abbe

Additions and Corrections 139

GENEALOGICAL RESEARCH
IN RHODE ISLAND 141
Jane Fletcher Fiske

Additions and Corrections 188

For my parents

Beulah Alfreda Watrous & Emerson Stanley Crandall

INTRODUCTION

Some years ago when the late Gilbert H. Doane, the longtime editor of *The New England Historical and Genealogical Register,* was speaking on his family research, he regretted the lack of a definitive guide to the sources for New England genealogy and wished his fellow scholars to undertake such a project in the pages of the *Register.* The result is printed here, the six major articles that were published in the *Register,* with some additions and corrections. The articles are intended to help any researcher, advanced or beginner, who is concerned with the history of New England. Their bibliographical coverage is extensive, and each article, as well, offers an historical survey of the state, identifying those major events, such as King Philip's War in 1675 or the American Revolution, that disturbed communities and caused people to migrate.

It is fitting that this immensely useful review of sources for New England history and genealogy should have been first published by the New England Historic Genealogical Society. Since its founding in 1845, the NEHGS has been dedicated to the study of the New England family. Its charter states that its purpose is to preserve and disseminate information on New England families. Over the past 138 years the Society has dedicated itself to this goal by building an unparalleled collection of primary and secondary sources on the New England people, by sponsoring major publications, and by offering a national lecture program on sources and resources for New England genealogical research.

Today, the Society's library consists of a permanent collection of more than 400,000 volumes, as well as a lending library of some 30,000 books. Its archives have over a million items, and include the papers of many of the major genealogical scholars of the nineteenth and twentieth centuries.

The great collections at the Society, as well as the six New England articles that appear in this volume, illustrate the events and historical forces that influenced New England life from the earliest settlements in the seventeenth century to the present day. When the great Puritan migration began in the 1630s, people came to the shores of New England for the purpose of creating a new religious commonwealth, untainted by the "popery" of the Anglican Church. John Winthrop imagined that New England would become like a "City set upon a Hill," a beacon light to the Old World. Although he may have been concerned about sending a message back to England, many of his followers quickly forgot their Old World homes and families as they turned to the tasks of clearing the forest, constructing new homes, and establishing church and town government. In effect, they were creating a new civilization out of a "howling wilderness."

Today we are often so mesmerized by the heroic efforts of our New England forefathers in conquering the wilderness that we overlook the fact that at almost every level there was a high degree of continuity between Old and New England. One point that remains to be explored fully is the degree to which people moved back and forth between Old and New England. We know that many New England men returned in the 1640s to fight in the civil wars, but others returned to settle estates, to form business connections, and to care for their families. Sometimes they grew tired of the harsh conditions that prevailed in the New World. We know, too, that the first New Englanders brought with them the accumulation of centuries of English practices, and the towns of New England became extensions of an old civilization in a new setting. Moreover, scholars have recently discovered that clusters of Englishmen originating in a particular English county, where agriculture was practiced in a certain way, would impose the same kind of practice upon the new township that they founded in New England.

Nowhere is such persistence in English ways demonstrated more clearly than in the keeping of records. Well before the Great Migration Englishmen were deeply rooted in the habit of record keeping at the parish, county, and national level, as well as in the church. When Englishmen moved to America they continued this pattern of record keeping in the New World. Moreover, this cultural expression was reinforced by their Puritan zeal, which demanded a stable society of institutions, laws, and records. In the mind of the Puritan, orderliness was next to godliness because only in an orderly society could Puritanism thrive. To fail to maintain order through institutions and record-keeping was to invite the ever-present chaos embodied in the wilderness.

For the first New Englanders, then, Puritanism and the fear of the un-civilizing ways of the wilderness account in considerable measure for the amazing proliferation of records at every level of society. This penchant for recording events in public and private life distinguishes the colonial New Englander from his counterpart in the mid-Atlantic and southern colonies.

Such records allow the genealogist and historian to document even the first New Englanders in nearly every phase of their life cycle, once they had arrived in the New World. For example, in the records generated by Daniel Whittemore, a representative Puritan who settled in Charlestown, Massachusetts, his activities and those of his wife and children appear in the Charlestown church records, the vital records of the town, the county inferior court documents, the legislative proceedings of the General Court, and several times in the Charlestown selectmen's records.

For Daniel Whittemore's sons, grandsons, and great grandsons who lived and died in the eighteenth century, our ability to trace them during the course of their lives is enhanced by additional records that become available;

8

yet at the same time our research is made more difficult because New Englanders, during the eighteenth century, were much more inclined to migrate. In addition to the records that were generated in the seventeenth century, the genealogist intent on tracing an eighteenth-century man will find a whole new series of land, military, census, and tax records available. Beginning about 1725 Yankee sons and daughters began migrating in large numbers to the frontier areas of Connecticut, Massachusetts, New Hampshire, and Maine. In many cases they were taking up land that had been promised to them because their father or grandfather had fought in King Philip's War or King William's War. Or they were enticed to the area by land companies and speculators. Many became "proprietors" and were entered as such in the "proprietors records" maintained by the new town. Such records, which were kept in addition to the town meeting records and selectmen's records, turn out to be of immense value to the genealogist, frequently listing not only the name of the original proprietor, but his sons and daughters for two or three generations, as the land was distributed.

The frequent wars in the eighteenth century, including especially the French and Indian conflict and the American Revolution, generated a massive amount of new information on New Englanders. For the French and Indian wars official correspondence and muster rolls are remarkably well preserved in many instances. Information from some of the muster rolls has been extracted and is available in print, in particular the series published jointly by the New England Historic Genealogical Society and the Society of Colonial Wars for the Commonwealth of Massachusetts. For the American Revolution, information is available on participants through numerous sources, including the muster rolls and pension applications. Of course, some of this data has been distilled and is available in print to the genealogist through the work of various patriotic organizations, such as the Daughters of the American Revolution, the Sons of the American Revolution, and the Sons of the Cincinnati.

During the eighteenth century, as well, several colony-wide and statewide valuations and censuses were generated which had not been available previously. The 1771 valuation list for Massachusetts and Maine, the 1782 Rhode Island census, the 1790 federal census, and the 1798 direct tax for Maine and Massachusetts are a few of the major ones for this period.

By 1900 some New England families could boast of nine or more generations in the region. Many had established distinguished records of service to their communities and were proud of their heritage and accomplishment. As Judge James Russell of Charlestown reminded his son, "You are the fifth generation. In the year 1646, Richard Russell entered into public life. From that time to the present . . . the family have had every office of profit and honor which the people could give them." But the Russells were an exception to the average family in New England at the turn of the century, for they were a relatively stable group who remained near their ancestral seat in Charlestown. In general the opposite was true. By 1800 most New England families had migrated numerous times. The migrations

9

had begun in earnest in the second quarter of the eighteenth century. By that time the Indian threat had been substantially reduced, and at the same time land scarcity in the older communities was forcing the grandsons and great-grandsons of the original settlers to look to the frontiers of northern and eastern New England for places with adequate land to raise a family. By the turn of the century the emotional ravages of migration were being felt by most New England families. Those families which had lived for three or four generations in the same localities now had members living in such distant places as Machias, Maine, or Rutland, Vermont, or Yarmouth, Nova Scotia. And many New Englanders had already left the region altogether, joining the swelling flood of people who were settling in western New York, Ohio, and Illinois.

Because families were moving so frequently in the last quarter of the eighteenth century and the first quarter of the nineteenth century, this period is perhaps the most difficult for the genealogist. Fortunately, some new, or at least better, sources of family information emerged in the late eighteenth and early nineteenth centuries which aid the genealogist in his search. Beginning about 1795 the major cities and towns began to publish city directories. These publications are immensely valuable to the researcher because they provide name, occupation, and residence for most heads of households living in the community. Similarly, there was a proliferation of newspapers in the early nineteenth century which frequently printed obituaries of members of the community. Many of these newspapers are available in the microfiche series *Early American Imprints*. Also, much of their genealogical data has been abstracted and is now available in book form.

In addition to the new types of records that are available for documenting the lives of nineteenth-century New Englanders, the genealogist's job is made easier by the fact that during this era individuals became interested in preserving the history of families and localities. Already the first historical society to be established in this country, the Massachusetts Historical Society, had been founded in Boston in 1791. This was soon followed in the nineteenth century by the American Antiquarian Society, established in Worcester, Massachusetts, in 1812. Then in 1845 a group of individuals who were dedicated to "preserving and disseminating information about New England families" founded America's first genealogical organization, the New England Historic Genealogical Society. Now Americans had an organization which was created expressly for the purpose of genealogical research. Its leaders soon began to gather primary records on New England families and to build a library of printed histories on New England families and localities.

During its early years one of NEHGS's greatest services to genealogy was to encourage an interest in the research and publication of information on colonial and nineteenth-century New England. No doubt this society had much to do with the great proliferation of published local histories and genealogies which rightly characterize the second half of the nineteenth century as the "golden age of American genealogy." Of course, the emergence of other important New England historical agencies, like the Essex Institute in Salem, Massachusetts, and the New Hampshire, Connecticut, and Rhode Island historical societies, also contributed significantly to the flowering of genealogy during this era.

An important impetus to the creation of NEHGS and state historical societies was the influx of non-English immigrants to New England. In the 1840s the Irish came to New England in great numbers, pushed out of their homeland by the deadly potato famine and attracted to New England by the opportunity to work in the textile industry and as laborers on roads, canals, and railroads. The Irish were eventually followed by large migrations of French-Canadians, Jewish, Polish, and Italian populations, to name just a few of the ethnic groups that had settled in New England by 1900.

Already by the 1870s many New England towns had been transformed by the infusion of new Americans. Old Yankee bastions like Charlestown, Massachusetts, Manchester, New Hampshire, and Pawtucket, Rhode Island, now reflected the appealing sight, sound, and character of the Old World as tens of thousands of immigrants worked out their destiny in New England.

For the family historian, the ethnic dimension adds a most interesting layer to genealogical research. At this time ethnic groups were frequently more stable than the Yankee population. They are traceable through Catholic sacramental records, vital statistics, and city directories. Catholic records have become in recent years a prime resource for documenting the movement of ethnic New Englanders, a secular use which is being increasingly appreciated by the Catholic clergy in the United States as they study the growth of the Church. Likewise, state and federal censuses, especially after 1850 when individuals rather than just heads of households were recorded, may quickly locate a family. By using city directories in conjunction with state and federal censuses, one can quickly locate the family in the correct ward and street. Such information may indicate the financial position as well as the politics of the family.

Ships' passenger lists and naturalization papers are also useful in documenting ethnic families. A ship's passenger list, when available, will often list the members of a family who came together to the New World and indicate the country of origin. Naturalization papers also provide important biographical details, including place of origin, age, marital status, and occupation.

One cannot overlook the wars of the nineteenth century that involved many New England families. The U.S. Civil War, especially, involved many New Englanders of ethnic background, and their participation will be well documented in muster rolls and pension applications. The records of the War of 1812, the Mexican War, and the Spanish-American War should also be studied if a family member served.

Most twentieth-century New Englanders have immigrant ancestors who came to the area in the nineteenth century or during the colonial period. The collective memory of the family no doubt dates back to the mid-nineteenth century or, perhaps, even to the late 1700s. This can usually be corroborated by documentation that exists for many twentieth-century families; certainly vital statistics, town and church records, and family mementos would be available.

Beginning in the nineteenth century, numerous layers of printed records were created by the states and the federal government. This fact is counterbalanced by the high mobility of nineteenth and twentieth-century families, especially Yankees. It was not at all unusual for a family in this period to move five or six times. If this movement occurred within a local area, it can easily be documented through city directories or census records. But all too often the family moved out of the state and frequently out of New England altogether. To find these more elusive families one must learn the paths of migration and contact family members who might know where other members have resettled. Sometimes the answer will come in an entirely unexpected and serendipitous fashion, perhaps while one is looking through a telephone directory on a business trip in a city many hundreds of miles from New England.

One's success in tracing his family will be subject to many variables. It is hoped that the multitude of sources to which one is introduced in this volume will make the family search a successful one.

R.J.C.

GENEALOGICAL
RESEARCH IN
NEW ENGLAND

MAINE GENEALOGY:
SOME DISTINCTIVE ASPECTS

John Eldridge Frost

I

The reputation that New England has long enjoyed of a richness in surviving records is doubtlessly merited. Its colonial performance in record keeping was distinguished, and one state, Massachusetts, pioneered in introducing the civil registration of vital statistics. Nevertheless, the recording in New England of births, marriages and deaths has varied greatly in both states and periods. Vital records generally decline in comprehensiveness as we move from densely settled areas to remote rural areas, with less developed and less adequately supported local governments. Maine entered upon its bleakest period in vital statistics when it broke away from Massachusetts in 1820 and achieved statehood.

Despite its long history Maine was the last state to be created in New England and the last to have its boundaries determined. No other retained its frontier for so long. No other has passed through so many governmental changes influencing the location of records. For these reasons genealogical research in Maine is often challenging to the professional. The researcher makes some surprising discoveries affecting his methods and findings: (1) size of state, (2) diversity of population, (3) extent and nature of records relevant to genealogy, (4) significance of land records, and (5) recent growth in access tools.

Few visitors and relatively few residents are aware of the state's size. Maine is the largest state in New England; it is so large that New Hampshire, Vermont, Rhode Island, Connecticut, and even most of Massachusetts could be fitted into it. The land sweeps north from the familiar beaches and rocky shores until one-half of the state lies above a straight continuation of the international border. There is a common saying that only a meeting of the state legislature brings together representatives of all of its counties. Travel time is easier to grasp than area statistics. From Maine's southern tip at Kittery to Madawaska in the north is a seven-and-a-half-hour drive, longer than from Kittery to New York City. Consequently, the genealogist values here more than in smaller states a familiarity with the archives and existing record transcripts whether in print, typescript, manuscript, or microfilm.

Maine's diverse population also surprises the genealogist. The once-common stereotype of the Downeast Yankee is virtually obsolete. The state was far more homogeneous in 1790, when it is estimated that 93.1 percent of the population was of English origin, than in the years that followed. Even then, four thousand persons of Scottish origin and thirteen hundred of Irish origin, as well as four hundred Indians and five hundred free blacks, were found here.[1] The numbers trebled in the first half of the nineteenth century when a surplus population crossed the state line from New Hampshire and joined hundreds of immigrant families from the older communities of eastern Massachusetts, attracted by inexpensive land and the allurements of land promoters. In this movement were emigrants of many backgrounds: French from Quebec, English, Scotch-Irish and Acadian from New Brunswick and Nova Scotia, English and Scotch-Irish from New Hampshire, and primarily English from Massachusetts. There remain in the state families, such as Shapleigh, Frost, Nason, Jordan, Libby, and Bragdon, whose forebears came directly to Maine three centuries ago. The vast majority of the families came later and had their American origins elsewhere, a significant factor in Maine genealogy. Several familiar names associated with the state's history—Wheelwright, Sewall, Gardiner, Longfellow, Hamlin, and Washburn—are those of families from Massachusetts. Again, the number of Franco-Americans in Maine in 1790 was estimated at 115 persons, but by 1970 15 percent of the total population was of French descent.[2]

Additional to size and diversity of population, the surviving records— local, state, and federal—hold surprises. The genealogist accustomed to the centralized and well-indexed vital records of Massachusetts and New Hampshire discovers that prior to this century comparable alphabetized holdings for Maine are less than one-half, perhaps less than one-fourth, complete. Fortunately, available also in the State Archives are copies of the Latter Day Saints' microfilms of Maine vital records for approximately four hundred cities, towns, and plantations, together with some original records deposited for security. The films give a far broader (though still incomplete) coverage, but lack a master index. A published check list, *Microfilm List of Maine Town Records and Maine Census Records* (Augusta, Me., 1965), defines the Archives holdings. The recently revised Maine State Archives *Public Record Repositories in Maine* (Augusta, Me., 1976),[3] indispensable to genealogical research, gives both state and local holdings of vital records.

In Maine, the recording of births, marriages, and deaths began later than in Massachusetts, and certainly later than many of the occurrences

1. United States Bureau of the Census, *A Century of Population Growth* (Washington, D. C., 1909), 116. The free blacks are explained by a court decision of Massachusetts abolishing slavery in 1781.

2. See Table 21 in United States Bureau of the Census, *1970 Census of Population: Characteristics of the Population, Part 21: Maine* (Washington, D. C., 1973), 263. Statistics in this table reveal that French is the mother tongue of over 14 percent of the Maine population.

3. Includes for towns: date of incorporation, covering dates for town records, town reports, and vital records, with extensive notes on the condition of the records, and whether a microfilm copy is in the Archives. Includes for counties: address of shire towns, covering dates for records of the commissioners, deeds, probate, treasurer, and the courts.

noted.[4] Often the earliest records are arranged by family, indicative of a census. Only 5 Maine towns possess vital records of seventeenth-century vintage as compared with 210 communities that began their records in the eighteenth century. Seventeenth-century entries (in Biddeford from 1653, Kittery from 1674, Kennebunkport from 1678, York from 1681, and Wells from 1694)[5] are of considerable interest, even though later than the settlement of the towns.

In 1864 state legislation required town clerks to record annually births, marriages and deaths and to forward returns to Maine's Secretary of State.[6] A few towns responded immediately while others began later. Although most returns were shortly discontinued, the records generated (and now in the State Archives) are especially useful. In 1892 vital statistics again were legislated and the State Board of Health became the depository.

While vital records are extensive for the colonial period, possibly reflecting Massachusetts practices, after statehood records became meager. Births and deaths were then rarely recorded. Occasionally a few tombstone transcripts, and sometimes data on his own family, were entered by the town clerk. The records most consistently kept were publishments or intentions of marriage which generally though not necessarily indicate that a marriage occurred. Cities, such as Portland, Auburn, Lewiston, and Waterville, usually have the most extensive records.

Publication of the state's vital records began in 1896 when Pepperrellborough, now the city of Saco, by a vote of the city council to assure preservation, printed its pre-1840 vital statistics. In the next year the Maine Genealogical Society published Gorham's before 1820. In Massachusetts historical societies had already sponsored the publication of similar records for several towns prior to 1850. Maine extended this example in 1909; by 1967 the Maine Historical Society had issued the pre-1892 vital records of eighteen towns.[7] The immense significance of the Maine project is only now fully appreciated. Much of the information could not now be assembled. Sources (indicated for each item) are as varied as diaries, church records, newspaper notices, gravestones, family

4. In 1639 by an enactment of the General Court, Massachusetts Bay required that each town record dates of births, marriages and deaths, adding in 1692 the names of parents to birth and death records. In Plymouth marriages had been recorded from 1633.

5. A yet earlier volume of vital records than is indicated by the microfilm list exists for Wells. A transcript (16pp.) in the Maine Historical Society is entitled: "Births, Marriages and Deaths | from the First Book | of the Town Records of | Wells." This records births for two families, Littlefield and Bolles, from the 1640s, but the two families are presented as units including birth dates for parents born in England. Probably these family records, which start the volume, were entered in the 1680s when extensive registration of births begins.

6. In Chapter 244 of Maine. Laws, Statutes, etc. 43rd Legislature, 1864, *Acts and Resolves* (Augusta, Me., 1864), 182-183. This was emended by the 44th Legislature, 1865. Final mandatory legislation, effective 1 Jan. 1892, is in Chapter 118 of Maine. Laws, Statutes, etc. 65th Legislature, 1891, *Acts and Resolves* ([Augusta, Me., 1891]), 127-131.

7. Augusta, Belfast, Bowdoin, Bristol, Clinton, Farmingdale, Gardiner, Georgetown, Hallowell, Lebanon, Nobleboro, Otisfield, Phippsburg, Pittston, Randolph, Topsham, West Gardiner, Winslow.

Bibles, private records, and the entries of town clerks. While the state sponsored the publication, extremely competent editorial service was voluntary. Verbatim transcripts, without amplification, for some other towns have been published in serials; the longest, that of York (1681-1891), appears in the *Register* (1955-1969).

The state's church records, auxiliary to the vital records, merit but await scholarly study. Registers are abundant, but vary unexpectedly in the extent of information furnished and the periods covered. No total census of what survives exists. Only the largest denominations can be mentioned here. The Congregational Church, the sole religious body with extensive colonial records, has well-kept marriage and baptismal entries. The latter are especially useful because of the prevalence of infant baptism. The largest number of registers that have been transcribed are Congregationalist, and a dozen have been printed at some length. Methodist registers begin late in the nineteenth century and yield many dates of marriages for which only publishments or intentions appear in the town clerk's books. However, no transcripts of Methodist registers have been observed. Baptist registers are not anticipated but some exist in Maine. Often Baptist (and sometimes Methodist) clergy maintained private records of marriages they had performed; transcripts of several are in libraries. The denominations named rarely recorded burials but sometimes entered deaths. Roman Catholic and Episcopal churches followed orthodox recording procedures but few transcripts of their registers have been encountered. Additionally, three registers are available in print for the Society of Friends.[8]

County marriage returns to the county clerk, mandated by the legislature in 1828,[9] have never been fully assessed. Although the legislation applied only to marriages by the clergy, civil marriages are frequently included. Some county returns patently appear incomplete, while others, such as those of Kennebec and Penobscot, are impressively large. Many returns antedate the establishment of the counties, and county commissioners' returns for York and Lincoln precede statehood. Conceivably, additional returns may be discovered. The following holdings (MSA: Maine State Archives; CCC: Clerk of County Courts) have been located:

> Androscoggin. 1 vol. MSA. c. 1851-1884.
> Aroostook. 2 vols. Original formerly with CCC, Houlton, not located in 1977, but filmed copy is held by Genealogical Library of the Latter Day Saints, Salt Lake City, Utah; CCC, Houlton, has index in 6 boxes. 1839-1892.
> Cumberland. County Commissioners Records, vol. 2, in Portland, contains marriage returns 1763-1786 from a half dozen towns. Original

8. The Congregational registers of Pepperrellborough (Saco), Buxton, and Falmouth were issued as volumes, but those for Arundel (Kennebunkport), Berwick, Biddeford, Dresden, North Yarmouth, South Berwick, Wells, and Windham appeared in serials, as did also those for the Society of Friends in China, North Berwick, and Vassalboro.

9. In Chapter 391, Section 2 of Maine. Laws, Statutes, etc. 8th Legislature, 1828, *Public Acts* (Augusta, Me., 1828), 1157-1158.

returns for 1787-1795 were not located in 1977, but the Maine Historical Society has a manuscript transcript (322 pp.; indexed).

Franklin. 4 vols. CCC, Farmington. Vol. 1 (presumably, 1838-1847) not located, 1977. Vols. 2-4 cover 1848-1891.

Hancock. 1 vol. CCC, Ellsworth. 1842-1891.

Kennebec. 5 vols. MSA. 1828-1887.

Knox. 1 vol. MSA. 1859-1887.

Lincoln. County Commissioners Records, vol. 2, with the CCC, Wiscasset, contains marriage returns, 1759-1777. An indexed typescript of the preceding, prepared by the Daughters of the American Revolution, is in the Maine Historical Society. Also in the CCC, Wiscasset are 3 vols. of marriage returns, 1780-1865, and Hezekiah Prince's record book as a Justice of the Peace which includes marriages in St. George, 1804-1816. A master index for Lincoln County marriages, 1760-1865, is being developed in the office of the CCC, Wiscasset.

Oxford. In boxes. MSA. 1830-1875.

Penobscot. 7 vols. MSA. 1827-1888.

Piscataquis. 3 vols. MSA. 1839-1889. An additional volume contains marriage intentions for Dover, 1844-1865.

Sagadahoc. 1 vol. MSA. 1852-1887.

Somerset. 3 vols. CCC, Skowhegan. 1834-1889. Also in the Commissioners Records are marriage returns: vol. 1, 1828-1830; vol. 3, 1837-1846.

Waldo. 3 vols. MSA. 1828-1887. A typed and indexed copy for 1828-1849, made by the Daughters of the American Revolution, is in the Maine Historical Society.

Washington. 1 vol. MSA. 1827-1890.

York. 3 vols. CCC, Alfred. 1771-1794; 1833-1887. In the same office the Sessions Records, vol. 16, contains marriage returns, 1825-1836. "Marriages in the County of York, Me., 1686-99" appears in the *Register,* 28 (1874): 117-119. "York County Marriage Returns, 1771-1794" appears in the *Register,* 63 (1909): 167-178, and was reprinted by George Walter Chamberlain (Malden, Mass., 1909). "Gleanings from York County Files . . . Marriages, Compiled from the Court Records" appears in *The Maine Historical and Genealogical Recorder,* 4 (1887): 60-62, 693, but covers only 1787-1788.

The county returns most often consulted by genealogists are wills, administrations, and deeds. In general, Maine's holdings[10] are:

County	Shire Town	Formerly	County Est.	Probate From	Deeds From
Androscoggin	Auburn	Cumberland/ Oxford/Kennebec/Lincoln	1854	1854	1854
Aroostook	Houlton/ Fort Kent	Penobscot/ Washington	1839	1839	1839/ Northern District, 1846

10. Some variation is often found in dates when probate and deeds begin, depending on whether the date used is that of the document or of its registration. Since for the genealogist the date of the document holds prior significance it is used here when known.

				County Probate Deeds	
County	Shire Town	Formerly	Est.	From	From
Cumberland	Portland	York	1760	1908[11]	1760
Franklin	Farmington	Kennebec/ Oxford/Som- erset	1838	1838	1838
Hancock	Ellsworth	Lincoln	1789	1790	1790
Kennebec	Augusta	Cumberland/ Lincoln	1799	1799	1799[12]
Knox	Rockland	Lincoln/ Waldo	1860	1860	1860[12]
Lincoln	Wiscasset	York	1760	1760	1761
Oxford	Paris/ Fryeburg	York/ Cumberland	1805	1805	Eastern District, 1806; West- ern, 1799
Penobscot	Bangor	Hancock	1816	1816	1814[13]
Piscataquis	Dover-Fox- croft	Penobscot/ Somerset	1838	1838	1838
Sagadahoc	Bath	Lincoln	1854	1854	1826[14]
Somerset	Skowhegan	Kennebec	1809	1809	1809
Waldo	Belfast	Hancock	1827	1837	1789[15]
Washington	Machias	Lincoln	1789	1785[16]	1784[16]
York	Alfred		1652	1640	1642

Some of the above are in print. A transcript of the deeds from 1642 to 1737 appears for a period when York was Maine's only functioning county: *York Deeds* (18 volumes in 19; Portland, Me., 1887-1910). Probate records become *Maine Wills,* 1640-1760 (Baltimore, Md., 1972 [orig. publ. Portland, Me., 1887]), compiled by William M. Sargent, and *The Probate Records of Lincoln County, Maine: 1760 to 1800* (Port- land, Me., 1895), compiled by William D. Patterson. In addition, York County court records, 1639-1727, emerge as the *Province and Court Records of Maine* (6 volumes; Portland, Me., 1928-1975), edited in turn by Charles Thornton Libby, Robert E. Moody, and Neal W. Allen. These are especially important since most Maine surnames of the period appear in some capacity: plaintiff, judge, juryman, or witness.

Records of genealogical interest from the state government are chiefly civil or military. Vital statistics have been mentioned, and land office papers will require special attention. Most judicial records of the counties (save York and Lincoln at Alfred and Wiscasset respectively) are in Augusta; most military records prior to statehood are in the Massachu- setts Archives in Boston and the National Archives in Washington. Some

11. Probate records destroyed in two fires, 4 July 1866 and 24 Jan. 1908. Index only for 1900-1908 survives.

12. Plus transcripts from earlier county designations for this area.

13. Includes deeds for Hancock County Northern District (an earlier designation), 1814-1816.

14. Includes deeds for Lincoln County Western District (an earlier designation), 1826-1853.

15. Includes bound transcript of earlier Hancock County deeds for this area.

16. Includes records of Lincoln County Eastern District (an earlier designation).

militia rolls and rolls for Army service in the War of 1812,[17] together with militia rolls and rosters formerly in the office of Maine's Adjutant General are in the Maine State Archives.

United States Government items pertinent to genealogy, located both within and outside the National Archives, are described in folders issued by the Archives (General Information leaflets five and six). The United States Superintendent of Documents offers a detailed guide to the Archives holdings relevant to genealogy. Census returns and pension applications are most often consulted. The census schedules from 1790 through 1880 are available on microfilm at the State Archives; so are the census mortality schedules (recording deaths by month and year only, with age, for the year preceding the census tabulations of 1850, 1860, and 1870). Little that is unique to Maine about these records can be noted[18] save that the York County census return for 1800 is described as incomplete. Remnants of a special state census of 1837 (to determine apportionment of federal funds arising from the sale of western lands) are in the State Archives and the Maine Historical Society.[19]

For the genealogist working in eastern and northern Maine the complexity of land records requires specialized knowledge to identify plot and range designations. Wide variations over years preclude generalization on land practices in the state. Land was distributed in an involved and inconsistent manner. Long before the Revolution, liberal grants and patents had disposed of thousands of Maine acres, presaging what lay ahead. Between 1783 (when it created the Committee for the Sale of Eastern Lands) and 1853, threescore and ten years later, when Massachusetts sold to Maine the balance of its Downeast holdings, the Bay State had disposed of, by sale, lottery, and grant, about one-half of the state of Maine.

II

The printing of family histories in the Pine Tree State began about the middle of the last century. A brief account of one Maine family, the Prebles of Portland, formerly of York, was issued in 1850; a pedigree chart of the Thorntons of Saco appeared in the same year. Two years later an extensive record of the Frosts of Eliot was published. The three appear

17. MS. service records for the War of 1812 appear to be a transcript in the same handwriting. The researcher would logically find the original records in Boston and Washington.

18. Worth noting is a special feature of the 1800 census of Hancock and Kennebec Counties, a column headed "From whence emigrated" and for Kennebec another column for year of emigration. Though the column for Hancock County was used by only one of the two census enumerators, the record covers many towns later in Penobscot and Waldo Counties. The data for Hancock, Waldo and Penobscot Counties was extracted by Walter Goodwin Davis and published as "Part of Hancock County, Maine, in 1800," in the *Register*, 105 (1951): 204-213, 276-291.

19. Maine State Archives has Portland, Bangor, and unincorporated areas, with heads of household and number in age categories listed; Maine Historical Society has a draft for Eliot listing all names and ages (and many relationships), arranged by school districts.

to have been printed for private distribution rather than commercial marketing. Surviving correspondence for the Frost volume indicates a substantial dependence on family archives: transcripts of wills and deeds, earlier social correspondence, and other family papers. Few inaccuracies have been detected but the work could have been enriched by exploring public source material.

The need for more varied sources arose when private archives had disappeared, destroyed by fire, a common rural disaster, or scattered by the emigration to the developing west and the gravitation of youth to major cities. The Centennial in 1876 sparked a countertrend, inspiring a more widespread appreciation of the heritage that remained and could be assembled, preserved and absorbed. It stimulated a generation not only to produce local and family histories but also to edit and disseminate source material of widespread interest.

Three serials issued in Maine in the nineteenth century contain excerpts from vital records and ecclesiastical registers, brief family histories, capsule biographies, tax and military lists, tombstone transcripts, and other content of genealogical concern. These are *The Maine Genealogist and Biographer* (3 volumes; Augusta, Me., 1875-1878), focusing on Kennebec County; *The Maine Historical and Genealogical Recorder* (9 volumes in 3; Baltimore, Md., 1973 [orig. publ. 9 volumes; Portland, Me., 1884-1898]), concentrating on Cumberland and York Counties; and the *Bangor Historical Magazine* (9 volumes; Bangor, Me., 1885-1895) "devoted principally to the history of eastern Maine" but emphasizing Penobscot County. William Berry Lapham, a physician and historian of several Maine towns, founded and edited the *Genealogist and Biographer*. Stephen M. Watson, librarian of the Portland Public Library, edited the *Recorder*. The Bangor publication was initiated by Joseph W. Porter, a farmer, lumberman and legislator. Early in the twentieth century, John Francis Sprague, a lawyer, published *Sprague's Journal of Maine History* (14 volumes; Dover, Me., 1913-1926) which includes records of genealogical interest. These were the principal publications of group records that exceeded local interest until the appearance of the *Genealogical and Family History of the State of Maine* (4 volumes; New York, 1909), statewide in scope and part of a series covering many states. George Thomas Little, librarian of Bowdoin College, compiled the Maine volumes. Subsequent research has made obsolete Little's coverage of early generations but his treatment of contemporary generations has continued value.

Two genealogical organizations arose in the Centennial years and vanished. The Maine Genealogical and Biographical Society founded at Augusta in 1875 may well have been inspired by patriotic fervor. The small Society sponsored Lapham's serial which it may scarcely have outlasted. The Maine Genealogical Society founded at Portland in 1885 had a stronger growth. Its 76 members of 1886 had expanded to 280 by 1904; during that time its holdings reached 2,619 books and 2,486 pamphlets. Additionally, it had published Lincoln County's early probate records and reinstituted the suspended *York Deeds.* In 1922 it merged with the Maine Historical Society giving the latter a competent genealogical collection.

In 1928, the Maine Historical Society began publishing records of the courts of common pleas and general sessions. Charles Thornton Libby was selected as first editor. At the close of his freshman year, Libby had left Harvard College to compile the genealogy of a typical Maine family about which little had appeared in print. The work was distinguished for its high standards of comprehensiveness and detail. In his new role, as editor of the court records, Libby began to amass files on countless individuals and families. The concept emerged of a repository noting every appearance in primary sources of all who had lived in colonial Maine and New Hampshire. Meanwhile, the president of the Maine Historical Society, Walter Goodwin Davis, visualized the end result as a published dictionary, with definite time limits, rather than a permanently expanding file. Davis assumed oversight of this project, the *Genealogical Dictionary of Maine and New Hampshire,* even writing some sections. After the first part had appeared, a brilliant professional genealogist, Sybil Noyes, was employed on a full-time basis to complete the work.[20] Publication was in five parts, spread over twelve years. Each section was eagerly awaited by genealogists and historians. So daring a concept required such commitment that no comparable dictionary has been produced for other states. It remains unique.

The *Genealogical Dictionary* was of even greater significance than was at first apparent. It contributed to the emerging worldwide genealogical revolution that stressed (1) a return to source material, (2) a critical approach to both secondary and source material, and (3) a democratic scope embracing all peoples.

The concise format of the dictionary reflects its role. It is a guide and index to source material, much of which is in print. A thorough genealogist will explore the cited sources and their historical background for relevant information. Such interpretation and expansion of the dictionary is an art, as two widely differing examples, significant to genealogy, demonstrate. In the first, published in a scholarly journal,[21] Neal W. Allen discusses a minor but highly litigious pioneer who migrated from Massachusetts to Newichawannock (South Berwick, Me.) by 1685 and to Spruce Creek (Kittery, Me.) by 1690. The account of Nathaniel Kene in the genealogical dictionary measures exactly two and one-half inches in length, but Professor Allen's account requires twelve pages. Allen's exploration of the sources makes Kene real. We read of his quarrels with neighbors and involvement in physical assault, and watch him acquitted

20. Although it covered two states, the dictionary was a Maine production, published, financed, and written there by three natives of the state.

21. Neal W. Allen, "Nathaniel Kene of Spruce Creek; a Portrait from the Court Records," *Old-Time New England,* 53 (1963): 89-101.

of manslaughter. Allen successfully transfers the frontier from the West to the East and points out Kene's efforts to rise in the world by any mee as at hand. Should his descendants after reading it disown Kene, they would be losing a colorful forebear. In the second example novelist Kenneth Roberts discusses no less entertainingly through six pages of *Trending into Maine* a courageous ancestor, often at odds with the government, who was awarded but three inches of space in the volume by Libby, Noyes and Davis.

Despite its detail, the bi-state dictionary should not be the sole compendium consulted on the pioneers. Charles H. Pope's *The Pioneers of Maine and New Hamphire, 1623 to 1660; a Descriptive List Drawn from Records of the Colonies, Towns, Churches, Courts and Other Contemporary Sources* (Baltimore, Md., 1973 [orig. publ. Boston, Mass., 1908]) often develops data that is given a concise factual treatment by Libby, Noyes and Davis. Wilbur D. Spencer's *Pioneers on Maine Rivers* (Baltimore, Md., 1973 [orig. publ. Portland, Me., 1930]) provides an intimate view of the settlement of individual areas. The genealogist may also discover that the classic writers covering New England (e.g., John Farmer, James Savage, and Henry Whittemore) present clues leading to additional information.

The significant growth in bibliography during the decades of the sixties and seventies enables the genealogist to cope with an influx of Bicentennial publications. It fills a gap that has widened annually since the closure date (1891) of Joseph A. Williamson's classic coverage of the state. The *Bibliography of the State of Maine* (Boston, Mass., 1962) relies heavily on the resources of the Bangor Public Library. Local history holdings in print for the two largest American libraries, the Library of Congress and the New York Public Library, expand this record.[22] The *Maine History News* and the *Maine Historical Society Quarterly* give limited updating.[23] A new bibliography of the state by John D. Haskell, Jr. (comparable to Haskell's recent bibliography for Massachusetts) will become the principal source for locating Maine material. A series of bibliographical guides issued by the Maine Historical Society (and edited by its director, Gerald E. Morris) touches many facets of Maine life. In this series J. E. Frost's *Maine Genealogy: a Bibliographical Guide* (Portland, Me., 1977) concentrates on printed material and on relating genealogy to a variety of activities: cartography, journalism, record transcription, local history, and biography. Brief topical bibliographies, easily and inexpensively produced, have recently become a library trend. An example is the seven-page annotated *Genealogy of French Canada, Acadia, & Franco-America*

22. Marion J. Kaminkow, ed., *United States Local Histories in the Library of Congress* (5 volumes; Baltimore, Md., 1975-1976); New York Public Library. Research Libraries, *United States Local History Catalog* (2 volumes; Boston, Mass., 1974).

23. Eric S. Flower's "Maine Local Histories 1960-1975" began publication in the *Maine History News*, vol. 12, no. 1 (Jan. 1977), and a "Publications Listing," noting the output of many local historical societies, began in vol. 11, no. 4 (Oct. 1976). The *Quarterly* includes a selective list of newspaper and periodical articles (on specific topics) and new books.

at the Maine State Library (Augusta, Me., 1977), prepared by the library staff.[24]

Recent progress in data processing has revolutionized census exploration. Although a printed and indexed 1790 census of Maine has been available since 1908, access to later censuses involved tedious and repetitive searching until the computer made viable mass indexing. By mid-1977 Accelerated Indexing Systems, Inc., had issued indexes[25] to the United States population schedules of Maine for 1800, 1810, and 1820. Additional indexes for later decades are projected for this year. Another innovation uses the census to explore the movement of population to other states. Two studies of migration from Maine to Florida and California may have pioneered this technique.[26] Such investigations are of obvious genealogical, historical, and sociological value.

Records of military service have been widely indexed[27] though some gaps exist. Surviving records of Maine's colonial military service are located primarily in the Massachusetts Archives. Muster rolls have appeared in a variety of publications, most extensively for all ranks and ratings (though during but one campaign) in Henry S. Burrage's *Maine at Louisburg in 1745* (Augusta, Me., 1910). While Nancy S. Voye's *Massachusetts Officers in the French and Indian Wars 1748-1763* (Boston, Mass., 1975) lists only officers from Massachusetts and Maine, a microfilmed index of both officers and enlisted men (covering Archives volumes 91-99) is available in the Massachusetts Archives. Maine appears again in *Massachusetts Soldiers and Sailors of the Revolutionary War* (17 volumes; Boston, Mass., 1896-1908), and in *Records of the Massachusetts Volunteer Militia Called out by the Governor of Massachusetts to Suppress a Threatened Invasion during the War of 1812-14* (Boston, Mass., 1913).[28] A recent reprint of Mary Ellen Baker's important *Bibliography of Lists of New England Soldiers* (Boston, Mass., 1977 [orig. publ. Boston, Mass., 1911]) becomes essentially a new publication because of addenda by Robert MacKay.

Apart from the national pension lists, two books deal specifically with Maine pensioners: Charles J. House's *Names of Soldiers of the American*

24. An item not included but useful in Maine because of migration patterns is *Tracing Ancestors through the Province of Quebec and Acadia to France* (Salt Lake City, Utah, 1969), originally a paper presented at the World Conference on Records by Roland J. Auger, Acting Archivist of the Province of Quebec and editor of the *French and Acadian Genealogical Review*.

25. A note of caution on the use of computerized indexes is interjected. The rapidly produced mass products generated without "see" and "see also" references depend on an exercise of imagination by the user to detect variant spellings.

26. Both were compiled by Frank Mortimer Hawes and appeared in the *Register:* "New Englanders in the Florida Census of 1850," 76 (1922): 45-54, and "Natives of Maine in the California Census of 1850," 91 (1937): 319-340.

27. For a brief summary see "Military Service and Wars," in J. E. Frost's *Maine Genealogy: a Bibliographical Guide*, 37-38.

28. Note that the Maine Archives has the militia rolls and rolls of Maine men serving in the United States regular army for the War of 1812, even though the war antedated statehood, but see also footnote 17.

Revolution who Applied for State Bounty ... as Appears of Record in Land Office (Baltimore, Md., 1967 [orig. publ. Augusta, Me., 1893]) and Charles A. Flagg's *An Alphabetical Index of Revolutionary Pensioners Living in Maine* (Baltimore, Md., 1967 [orig. publ. Dover, Me., 1920]). Service in Maine's bloodless war is recorded in *Aroostook War. Historical Sketch and Roster of Commissioned Officers and Enlisted Men Called into Service for the Protection of the Northeastern Frontier of Maine* (Augusta, Me., 1904). Civil War service from the state was listed in the published annual reports and supplement of the Maine Adjutant General's Office, 1862-1867. The same office issued for World War I a *Roster of Maine in the Military Service of the United States and Allies in the World War, 1917-1919* (2 volumes; Augusta, Me., 1929). Service from Maine in the Mexican and Spanish-American Wars lacks printed coverage. Valuable though it would be to the genealogist, no index exists for service in the Maine militia in times of peace.

Some patriotic societies in the state have issued membership and ancestral registers, notably the Society of Colonial Wars in the State of Maine (1905, 1947), the Maine Daughters of the American Revolution (1948, 1975), and the Piscataqua Pioneers (1919, 1967). The Daughters of the American Revolution and the Daughters of the American Colonists have made major genealogical contributions through their yearbooks and special publications.

A few older guides, indexes, and lists have not been superseded. Outstanding among these is *A Reference List of Manuscripts Relating to the History of Maine,* edited by Elizabeth Ring (3 volumes; Orono, Me., 1938-1941) and produced by the University of Maine under Federal Emergency Relief Administration sponsorship. This list includes a section on manuscript genealogies and many individual items pertinent to family history. The Works Progress Administration spawned a Maine portrait survey: *American Portrait Inventory. American Portraits (1645-1850) Found in the State of Maine* (Boston, Mass., 1941). Not to be overlooked is Marquis F. King's *Changes in Names by Special Acts of the Legislature of Maine 1820-1895* (n.p., 1901). Colonial names abound in William H. Whitmore's *The Massachusetts Civil List for the Colonial and Provincial Periods, 1630-1774* (Baltimore, Md., 1969 [orig. publ. Albany, N. Y., 1870]) which includes Maine. The record of civil office holders is often continued in the county histories.

Town registers for more than one hundred seventy-five Maine towns were issued between 1900 and 1911 as a commercial venture by H. E. Mitchell.[29] A few New Hampshire towns were covered by the same compiler but essentially the town register was an unique Maine product. Included is an alphabetized census of all inhabitants and a civil list of local officeholders.

29. See James B. Vickery, "A Bibliography of Local History—the Town Registers of Maine," in *Maine Historical Society Newsletter,* 5 (1965): 6-11, and an alphabetized list in Frost's *Maine Genealogy: a Bibliographical Guide,* 42-43.

A nearly indispensable reference handbook (available in paperback) is Stanley Bearce Attwood's *The Length and Breadth of Maine* (Orono, Me., 1973 [orig. publ. Augusta, Me., 1946]). This potpourri of information gives the genealogist: (1) maps of the counties which indicate (i) township contours, and (ii) names of surrounding towns, vital in radial searching, and (2) a gazetteer naming and locating rivers, brooks, lakes, ponds, falls, mountains, hills, capes, river basins, notches, narrows, and cities, towns, and unorganized townships under both current and superseded names.

Some especially useful unpublished indexes might easily elude the researcher. One of these is a catalogue of the graves of three thousand Revolutionary War soldiers buried in Maine which was compiled as a Bicentennial project of the Maine Old Cemetery Association. Records assembled for this project are in the Special Collections division of the Raymond H. Fogler Library of the University of Maine at Orono. Select data, including name, date and place of birth and death, and location of interment, are being computerized. Inevitably incomplete, the survey nevertheless has uncovered names of hundreds of veterans hitherto untraced. No comprehensive listing had been attempted since the Daughters of the American Revolution's Golden Jubilee Project of 1940.

Transcripts of tombstone records throughout the state are being gathered for the Inscriptions Project of the Maine Old Cemetery Association. This growing collection, typed and indexed, totaling by 1977 seven substantial volumes, has been deposited for public access at the Maine State Library in Augusta. Arrangement of the material is first by town and second by cemetery or private plot. Also at the State Library are the records of the Surname Indexing Project of the same organization which (until computerized or microfilmed) are available only by appointment. Within the past five years ninety thousand Maine tombstone inscriptions have been assembled and arranged alphabetically. Despite some overlap, contents of the two projects differ considerably.

A continuation of the Maine entries of the *Index to American Genealogies* (commonly called Munsell's Genealogical Index), which had ceased coverage in 1908, has been maintained in volumes and card files by the State Library. The inclusion of internal (or contents) coverage of serials and monographs makes this record significant since the Newberry Library's similar index ended in 1918.

Vital records transcripts in the Maine Historical Society, and often elsewhere too, are indexed in J. E. Frost's "Guide to Maine Vital Records in Transcript." The term "vital records" is broadly interpreted to include journal and periodical notices, private records of clergy and laity, family Bible excerpts, gravestone transcripts, registers of interment, and the town clerk's official record. Manuscripts and typescripts as well as published items are noted. Completed in 1963, this typescript volume at the Maine Historical Society's library is now being updated.

A little in advance of the recent popular interest, Maine evinced a resurgent genealogical commitment. The *Maine Sunday Telegram* in Portland has long carried a weekly column of queries and responses. From 1970 the *Maine Genealogical Inquirer* served for several years as a medium of genealogical communication. In June of 1977 a new bi-monthly periodical, *Downeast Ancestry,* was initiated in Machias. The newsletter of the Maine Old Cemetery Association (founded by Dr. Hilda Fife in 1969) has contents of genealogical interest. The *Maine History News,* organ of the Maine League of Historical Societies and Museums, keeps the genealogist alert to activities of local historical organizations. The periodicals *Downeast* and the *Maine Historical Society Quarterly,* and numerous recent local histories, expand the background material. Within the present decade a branch library of the Latter-Day Saints was opened in Farmingdale, making available to readers there the extensive genealogical holdings on microfilm of the Mormon Church. The Maine State Archives was established in 1965. A new Maine Genealogical Society, which meets at various locations within the state, was founded in 1976.

The largest collections of published genealogies within the state are in the State Library, the Maine Historical Society, and the Bangor Public Library. Some valuable small collections of manuscript genealogies are held by local historical societies; that at York is perhaps the largest. A booklet called *The Special Collections* describes documents and family papers in the state university's library at Orono. The University of Maine's Fogler Library, with the state's largest newspaper holdings in microfilm, has polled local libraries and compiled a typescript: "Maine Newspapers in the Smaller Maine Public Libraries." The Mantor Library of the University of Maine at Farmingdale produced in 1977 an index (compiled by David Young) to obituaries in three Maine newspapers of the nineteenth century. While newspapers have obvious genealogical value, so do Maine town reports which after 1892 frequently contain extracts of vital statistics in brief form. Although the largest collection of town reports appears to be in the Fogler Library, substantial holdings are also in the State Library and in the Hawthorne-Longfellow Library of Bowdoin College in Brunswick.

The two principal centers of genealogical research in Maine are Augusta and Portland. In Augusta the Maine Cultural Building houses the State Archives, Library, and Museum. The Archives has the largest centralized grouping of vital records in the state, backed by land, military, and judicial resources described in four pamphlets: *Records Available for Genealogical Research, Records Relating to Local History, Military Records,* and *Land Records.* The adjacent State Library has town, county and local histories, registers and yearbooks of organizations, general catalogues listing college graduates, school and business reports, the Maine Old Cemetery Association transcripts, and the Maine update of the Munsell index. In Portland the Maine Historical Society (fourth oldest in the nation) has the state's largest assemblage of historical manuscripts and of indexed transcripts of vital records, tombstone inscriptions, and family Bible records; it has a library strong in local history, genealogy, and maps.

Outside the state Boston is a third research center. The New England Historiç Genealogical Society has rich manuscript holdings of Maine genealogies and the unique Direct Tax Records of Maine in 1798. A perusal of the manuscript material in the Society's library, the State Archives, and the Massachusetts Historical Society quickly reminds the reader that Maine shares with Massachusetts more than a century of its heritage.

CHECK LIST OF SOME MAINE GENEALOGIES

De Alva S. Alexander, *The Alexanders of Maine*. Buffalo, N. Y., 1898.

Mary L. Benjamin, *A Genealogy of the Family of Lieut. Samuel Benjamin . . . of Livermore, Maine*. [?Winthrop, Me.], 1900.

Grace M. Limeburner, *Seth Blodgett (of Brooksville, Maine) 1747-1817; his Ancestors and his Descendants*. Rutland, Vt., 1933.

John A. Bolles, *Genealogy of the Bolles Family in America*. Boston, Mass., 1865.

George E. Williams, *A Genealogy of the Descendants of Joseph Bolles of Wells, Maine*. West Hartford, Conn. [c1970].

Charles E. Banks, *The Bonython Family of Maine*. [Boston, Mass., 1884] Repr. from the *Register*.

Eric G. Bonython, *History of the Families of Bonython*. [Netley, S. A.], 1966.

William B. Lapham, *Bradbury Memorial*. Portland, Me., 1890.

Kenneth S. McCann, *Genealogy and History of the Portland, Me., Bruns Families . . . 1739-1956*. Glen Burnie, Md. [1956].

George H. Butler, *Thomas Butler and his Descendants . . . of Butler's Hill, South Berwick, Me., 1674 to 1886*. New York, 1886.

Helen G. Buzzell, *Buzzell, Orr, and Related Families of Massachusetts and Maine*. Maplewood, N. J., 1964.

Sydney H. Carney, Jr., *Genealogy of the Carney Family . . . of Pownalboro, Maine, 1751-1903*. New York, 1904.

William M. Emery, *Chadbourne-Chadbourn Genealogy*. [Fall River, Mass., 1904.]

Milton Ellis and Leola C. Ellis, *John Chaplin, 1758-1837, of Rowley, Mass. and Bridgton, Me., his Ancestry and Descendants*. [Westbrook, Me., 1949.]

Julia C. Washburn and William B. Lapham, *Records of the Descendants of Rev. Nathaniel Chase of Buckfield, Maine*. Augusta, Me., 1878.

Frank H. Chick, *The Chick Family, Hancock and Penobscot Counties, Maine*. [Edmonds, Wash., 1964.]

Cecil H. C. Howard, *Genealogy of the Cutts Family in America*. Albany, N. Y., 1892.

Walter G. Davis, *The Ancestry of Nicholas Davis, 1753-1832, of Limington, Maine*. Portland, Me., 1956.

Rufus Emery, *Genealogical Records of Descendants of John and Anthony Emery, of Newbury, Mass., 1590-1890*. Salem, Mass., 1890.

Charles A. Fernald, *Universal International Genealogy and of the Ancient Fernald Families.* [?Boston, Mass., 1910.] See Davis, *The Ancestry of Joseph Waterhouse,* [35]-55 on this book.

John E. Frost, *The Nicholas Frost Family.* [Milford, N. H., 1943.]

Norman S. Frost, *Frost Genealogy in Five Families.* West Newton, Mass., 1926.

[Usher Parsons], *Genealogy of the Frost Family, Eliot, York County, Maine.* N.p., 1852.

John S. Goodwin, *The Goodwins of Kittery, York County, Maine.* Chicago, Ill. [1898].

Philip C. Greene *(sic)*, *The Green Family of Otisfield, Maine.* New York, 1976.

Samuel K. Hamilton, *The Hamiltons of Waterborough (York County, Maine) their Ancestors and Descendants.* [Boston, Mass.], 1912.

Frederick S. Hammond, *History and Genealogies of the Hammond Families in America.* Two volumes, Oneida, N. Y., 1902-1904.

John T. Hassam, *Some of the Descendants of William Hilton.* Boston, Mass., 1877. Repr. from the *Register.*

Margaret I. Gregory, *A Complete Record of the Family of George and Jessie McQueen Innes, Immigrants to Maine 1873.* [?Rockland, Me.], 1965.

Joseph C. Jefferds, Jr., *Simon Jefferds . . . and Some of his Descendants.* 2nd ed. Charleston, W. Va. [?1975].

Charles N. Sinnett, *Jacob Johnson, of Harpswell, Maine, and his Descendants East and West.* Concord, N. H., 1907.

Tristram F. Jordan, *The Jordan Memorial.* Boston, Mass., 1882.

James R. Joy, *Thomas Joy and his Descendants in the Lines of his Sons Samuel of Boston . . . Ephraim of Berwick . . .* New York, 1900.

Harry A. Davis, *The Junkins Family.* Washington, D. C., 1938.

Hiram B. Lawrence, *Memorials of Robert Lawrence, Robert Bartlett, and their Descendants.* [?Holyoke, Mass., 1888.]

Tristram F. Jordan, *An Account of the Descendants of Capt. William Leighton of Kittery, Maine.* Albany, N. Y., 1885.

Charles T. Libby, *The Libby Family in America, 1602-1881.* Portland, Me., 1882.

Charles C. Lord, *A History of the Descendants of Nathan Lord of Ancient Kittery, Me.* Concord, N. H., 1912.

Charles E. Lord, *The Ancestors and Descendants of Lieutenant Tobias Lord.* [Boston. Mass.], 1913.

Harold M. Lord, *The Windham, Maine Branch of the Nathan Lord Family of Kittery, Maine.* N.p., n.d.

Harry A. Davis, *The McIntire Family.* York, Me., 1939.

Robert H. McIntire, *Ancestry of Robert Harry McIntire and of Helen Annette McIntire, his Wife.* Norfolk, Va., 1950.

————, *Descendants of Micum McIntire.* Rutland, Vt., 1940.

William M. Sargent, *Merrill Family.* Portland, Me., 1886. Repr. from the *Maine Historical and Genealogical Recorder.*

————, *The Mitchell Family of North Yarmouth, Maine.* Yarmouth, Me., 1878.

Emma E. N. Brigham, *Neal Family.* Springfield, Mass., 1938.

Walter G. Davis, *The Ancestry of Joseph Neal, 1769-c. 1835, of Litchfield, Maine.* Portland, Me., 1945.

Nowell and Allied Families. New York, 1941. Compiled and privately printed for Mrs. James A. Nowell by the American Historical Company, Inc.; copy in rare book division of the Library of Congress.

Cecil H. C. Howard, *The Pepperrells in America.* Salem, Mass., 1906. Repr. from the *Historical Collections of the Essex Institute.*

Thomas A. Perkins, *Jacob Perkins of Wells, Maine, and his Descendants, 1583-1936.* Haverhill, Mass., 1947.

Charles N. Sinnett, *Our Perry Family in Maine.* Lewiston, Me., 1911.

Marquis F. King, *Lieut. Roger Plaisted of Quamphegon (Kittery), and Some of his Descendants.* Portland, Me., 1904.

A Genealogical Sketch of the Preble Families, Resident in Portland, Me., A.D. 1850. Portland, Me., 1850.

William P. Jones, *John Preble of Machias (1771-1841) and his Descendants.* Somerville, Mass., 1929.

George H. Preble, *Genealogical Sketch of the First Three Generations of Prebles in America.* Boston, Mass., 1868.

Worrall D. Prescott, *A Genealogical Record concerning Capt. Samuel Reed . . .* [New York], 1953.

Winifred L. Holman, *Remick Genealogy.* [Concord, N. H.], 1933.

Henry S. Webster, *Thomas Sewall; Some of his Ancestors and All of his Descendants.* Gardiner, Me., 1904.

Ralph S. Bartlett, *Alexander Shapleigh of Kittery, Maine, and Some of his Descendants.* [Boston, Mass., 1941.] Repr. from the *Register.*

Hannah C. S. Tibbetts and Frederick E. Shapleigh, *The Descendants of Alexander Shapleigh.* [Kennebunk, Me., 1968.]

John S. Emery, *Genealogy of the Original Simpson Family, of York and Hancock Counties, Me.,* Bangor, Me. [1891]. Repr. from the *Bangor Historical Magazine.*

Charles N. Sinnett, *Sinnett Genealogy.* Concord, N. H., 1910.

Lora A. W. Underhill, *Descendants of Edward Small of New England.* Three volumes, Boston, Mass., 1934.

Edwin E. Smith, *James Smith, Berwick, 1668, Some of his Descendants.* Kennebunk, Me., 1940.

Leonard B. Chapman, *Monograph on the Southgate Family of Scarborough, Maine.* Portland, Me., 1907.

Walter G. Davis, *The Ancestry of Annis Spear, 1775-1858, of Litchfield, Maine.* Portland, Me., 1945.

————, *The Ancestry of Sarah Stone, Wife of James Patten of Arundel (Kennebunkport), Maine.* Portland, Me., 1930.

Alonzo W. Sturges, *From 1530 to 1900; Complete Lineage of the Sturges Families of Maine.* Lewiston, Me., 1900.

Thomas C. Amory, *Materials for a History of the Family of John Sullivan of Berwick* . . . Cambridge, Mass., 1893.

Harriet S. Tapley, *Genealogy of the Tapley Family.* Danvers, Mass., 1900.

Charles N. Sinnett, *Our Thompson Family in Maine, New Hampshire and the West.* Concord, N. H., 1907.

Josiah H. Thompson, *Autobiography of Deacon John Thompson, of Mercer, Maine, with Genealogical Notes of his Descendants.* Farmington, Me. [1920].

Rufus B. Tobey and Charles H. Pope, *Tobey (Tobie, Toby) Genealogy.* Boston, Mass., 1905.

Walter G. Davis, *The Ancestry of Lieut. Amos Towne, 1737-1793, of Arundel (Kennebunkport), Maine.* Portland, Me., 1927.

Worrall D. Prescott, *A Genealogical Record concerning Phebe (Reed) Trott and John Trott* . . . [New York], 1954.

F. K. Upham, *Genealogy and Family History of the Uphams of Castine, Maine.* [Newark, N. J.], 1887.

John H. Sheppard, *Reminiscences of the Vaughan Family.* Boston, Mass., 1865.

Ernest G. Walker, *Walkers of Yesterday.* [Washington, D. C., c1937.]

Orin Warren, *Warren; a Genealogy of the Descendants of James Warren* . . . *Kittery, Maine.* Haverhill, Mass., 1902.

Vanetta H. Warren, *Adriel Warren of Berwick, Maine; his Forbears and Descendants.* Boston, Mass., 1964.

————, *Supplement.* Weston, Mass., 1976.

Lilian Washburn, *My Seven Sons.* Portland, Me., 1940.

Walter G. Davis, *The Ancestry of Joseph Waterhouse, 1754-1837, of Standish, Maine.* Portland, Me., 1949.

Charles E. Waterman, *The Maine Watermans.* Mechanic Falls, Me., 1906.

William M. Sargent, *The Weare Family, of Hampton, New Hampshire, and North Yarmouth, Maine.* Yarmouth, Me., 1879.

George W. Chamberlain, *Descendants of Michael Webber of Falmouth, Maine* . . . Wellesley Hills, Mass. [c1935].

George B. Sedgley, *The Wellcome Family of Freeman, Maine.* Phillips, Me., 1939.

Charles K. Wells, *The Wells Family of Wells, Maine.* Milwaukee, Wisc., 1874.

Foster C. Whidden and Rae M. Spencer, *The Story of Some Descendants of Rendol and Sarah Whidden of Calais, Maine.* [?Marblehead, Mass., 1968].

[Sidney A. Wilder and Gerald G. Wilder], *Joseph Wilder and his Descendants.* Pembroke, Me., 1902.

Emery S. Wilson, *A Brief Account of the Wilsons who First Settled in Cherryfield, Maine.* Camilla, Ga., 1970.

Fred A. Wilson, *The Early History of the Wilson Family of Kittery, Maine.* Lynn, Mass., 1898.

————, *The Genealogy of the Family of Elihu Parsons Wilson of Kittery, Me.* [Nahant, Mass., 1894.]

————, *The Genealogy of the Family of Nathaniel Wilson of Kittery, Me.* [Nahant, Mass., 1894.]

Cyrus Woodman, *The Woodmans of Buxton, Maine.* Boston, Mass., 1874.

Frank E. Woodward, *Descendants of Samuel Woodward of Bristol, Maine.* Portland, Me., 1887. Repr. from the *Maine Historical and Genealogical Recorder.*

Doris Y. H. Smith and Mary L. H. Littlefield, *Some of the Descendants of Rowland Young of York, Maine.* N.p., 1975.

SOME GROUP GENEALOGIES

George T. Little, *Genealogical and Family History of the State of Maine.* Four volumes, New York, 1909.

Henry C. Quimby, *New England Family History.* Four volumes, New York, 1907-1912. Covers largely Maine families.

G. T. Ridlon, *Saco Valley Settlements and Families.* Portland, Me., 1909. Gen.: [443]-1218.

Mildred N. Thayer and Mrs. Edward W. Ames, *Brewer, Orrington, Holden, Eddington; History and Families.* [Brewer, Me., 1962.]

GENEALOGIES IN SOME MAINE TOWN HISTORIES
BETHEL

Eva Bean, *East Bethel Road.* Bethel, Me., 1959. Gen.: [159]-380.

BLUEHILL

R. G. F. Candage, *Historical Sketches of Bluehill, Maine.* Ellsworth, Me., 1905. *Passim.*

BOOTHBAY

Francis B. Greene, *Family History of the Boothbay Region . . . from the First Permanent Settlement in 1730 to Recent Times.* Boothbay Harbor, Me., 1932.

BROOKS

Seth W. Norwood, *Sketches of Brooks History.* [Dover, N. H., 1935.] Gen.: [286]-345.

BRUNSWICK

George A. Wheeler and Henry W. Wheeler, *History of Brunswick, Topsham, and Harpswell.* Boston, Mass., 1878. Gen.: 827-862.

BUCKFIELD

Alfred Cole and Charles F. Whitman, *A History of Buckfield, Oxford County, Maine.* Buckfield, Me., 1915. Gen.: 520-722.

BUXTON

J. M. Marshall, *A Report . . . of the First Centennial Anniversary of the In-corporation of the Town of Buxton, Maine.* Portland, Me., 1874. Gen.: 142-246.

CHINA

Marion T. Van Strien, *China, Maine: Bicentennial History.* [Weeks Mills, Me., 1975.] Gen. (separate paging): 1-[124].

CORNISH

Leola C. Ellis and Kera C. Millard, *More about Early Cornish.* [Cornish, Me., 1975.] Gen.: 139-215.

DRESDEN

Charles E. Allen, *History of Dresden, Maine.* [Augusta, Me.], 1931. Gen.: 540-575.

DURHAM

Everett S. Stackpole, *History of Durham, Maine.* Lewiston, Me., 1899. Gen.: 148-290.

ELIOT

Old Eliot, ed. by J. L. M. Willis. Nine volumes, Eliot, Me., 1897-1909.

FARMINGTON

Frances G. Butler, *A History of Farmington, Franklin County, Maine.* Far-mington, Me., 1885. Gen.: 345-621.

FOXCROFT

Mary C. Lowell, *Old Foxcroft, Maine.* Concord, N. H. [1935]. Gen.: 155-262.

GORHAM

Hugh D. McLellan, *History of Gorham, Maine.* Portland, Me., 1903. Gen.: 382-843.

GREENE

Walter L. Mower, *Sesquicentennial History of the Town of Greene, Andros-coggin County, Maine.* N.p., 1938. Gen.: [184]-568.

HALLOWELL

Emma H. Nason, *Old Hallowell on the Kennebec.* Augusta, Me., 1909. Gen.: 73-192.

HARPSWELL, see Brunswick.

HARRISON

Alphonso Martin [and others], *Centennial History of Harrison, Maine.* Port-land, Me., 1909. Gen.: [333]-727.

HOLLIS

Martin H. Jewett and Olive W. Hannaford, *A History of Hollis, Maine,*

Formerly Little Falls, Later Phillipsburg. Farmington, Me., 1976. Gen.: 165-193.

INDUSTRY

William C. Hatch, *A History of the Town of Industry, Franklin County, Maine.* Farmington, Me., 1893. Gen.: [471]-847.

ISLESBOROUGH

John P. Farrow, *History of Islesborough, Maine.* Bangor, Me., 1893. Gen.: [165]-303.

JAY

Benjamin F. Lawrence, *History of Jay, Franklin County, Maine.* Boston, Mass., 1912. Gen.: [63]-93.

KENNEBUNKPORT

Charles Bradbury, *History of Kennebunkport.* Kennebunk, Me., 1837. Gen.: 223-287.

KITTERY

Everett S. Stackpole, *Old Kittery and her Families.* Lewiston, Me., 1903. Gen.: 269-811.

LEE

Vinal A. Houghton, *The Story of an Old New England Town; History of Lee, Maine.* Wilton, Me., 1926. Gen.: [191]-211.

LEEDS

J. C. Stinchfield, *History of the Town of Leeds, Androscoggin County, Maine.* Lewiston, Me. [1901]. Gen.: 17-243.

LIMINGTON

Robert L. Taylor, *History of Limington, Maine, 1668-1900.* [Norway, Me., 1975.] Gen.: 146-[212].

LINCOLN

Dana W. Fellows, *History of the Town of Lincoln, Penobscot County, Maine.* Lewiston, Me. [1939]. Gen.: [267]-430.

LITCHFIELD

History of Litchfield and an Account of its Centennial Celebration. Augusta, Me., 1897. Gen.: 23-406h.

LIVERMORE

Ira T. Monroe, *History of the Town of Livermore, Androscoggin County, Maine.* Lewiston, Me. [1928]. Gen.: [57]-241.

MACHIAS

George W. Drisko, *Narrative of the Town of Machias.* Machias, Me., 1904. Gen.: [345]-578.

MATINICUS [Plantation, Knox County]

Charles A. E. Long, *Matinicus Isle, its Story and its People.* [Lewiston, Me.], 1926. Gen.: 125-235.

MONMOUTH

Harry H. Cochrane, *History of Monmouth and Wales.* [Winthrop, Me.], 1894. Gen. (separate paging) : [1]-216.

MORRILL

Theda M. Morse and Mr. and Mrs. Charles White, *A Genealogical History of the Families of Morrill, Maine.* Morrill, Me. [1957].

NEW VINEYARD

Dorothy C. Poole, *A New Vineyard.* Edgartown, Mass., 1976. Gen.: 172-211.

NEWCASTLE, see Sheepscot.

NORWAY

William B. Lapham, *Centennial History of Norway, Oxford County, Maine, 1786-1886.* Portland, Me., 1886. Gen.: [453]-627.

Charles F. Whitman, *A History of Norway, Maine from the Earliest Settlements to the Close of the Year 1922.* Norway, Me., 1924. Gen.: 339-538.

OTISFIELD

William S. Spurr, *A History of Otisfield, Cumberland County, Maine.* N.p., 1944. Gen.: [313]-661.

OXFORD

Marquis F. King, *Annals of Oxford, Maine.* Portland, Me., 1903. Gen.: [126]-298.

PARIS

William B. Lapham and Silas P. Maxim, *History of Paris, Maine.* Paris, Me., 1884. Gen.: 491-778.

PARSONSFIELD

J. W. Dearborn [and others], *A History of the First Century of the Town of Parsonsfield, Maine.* Portland, Me., 1888. Gen.: [365]-413.

RUMFORD

William B. Lapham, *History of Rumford.* Augusta, Me., 1890. Gen.: [285]-423.

ST. GEORGE

Albert J. Smalley, *St. George, Maine.* N.p. [1976]. Gen. (separate paging) : 1-98.

SANFORD

Edwin Emery, *The History of Sanford, Maine.* Fall River, Mass., 1901. Gen.: [391]-517.

SHEEPSCOT

David Q. Cushman, *History of Ancient Sheepscot and Newcastle*. Bath, Me., 1882. Gen.: [351]-437.

SORENTO, see Sullivan.

SULLIVAN

Leila A. C. Johnson, *Sullivan and Sorento since 1760*. Ellsworth, Me., 1953. Gen.: 141-397.

SUMNER

Centennial History of the Town of Sumner, Maine, 1798-1898. West Sumner, Me., 1899. Gen.: 53-202.

TOPSHAM, see Brunswick.

UNION

John L. Sibley, *A History of the Town of Union*. Boston, Mass., 1851. Gen.: 429-517.

WALES, see Monmouth.

WARREN

Cyrus Eaton, *Annals of the Town of Warren*. 2nd ed. Hallowell, Me., 1877. Gen.: 498-651.

WATERFORD

Henry P. Warren [and others], *The History of Waterford, Oxford County, Maine*. Portland, Me., 1879. Gen.: [227]-309.

WAYNE

[George W. Walton and others], *History of the Town of Wayne*, Kennebec County, Maine. Augusta, Me., 1898. Gen.: [284]-354.

WHITING

Gladys H. Forslund, *A History of Whiting, Maine*. [Calais, Me., 1975.] Gen.: 64-[95].

WILSONS MILLS

History of Wilsons Mills, Maine and the Megalloway Settlements. Wilsons Mills, Me., 1975. Gen.: 205-[286].

WINDHAM

Samuel T. Dole, *Windham in the Past*. Auburn, Me., 1916. Gen.: [285]-586.

WINTHROP

Everett S. Stackpole, *History of Winthrop, Maine*. Auburn, Me., [1925]. Gen.: 247-704.

David Thurston, *A Brief History of Winthrop*. Portland, Me., 1855. Gen.: 172-203.

WOODSTOCK

William B. Lapham, *History of Woodstock, Maine.* Portland, Me., 1882. Gen.: 169-268.

YARMOUTH

Katherine P. Kaster, *Cousins and Littlejohn's Islands, 1645-1893.* [Portland, Me., ?1942.] Gen.: 72-128.

YARMOUTH, NORTH

Old Times; a Magazine . . . of North Yarmouth, Maine. Eight volumes in two, Yarmouth, Me., 1877-1884.

John Eldridge Frost (Ph.D.), a native of Maine and until 1977 Associate Librarian of the New York University Libraries, is a member of the Genealogy Committee of the American Library Association.

ADDITIONS

The researcher — professional or amateur — logically starts with a literature search to discover and evaluate information in print. He must become familiar with the bibliographic coverage, even more so if it is geographically scattered. For Maine two indispensable indexes illustrate this principle. In Augusta is the Maine State Library's continuation of Maine entries in Munsell's *Index to American Genealogies.* Card files and bound typescripts cover the years 1908 through 1950. In Portland is the Maine Historical Society's *Name Index to Maine Local Histories*[1] by Marie Estes. The compiler lists alphabetically by surname families whose genealogies appear in Maine local histories before 1970. The Augusta and Portland lists are complementary, and both should be consulted.

During the past five years genealogies associated with Maine — usually less comprehensive in scope than their predecessors — have continued to appear. If it were possible to add only five titles to the check lists of monograph genealogies in the preceding article I would select some old, some new, that cover families long resident in Maine. One of them was written by a Maine Commissioner of Insurance, W. D. Spencer.

Helen Bourne Joy Lee, *The Bourne Genealogy.* Chester, Conn., 1972.

A. J. Hodsdon, *Genealogy of the Descendants of Nicholas Hodsdon-Hodgdon of Hingham, Mass., and Kittery, Maine, 1635-1904.* Haverhill, Mass., 1904.

Benjamin N. Goodale, *Material for a Genealogy of the Scammon Family in Maine.* Salem, Mass., 1892.

Wilbur D. Spencer, *The Maine Spencers.* Concord, N.H., 1898.

Ruth Varney Held, *Charles Varney and Rachel Parker of Berwick, Maine.* San Diego, Calif., ᶜ1967.

No longer do the Preble and Thornton pedigrees, both of 1850 vintage, vie for the record of the earliest published genealogy in the state. While searching for other material, I uncovered a Herrick genealogy that precedes them by four years, *viz., A Genealogical Register of the Name and Family of Herrick, from the Settlement of Henerie Hericke in Salem, Massachusetts 1629, to 1846, with a Concise Notice of Their English Ancestry.* Printed in Bangor, Maine, by Samuel S. Smith in 1846, the book is written by Maj. Gen. Jedediah Herrick (1780-1847), a veteran of some distinction of the War of 1812 who was later sheriff of Penobscot County. The printing must have been small for copies are scarce.

An increase in indexes is a new and significant trend. Accelerated Indexing Systems continues to index the U.S. censuses of Maine, adding 1840 and 1850 in 1978. Indexed coverage now extends from 1790 through 1850.

---

1. Unlike its New Hampshire counterpart (see *Historical New Hampshire,* 1946, 1980) the Estes list is not in print.

In 1977 David Young and Rebecca Burnham at the University of Maine—Farmington — issued as a bicentennial project an index to selected obituaries from three Maine newspapers[2] as a potential source for locating death records of Revolutionary War veterans. In the same year Fr. Yourville La Bonté completed the *Necrologies of Franco-Americans Taken from Maine's Newspapers 1966-76.* In 1980 and 1981 Ruth and Charles Candage produced several volumes of indexed marriage and death notices (1846-1872) from Rockland newspapers with a broad radial coverage. In 1982 David Colby Young and Robert Taylor completed an index to Maine and New Hampshire death notices in a Baptist newspaper, the *Morning Star* (1821-1851), an astonishing 346-page typescript listing many deaths unrecorded in the usual sources.

A new volume of Maine vital records under totally different auspices is a surprise. In 1980 the Society of Mayflower Descendants published at Warwick, R.I. the vital records of North Yarmouth, Maine to 1850. Additionally, vital records of Stockton Springs appeared in 1978, Fairfield in 1981, and Bucksport in 1982. Catholic church records have bounded ahead with Fr. La Bonté's transcripts of eight marriage registers[3] to the present, a major contribution to Franco-American genealogy.

The Maine Old Cemetery Association [MOCA] has issued on microfilm two series of their cemetery transcripts. By closing and microfilming a part, the records become available for sale and distribution; hard copy continues to accumulate in the State Library for later series. A MOCA publication lists in detail the areas covered. Project SIP [the Surname Indexing Project] has become independent of MOCA and is housed and serviced in the Reference area of the Maine State Library. A newly completed index at the Maine Historical Society in Portland is rapidly covering the MOCA-owned records of an important tombstone business in Skowhegan and Bath.

A recent development in Augusta is the Archives microfilming of Maine's County Marriage Returns, whenever they are found in records deposited there.[4] This greatly facilitates their use. The Maine State Library in 1980 issued an expanded revision of its popular bibliography *Genealogy of French Canada, Acadia and Franco-Americans at the Maine State Library.*

The continued joint publication by the Society of Colonial Wars in the Commonwealth of Massachusetts and the New England Historic Genealogical Society (and additionally the Commonwealth of Massachusetts for one volume) of a series on Massachusetts service in the colonial wars and the Revolution is of equal relevance to Maine and Massachusetts. To Voye and MacKay listed earlier we add:

Myron O. Stachiw, ed., *Massachusetts Officers and Soldiers 1723-1743, Dummer's War to the War of Jenkins Ear.* Boston, 1979.

2. The *Kennebec Journal,* 1825-54, the *Oxford Observer,* 1826-28, and the *Oxford Democrat,* 1835-55.
3. Auburn, Biddeford, Brunswick, Lewiston, Lisbon, Sanford, Waterville, and Westbrook.
4. Includes Androscoggin, Kennebec, Knox, Penobscot, Piscataquis, Sagadahoc, Somerset, Waldo, Washington, York.

Mary E. Donohue, *Massachusetts Officers and Soldiers 1702-1722, Queen Anne's War to Dummer's War.* Boston, 1980.

Carole Doreski, *Massachusetts Officers and Soldiers in the Seventeenth Century Conflicts.* Boston, 1982.

Soldiers, Sailors and Patriots of the Revolutionary War — Maine, by Carleton E. and Sue G. Fisher is the product of a totally fresh searching of extant sources. The Fishers expand the list covered in *Massachusetts Soldiers and Sailors of the Revolutionary War* and add the neglected "patriots" who have provided gateways to many memberships in patriotic societies. This will probably be the most frequently used of any of the books covered in the five-year span.

An article by Winifred Lovering Holman and Mary Lovering Holman several years ago merits inclusion in any survey of Maine genealogy. "Suffolk County Probate (1686-1692)," in *The American Genealogist* 12 (1936): 175-184, 222-234; 13 (1936): 98-106; and 14 (1937): 34-45 lists probates during Sir Edmund Andros's Dominion of New England. During these seven years all estates of £50 or more were probated in Boston. Eight or nine Maine estates appear here. In turn, this listing underscores the necessity to utilize all early Maine records in the Massachusetts Archives.

It is cheering to close on the happy note that the "lost" is no longer missing. Original marriage returns in Cumberland County were reported earlier as not found. In four volumes (lettered A, B, C, D) these are located (1982) in the Cumberland County Probate Office in Portland.

NEW HAMPSHIRE GENEALOGY:
A PERSPECTIVE

David C. Dearborn

The northern New England states challenge the skill and ingenuity of the best American genealogists. Unlike Connecticut, Rhode Island, and Massachusetts, which exhibit fairly stable patterns of family settlement and migration, Maine, Vermont, and New Hampshire were exposed to frontier conditions into the nineteenth century and present to genealogists the double problems of high mobility and diverse origins.

From the beginning New Hampshire's genealogical history has been influenced by the frontier and its New England neighbors. Founded as a business venture by merchants and speculators rather than as a haven for religious dissenters, New Hampshire received its start at Dover, Portsmouth, and Gosport, a fishing village on the Isle of Shoals, in the 1620s. Soon, however, religious dissenters from Puritan Massachusetts intruded upon the scene with the arrival of John Wheelwright's company of Antinomians at Exeter in 1638. At this time also, disaffected residents from Newbury, Watertown, and Dedham, Massachusetts, settled Hampton. These Massachusetts families began a continuous migration into the colony which persists almost to the present day.

Further settlements reveal this intermingling of New Hampshire and Massachusetts families. The Chase family, for example, came in 1647 to Newbury, Massachusetts, where the immigrant Aquila Chase lived and died. Three generations of his descendants remained in Massachusetts. But by the fourth generation, in the first half of the eighteenth century, many members of this family had moved to New Hampshire where they intermarried with the Blakes, Sanborns, and Haineses. During the eighteenth century the fourth and fifth generations of the Chase family followed the line of settlement north and west, pioneering Conway, Fitzwilliam, and Plymouth. As they moved west to the Connecticut River, they met and mingled with settlers who had migrated upriver from Connecticut, further complicating this family's genealogy. Married to the daughters of Connecticut men, they founded towns in Cheshire, Sullivan, and Grafton counties.

While the Chases were moving west, another pattern of New Hampshire settlement was emerging as ethnic families came into the colony. In the eighteenth century large numbers of Ulster Scots settled in New Hampshire, concentrating in the Londonderry area. For at least a generation they did not intermarry with Yankees, but by the Revolution, they had begun to assimilate into the native population. Similarly, the nineteenth century witnessed a massive migration of French Canadians from Quebec into New Hampshire. Families like the LeBlancs, Desrosiers, Chagnons, and LeFebvres were originally attracted by factory jobs in the textile mills of the river cities of Manchester and Nashua, where they lived in segregated communities and preserved their French traditions and Catholic faith. Like the Scotch-Irish before them, the French Canadians gradually entered the mainstream of New England life. Sons and daughters of the second and third generations have moved out of French Canadian neighborhoods in the mill cities and married many New Hampshire Yankees.

The family history for Ulster Scots is not easily documented. Their places of origin in Scotland and Ireland are obscure, making the identification of their European ancestry difficult. The paucity of vital, town, and church records in the Merrimack River Valley area perpetuates this problem here. For the French Canadians the difficult areas of research are discovering places of origin in Quebec and piecing together the records of unrelated families with the same popular surnames. Another complication is the anglicization of French names—changing LeBlanc to White, for example.

The Dearborns, a typical New Hampshire family, illustrate these genealogical problems. The first four generations are easily traced since they remained in Hampton, a town with good vital records. In the fifth generation, however, the Dearborns followed the frontier north and west, becoming less visible. In frontier communities like Effingham and Wakefield, many of them resist complete identification, for the recording of births, deaths, and marriages was sometimes neglected, and wills and deeds were seldom prepared. Moreover, many early town records have been lost through fire and carelessness. The ancestry of James Dearborn, Jr., a Revolutionary soldier of Effingham, cannot be traced through wills, deeds, or vital records, the sources upon which the genealogical sections of town histories are largely based. A tentative hypothesis is possible, but it cannot be proved. Simultaneously, as Dearborns moved into the Merrimack River Valley, they intermarried with Scotch-Irish families. Thus, Sarah[6] and Elizabeth Dearborn, daughters of Levi[5] of North Hampton, married McClarys of Epsom.

Typical of the Scotch-Irish, the European history of the McClarys is sketchy. It is known that they came to Ulster County, Ireland, from Dumfries, Scotland, and that Andrew McClary, the immigrant ancestor, sailed with his family to Boston in 1726. Like the Sullivans of Durham, New Hampshire, the McClarys acquired valuable property, took an active role in local politics, and assumed positions of leadership in the American Revolution. Understandably, then, this rising Scotch-Irish family would intermarry with Dearborns.

Because of linguistic, religious, and cultural differences, French Canadians and Yankees have been slower to intermarry than Yankees and Scotch-Irish. But proximity and the passage of time have brought them closer to the mainstream of New England life. For example, marriage records for the period 1901 to 1937 in the New Hampshire Department of Health reveal that 7 of 112 male Dearborns married French Canadians. These marriages took place in such scattered communities as Haverhill, Portsmouth, Laconia, and Milford, indicating that assimilation has been widespread.

Like most seventeenth-century New Hampshire settlers, the Dearborns, by the fifth generation, exhibited characteristic patterns of migration. Branches of the family could be found throughout central and southeastern New Hampshire, southern and central Maine, and central Vermont. A few early pioneers had already gone to upstate New York, Pennsylvania, and even Ohio. Typical, too (except for one individual who appeared in Taunton, Massachusetts), no pattern of Dearborn migration to southern New England emerged before 1800: the flow of people was north and west. After 1800, however, migration became more complex. Certainly many Dearborns followed the general movement west, appearing in the censuses of Illinois, Michigan, and Wisconsin. But with the growth of commerce and large cities, less predictable patterns of movement surfaced. New Hampshire Dearborns moved spontaneously in the nineteenth century to Boston, New York, Chicago, and even San Francisco—wherever opportunity called. The unpredictable nature of migration in the later nineteenth and twentieth centuries represents the greatest challenge to contemporary New Hampshire family genealogists.

Fortunately, there is a wealth of material to help the genealogist unravel the complexities of New Hampshire family history. This literature includes genealogical dictionaries, bibliographies, periodicals, census schedules, military records, newspapers, atlases and maps, biographical compendia, single-family genealogies, and town histories.

Certainly the first work to consult is the monumental *Genealogical Dictionary of Maine and New Hampshire* (Baltimore, 1972, 1976 [orig. publ. Portland, Me., 1928-1939]). Compiled by three of the best northern New England genealogists, Sybil Noyes, Charles T. Libby, and Walter G. Davis, it covers all settlers in both colonies through 1699 and frequently treats families for two or three generations. Moreover, its numerous lists, petitions, warrants, and other original documents are not found elsewhere. In this same genre is Charles H. Pope's *Pioneers of Maine and New Hampshire* (Boston, 1908). These two dictionaries offer a nearly complete survey of the first settlers of New Hampshire, and by suggesting the frequency and geographical distribution of every surname in seventeenth-century New Hampshire, these volumes can usually guide the researcher to further relevant material on later residents as well.

Several bibliographical surveys are also well worth mastering. Laird C. Towle's *New Hampshire Genealogical Research Guide* (Bowie, Md., 1973) evaluates many printed sources and original records and points out the availability of primary sources which have been microfilmed by the Genealogical Society of the Church of Jesus Christ of Latter-Day Saints (Mormon Church). This microfilmed material includes probate, land, and

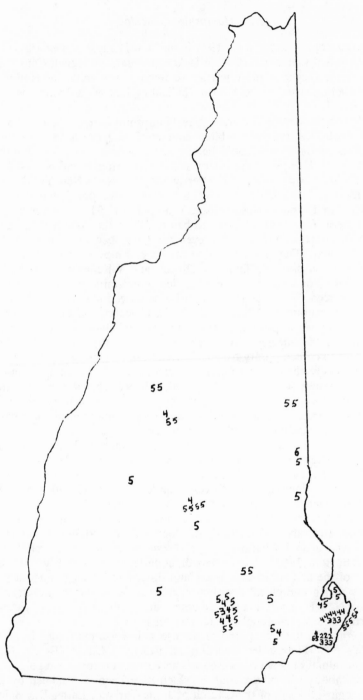

Five Generations of Dearborns in New Hampshire. The number represents the generation, as well as the approximate number of families involved.

town records (with the master file of all names at the New Hampshire State Library, Concord), and most of the manuscript holdings of the Library of the New Hampshire Historical Society. Walter G. Davis's article on Maine and New Hampshire in *Genealogical Research Methods and Sources,* edited by Milton Rubincam (Washington, D. C., 1960), discusses the racial and ethnic origins of the Granite State's present-day population and lists those town histories with genealogical sections. *Hammond's Check List of New Hampshire History,* edited by E. J. Hanrahan (Somersworth, N. H., 1971), a reprint of Otis G. Hammond's long unavailable *A Check List of New Hampshire Local History* (Concord, 1925), includes virtually every book and periodical on New Hampshire history through 1924. In this same vein are the *Author List of the New Hampshire State Library, June 1, 1902* (2 volumes; Manchester, 1904) and the *Supplement* (Manchester, 1904), as well as the section on New Hampshire in volume one of *United States Local Histories in the Library of Congress: A Bibliography* (Baltimore, 1975). Elmer M. Hunt's "Family Names in New Hampshire Town Histories," published in *Historical New Hampshire* in December 1946, is a bibliography by surname of the genealogical sections of New Hampshire town histories. It includes about three thousand families treated in the eighty-five town histories that were in the Library of the New Hampshire Historical Society in 1946. And although not a complete list of New Hampshire surnames, it suggests much of post-seventeenth-century distribution of family names throughout the state.

After consulting the genealogical dictionaries and major bibliographical guides, the genealogist would probably next want to examine the forty-volume *New Hampshire Provincial and State Papers* (Concord, 1867-1943). These contain abstracts of wills, administrations, and inventories as well as town and military records for the colonial period. The town records should be used in conjunction with *Hammond's Check List,* which names each community with references showing where it appears in the *Provincial and State Papers.* The Revolutionary War Rolls list each military company, including muster and payrolls.[1]

Quite useful as well is the state's periodical literature. *The New Hampshire Genealogical Record* (7 volumes; Dover, N. H., 1903-1910) was, during its short career, a genealogical magazine of the highest quality. Besides compiled family histories, this journal published church and vital records for several towns, including Portsmouth. The *Record* is especially

1. Subjects included in this series are: Vols. 1-7, Provincial Papers, 1623-1776; Vol. 8, State Papers during the Revolution, 1776-1783; Vols. 9, 11-13, Town Papers; Vol. 10, Provincial and State Papers, 1779-1792; Vols. 14-17, Rolls and Documents relating to Soldiers in the Revolutionary War; Vol. 18, Miscellaneous Provincial and State Papers; Vol. 19, Provincial Papers; Vols. 20-22, Early State Papers; Vol. 23, List of Documents in the Public Record Office in London relating to the Province of New Hampshire; Vols. 24-25, Town Charters; Vol. 26, The New Hampshire Grants (regarding settlement of Vermont); Vols. 27-28, Township Grants; Vol. 29, Documents relating to the Masonian Patent; Vol. 30, Miscellaneous Revolutionary Documents; Vols. 31-39, Probate Records, 1635-1771; Vol. 40, Court Records, 1640-1692.

useful for research in Strafford and Rockingham counties, as it published
a disproportionate number of essays on this area. *The Granite Monthly*
(62 volumes; Concord, 1877-1930), although strictly speaking not a
genealogical magazine, is rich in local history and biography. Both of these
journals have been subject-indexed in Donald Lines Jacobus's *Index to
Genealogical Periodicals*. Of interest also is *Historical New Hampshire,* a
magazine of state and regional history published by the New Hampshire
Historical Society since 1944. The biographical sketches in this journal
are particularly valuable to genealogists. "Family Names in New Hampshire Town Histories," the issue for December 1946, has already been
mentioned. In 1972 the Society published a consolidated index to volumes
1 to 25 (1944-1970) of *Historical New Hampshire*.

The federal censuses document both the internal migrations (as well
as the growth of individual families and surnames) and the removal of
many families to the west during the nineteenth century. The first United
States census for New Hampshire, taken in 1790, provides the names of
heads of households, counties and towns of residences, and number of
dependents, both male and female. Except for a few missing sections in
the 1800 and 1820 censuses, the series is complete through 1880. Both the
1790 and the 1800 censuses are indexed and in print. Two separate indexes exist for the 1800 census. The first, *An Index to the 1800 Federal
Census of the State of New Hampshire in Three Sections* (Danville, Ill.,
1967, 1972, 1973), is difficult to use, as it does not list the actual enumeration and indexes each of the three sections separately. John B. Threlfall's
*Heads of Families at the Second Census of the United States Taken in the
Year 1800: New Hampshire* (Chicago, 1973) lists the actual census with
an index, allowing users to avoid microfilm and to see, town-by-town, the
heads of families. It provides schedules of summaries of population by
county and town.

Probably as important as census records for locating New Hampshire
ancestors are the military records of its soldiers. They document soldiers'
actions and movements and reveal their towns of origin. Frequent disruptions in community life during war interrupted record-keeping, and
military papers such as muster rolls must supplement meager local records.
For the colonial and early national period, Chandler E. Potter's *The Military History of the State of New Hampshire, 1623-1861* (2 volumes in 1;
Baltimore, 1972 [orig. publ. Concord, 1866, and Manchester, 1868])
provides copies of many rosters and muster rolls, especially the seldom-
published records for the colonial wars, the War of 1812, and the Mexican
War. A recent reprint of this work contains indexes to both volumes. For
the Revolution, the *New Hampshire State Papers* offers the *Rolls of Documents Relating to Soldiers in the Revolutionary War* (volumes 14 to 17),
which includes muster rolls, pay rolls, and Association Test lists. The
Daughters of the American Revolution *Lineage Books* profile many New
Hampshire men who served in the American Revolution as well as some
of their descendants, indicating birth and death dates, marriages, and

places of residence. The *D.A.R. Patriot Index* (Washington, D. C., 1966) and its supplements provide the names of New Hampshire soldiers and other patriots who have been enrolled by descendants in the Daughters of the American Revolution since 1921. For the Civil War, August D. Ayling's well-indexed *Revised Register of the Soldiers and Sailors of New Hampshire in the War of Rebellion, 1861-1866* (Concord, 1895) lists all men who served in New Hampshire regiments, together with their service records.

While military records name individuals in segmented periods of time, newspapers give regular accounts of local figures. Unfortunately newspapers in New Hampshire did not exist until about 1750, and copies of these papers are not, for the most part, extant today. However, Otis G. Hammond's *Notices from the New Hampshire Gazette, 1765-1800* (Lambertville, N. J., 1970) gleans birth, marriage, and death records from one of these earliest newspapers. Most of these items concern Granite State residents, but also mentioned are prominent New Hampshire men who died out of the state. *Notices* has a name and place index.

Maps, atlases, and gazetteers may also serve the genealogist. The two major atlases are D. H. Hurd and Company's *Town and City Atlas of the State of New Hampshire* (Boston, 1892) and H. F. Walling and Charles H. Hitchcock's *Atlas of the State of New Hampshire* (New York, 1877). Hurd's treats each town on a separate plate, showing individual houses with the occupants' names and close-ups of the village centers. Larger cities, such as Portsmouth, Manchester, Nashua, and Concord, are covered by more detailed ward maps. This work also has a useful statistical section which lists the dates of settlement and incorporation of towns. Walling and Hitchcock's *Atlas* contains folio maps of each county and street maps of the larger cities, which, however, do not show individual houses. The earliest state gazetteers, Eliphalet and Phinehas Merrill's *A Gazetteer of the State of New Hampshire in Three Parts* (Exeter, 1817) and Jacob B. Moore and John Farmer's *A Gazetteer of the State of New-Hampshire* (Concord, 1823), are useful for locating extinct place names. The best gazetteer is Alonzo J. Fogg's *The Statistics and Gazetteer of New Hampshire* (Concord, 1874), which has, besides a full list of place names, statistical tables of population growth and distribution, occupation, education, wealth, and mortality (derived from the 1860 and 1870 federal census schedules). A recent gazetteer, Elmer M. Hunt's *New Hampshire Town Names and Whence They Came* (Peterborough, 1970) is arranged by region rather than by county and provides an etymology of place names. This source reveals that colonial governors Benning and John Wentworth named numerous towns after their friends and relatives.

Other frequently consulted genealogical tools are the various biographical compendia which focus on the lives of prominent local figures. Much of the information in these works—largely produced in the late nineteenth century—was supplied by the subjects themselves. The obvious appeal of these directories (or "mugbooks," as they are commonly called by genealogists) is the concentration of genealogical data not otherwise available, and if used critically for their biographical content and only as guides to descent, they are an invaluable aid in compiling a family history. The most comprehensive of these is Ezra S. Stearns's *Genealogical and Family History of the State of New Hampshire* (Chicago, 1908), a massive, four-volume compendium of the ancestry of numerous nineteenth-century New Hampshire men. It provides graphic evidence that many present-day New Hampshire families originated from outside the state, especially from Essex and Middlesex counties, Massachusetts.

Specialized directories of New Hampshire business, political, and professional figures also contain a wealth of information on the family and often trace patrilineal descents from immigrant ancestors. These studies include Hobart Pillsbury's *New Hampshire: Resources, Attractions, and Its People* (biographical volume; New York, 1929); Everett S. Stackpole's *History of New Hampshire* (volume 5; New York, 1916); *Representative Citizens of the State of New Hampshire* (Boston, 1902); George H. Moses's *New Hampshire Men* (Concord, 1893); Richard Herndon's *Men of Progress: Biographical Sketches and Portraits of Leaders in Business and Professional Life in and of the State of New Hampshire* (Boston, 1898); *Sketches of Successful New Hampshire Men* (Manchester, 1882); George F. Willey's *State Builders: An Illustrated Historical and Biographical Record of the State of New Hampshire at the Beginning of the Twentieth Century* (Manchester, 1903); Henry H. Metcalf's *One Thousand New Hampshire Notables* (Concord, 1919); and its sequel, *New Hampshire Notables* (1932). In addition, the index volume to the *Dictionary of American Biography* has a list of subjects arranged by birthplace.[2]

Other biographical directories are based on occupation rather than locality. Thus Nathan F. Carter's *The Native Ministry of New Hampshire* (Concord, 1906) is a meticulous record of all clergymen born in the state between 1658 and 1879 and is cross-indexed by surname, location, denomination, and order of age. It is especially useful for nineteenth-century clergy. For pre-Revolutionary ministers, Frederick L. Weis's *The Colonial Clergy of New England* (Lancaster, Mass., 1936) lists all clergymen who practiced within New Hampshire. Charles H. Bell's *The Bench and Bar of New Hampshire* (Cambridge, Mass., 1894) treats 871 New Hampshire lawyers and judges of the eighteenth and nineteenth centuries. Henry H. Metcalf's *New Hampshire Agriculture: Personal and Farm Sketches* (Concord, 1897) describes 125 prominent New Hampshire farmers. Granville P. Conn's *History of the New Hampshire Surgeons in the War of the Rebellion* (Concord, 1906) profiles 258 surgeons practicing in New Hampshire during the mid-nineteenth century. And Bela Chapin's *The Poets of New Hampshire* (Claremont, 1883) treats about 300 Granite State poets, including Jeremy Belknap, Mary Baker Eddy, Horace Greeley, and Daniel Webster.

2. Of the approximately 15,000 figures treated in the *Dictionary of American Biography*, 325, or about 1/46th of the total, were New Hampshire natives.

State histories are yet another source of biographical information. The earliest, Jeremy Belknap's *The History of New Hampshire* (3 volumes; Philadelphia, 1784; Boston, 1791, 1792) reproduces various original records and recounts the lives of many prominent New Hampshire men.[3] It has served as a model for later histories of New Hampshire, including John N. McClintock's *Colony, Province, State, 1623-1888. History of New Hampshire* (Boston, 1889); Hobart Pillsbury's *New Hampshire: Resources, Attractions, and Its People* (5 volumes; New York, 1927); and Everett S. Stackpole's *History of New Hampshire* (5 volumes; New York, 1916).

Probably the second most valuable source for New Hampshire family history is the published genealogy. Even though for the colonial period probably no more than 25 percent of New Hampshire families have been fully treated (and if the post-Revolutionary period is included, this figure will be substantially reduced), nonetheless, certain lines of most early New Hampshire families appear in this literature. These works, like other secondary works, vary in quality. However, the excellent scholarship of V. C. Sanborn, Agnes P. Bartlett, Henry W. Hardon, Walter G. Davis, Eugene F. Weeden, and George W. Chamberlain has much improved the standard of New Hampshire family histories. The best early compiled genealogy is John Wentworth's massive, three-volume *The Wentworth Genealogy* (Boston, 1878), which discusses the state's most powerful colonial family and its marital connections on both sides of the Atlantic. Its value is greatly increased by a detailed treatment of families linked by marriage and by the inclusion of a comprehensive index. Other carefully compiled genealogies are Elizabeth K. Folsom's *Genealogy of the Folsom Family* (2 volumes; Baltimore, 1975 [orig. publ. Rutland, Vt., 1938]); Katharine F. Richmond's *John Hayes of Dover, New Hampshire: A Book of his Family* (2 volumes; Tyngsboro, Mass., 1936); and Arthur H. Locke's *A History and Genealogy of Captain John Locke* (Rye, 1973 [orig. publ. Concord, 1916]). Such genealogies trace all male lines and provide vital biographical detail, such as birth and death dates, places of residence, occupations, and records of achievement. Frequently they document the lines of married daughters and their descendants for one or two generations. And they critically evaluate the available genealogical material, both published and unpublished. They also offer a comprehensive name index.

But certainly the most important source for New Hampshire genealogy is the town histories. Ranging from brief biographical descriptions of notable citizens to complete genealogical surveys of communities, the family history sections of these works rely upon gravestone inscriptions, Bible records, and family traditions. Since vital records are missing for many New Hampshire communities, the authors frequently produced sketches resembling biographical compendia. Consequently the users of

3. Belknap's work has appeared in various editions, most recently in a facsimile reprint of 1970.

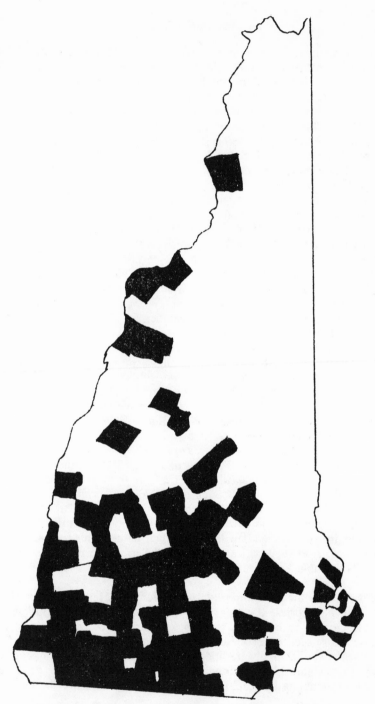

Geographical Distribution of New Hampshire Town Histories.

these histories should be aware of lines of descent without documentation. (It should be noted that a few town histories, such as John C. Chase's *History of Chester, including Auburn* [Derry, 1926], have printed abstracts of vital records.) The completeness of the genealogical sections vary from history to history, some failing to provide obvious genealogical data such as dates of birth and death and names of spouses. This is especially true of early town histories, such as Charles H. Bell's *History of the Town of Exeter* (Exeter, 1888); J. P. Jewett's *History of Barnstead* (Lowell, Mass., 1872); Daniel Lancaster's *The History of Gilmanton* (Gilmanton, 1845); Elliott C. Cogswell's *History of Nottingham, Deerfield, and Northwood* (Somersworth, 1972 [orig. publ. Manchester, 1878]). On the whole, however, New Hampshire town histories provide some information on nearly every original inhabitant of a community. Works such as Ezra S. Stearns's *History of Plymouth* (Plymouth, 1906) treat even the ancestry of the original settlers (in some cases back to the European immigrant) and trace the migrations for several generations of those who left the town.

Those one hundred towns having histories with genealogical sections are concentrated in southern New Hampshire. The histories of the four original communities—Dover, Hampton, Exeter, and Portsmouth—vary considerably in the thoroughness of their genealogies. Dover's and Hampton's identify most of the first inhabitants, while Exeter's focuses mainly on its most important families. The historians of Portsmouth, however, have not even attempted a genealogical treatment of its families—due perhaps to the size and mobility of this port's population.[4] And of towns along the Merrimack River, Bedford is perhaps the easiest community in New Hampshire in which to trace one's ancestry. Its three histories (the latest published in 1971) each offer first-rate genealogical registers.

But the settlements of southwestern New Hampshire, particularly Hillsborough, Cheshire, and Sullivan counties, have by far the greatest number of histories of interest to the genealogist. Particularly well done is the Surry-Walpole-Langdon-Acworth-Charlestown area. The adjoining towns of Rockingham (Bellows Falls) and Springfield, Vermont, also have good genealogical treatments. The result is a kind of genealogical oasis along this stretch of the upper Connecticut River.

Moving north, town histories for the communities in Carroll and Coös counties are almost nonexistent, forcing one to rely on county histories, censuses, and other kinds of genealogical information. The sparsity of population in this area discouraged a historical and genealogical conscious-

4. Some of Portsmouth's vital and church records have been published in the *Register* and the *New Hampshire Genealogical Record*. There is also a manuscript by Agnes P. Bartlett at the New Hampshire Historical Society which treats about 240 early Portsmouth families.

Langdon B. Parsons's *History of the Town of Rye* (Concord, 1905), a community that was formerly a part of Portsmouth, covers its genealogical history, although it leaves out numerous facts, such as maiden names of wives, kinship connections, and vital dates. Unfortunately the other communities in Rockingham and Strafford counties have few town histories with significant genealogical content.

ness. Although the first excursion by a European into the White Mountains occurred in 1642, when Darby Field climbed Mount Washington, the French and Indians, as well as a rigorous climate, impeded permanent settlement until the late eighteenth century.

Finally, anyone seeking an ancestor in an area without a genealogical town history should search for information in a neighboring community. Many families lived miles from their town centers and conducted their business in nearby villages. Since individuals moved and married across town lines, the histories of surrounding communities will frequently contain pertinent genealogical information.[5]

Whether using single family genealogies, town studies, or biographical compendia, the New Hampshire genealogist has access to a variety of printed sources. Predictably, the volume of material does not compare with that for the southern New England states, which have a more orderly and better documented history. Still, a massive amount of data exists, and a knowledge of this material will probably allow the researcher to unravel a significant portion of his own New Hampshire ancestry. If not, such knowledge should show him at least what primary research will be required.

5. Among the best town histories are M. T. Runnels's *History of Sanbornton* (Boston, 1881); Albert Annett and Alice E. E. Lehtinen's *History of Jaffrey* (Jaffrey, 1934); Josiah L. Seward's *A History of the Town of Sullivan, 1777-1917* (Keene, 1921); Frank B. Kingsbury's *History of the Town of Surry* (Surry, 1925); James R. Jackson's *History of Littleton* (3 vols.; Cambridge, Mass., 1905); William H. Child's *History of the Town of Cornish* (Concord, 1911); John R. Eastman's *History of the Town of Andover, 1751-1906* (Concord, 1910); George W. Browne's *The History of Hillsborough, 1735-1921* (2 vols.; Manchester, 1921-1922); William Little's *The History of Weare, 1735-1883* (Lowell, Mass., 1888); John F. Norton's *The History of Fitzwilliam, from 1752 to 1887* (New York, 1881); Benjamin Read's *The History of Swanzey, from 1734 to 1890* (Salem, Mass., 1892); and George A. Morison's *History of Peterborough* (2 vols.; Rindge, 1954).

For the town of Enfield, George M. Roberts's "The Vital and Cemetery Records of the Town of Enfield, New Hampshire" (1957 manuscript, New England Historic Genealogical Society, Boston) in effect replaces the town's vital records, destroyed by fire in the 1850s. In collecting his data, Roberts examined cemeteries, neighboring town records, tax lists, census schedules, probate, land, and Bible records, newspaper items, family genealogies, and local histories. The result is a well-documented list of most of Enfield's families.

David C. Dearborn is a reference librarian at the New England Historic Genealogical Society, Boston, and he is compiling a Dearborn family genealogy.

BIBLIOGRAPHY OF PUBLISHED SINGLE-FAMILY GENEALOGIES

Frederick C. Pierce, *Batchelder-Batcheller Genealogy*. Chicago, 1898.

Bernie Bean, *The Life and Family of John Bean of Exeter and his cousins*. Seattle, Washington, 1970.

Catherine B. Fahnestock, *Three Hundred Fifty Years of Bickfords in New Hampshire*. Cottonport, La., 1971.

Herbert I. Brackett, *Brackett Genealogy*. Washington, D. C., 1907.

E. E. Cates and M. Ray Sanborn, *The Cate-Cates Family of New England*. Frederick, Md., 1904.

Doane B. Colcord, *Colcord Genealogy*. Coudersport, Pa., 1908.

Henry W. Hardon, *Cole Family of Stark, New Hampshire*. New York, N. Y., 1932.

Louis S. Cox, *The Cox Family of Holderness, with partial genealogies of the Cox, Randall, Nutter, and Pickering families*. Brattleboro, Vt., 1939.

Cecil H. C. Howard, *Genealogy of the Cutts Family in America*. Albany, 1892.

Robert P. Dow, *The Book of Dow*. Rutland, Vt., 1929.

Alice S. Thompson, *The Drake Family of New Hampshire*. Concord, 1962.

Elizabeth K. Folsom, *Genealogy of the Folsom Family*. Two volumes, Baltimore, 1975 (orig. publ. Rutland, Vt., 1938).

Arthur Gilman, *The Gilman Family traced in the line of the Hon. John Gilman of Exeter, N. H.* Albany, N. Y., 1869.

George W. Chamberlain and Lydia G. Story, *The Descendants of Charles Glidden of Portsmouth and Exeter, New Hampshire*. Boston, Mass., 1974 (orig. publ. Boston, 1925).

William H. Gove, *The Gove Book*. Salem, Mass., 1922.

Andrew M. and Thomas V. Haines, *Deacon Samuel Haines of Westbury, Wiltshire, England, and his descendants in America*. North Hampton, 1902.

Katharine F. Richmond, *John Hayes of Dover, New Hampshire: A Book of His Family*. Two volumes, Tyngsboro, Mass., 1936.

Henry W. Hardon, *Huckins Family*. N.p., 1916.

Emily L. Noyes, *Leavitt, Descendants of John, the Immigrant, Through His Son, Moses*. Tilton, N. H., 1941.

————, *Leavitt, Descendants of John Leavitt, the Immigrant, Through His Son, Israel and Lydia Jackson*. Tilton, 1948.

————, Leavitt, Descendants of John Leavitt, the Immigrant, Through His Son, Josiah, and Margaret Johnson. Tilton, 1949.

————, Leavitt, Descendants of Thomas Leavitt, the Immigrant 1616-1696, and Isabella Bland. Tilton, 1953.

————, Leavitt, Descendants of John Leavitt the Immigrant through his son, Samuel and Mary Robinson. Tilton, 1956.

Arthur H. Locke, A History and Genealogy of Captain John Locke. Rye, N. H., 1973 (orig. publ. Concord, N. H., 1916).

Sylvia F. Getchell, Marden Family Genealogy. Newmarket, N. H., 1974.

Nathan W. Marston, The Marston Genealogy in Two Parts. South Lubec, Me., 1888.

Henry W. and Claribel Moulton, Moulton Annals. Chicago, Ill., 1906.

Emma E. Brigham, Neal Family. Springfield, Mass., 1938.

James C. Odiorne, Genealogy of the Odiorne Family. Boston, Mass., 1875.

David W. Odiorne, Genealogy of the Odiorne Family in America. Ann Arbor, Mich., 1967.

Henry W. Hardon, Peverly Family. Boston, Mass., 1927.

Jacob Chapman, A Genealogy of the Philbrick and Philbrook Families. Exeter, N. H., 1886.

[Robert H. Eddy], Genealogical Data respecting John Pickering of Portsmouth, N. H., and his Descendants. Boston, Mass., 1884.

————, Supplement to Genealogical Data respecting John Pickering of Portsmouth, N. H., and his Descendants. Boston, Mass., 1884.

Charles N. Sinnett, Richard Pinkham of Old Dover, New Hampshire, and his descendants. Concord, N. H., 1908.

William Prescott, The Prescott Memorial. Boston, Mass., 1870.

John R. Rollins, Records of families of the name Rawlins or Rollins in the United States. Lawrence, Mass., 1874.

V. C. Sanborn, Genealogy of the family of Samborne or Sanborn in England and America, 1194-1898. N.p., 1899.

Harriette F. Farwell, Shaw Records. Bethel, Me., 1904.

Gerald F. Shepard and Donald L. Jacobus, Shepard Families of New England. (Volume III) New Haven, Conn., 1973.

Azariah B. Sias, The Sias Family in America. Orlando, Fla., 1952.

————, Supplement to the Sias Family in America, 1677 to 1952. Orlando, Fla., 1957.

————, Volume III, Supplement 2 to the Sias Family in America, 1677 to 1952. Orlando, Fla., 1967.

Harold M. Taylor, *Anthony Taylor of Hampton, New Hampshire, and some of his descendants, 1635-1935*. Rutland, Vt., 1935.

————, *Anthony Taylor of Hampton, New Hampshire: Additions*. Rutland, Vt., 1935.

Joseph Dow, *Tuck Genealogy*. Boston, Mass., 1877.

George F. Tuttle, *The Descendants of William and Elizabeth Tuttle*. Rutland, Vt., 1883 (For descendants of John Tuttle of Dover, N. H.).

Josephine C. Frost, *Underhill Genealogy*. (Volume IV) N.p., 1932 (For descendants of Sampson Underhill of Chester, N. H.).

George E. Hodgdon, *Reminiscences and Genealogical Record of the Vaughan Family of New Hampshire*. Rochester, N. Y., 1918.

Jacob Chapman, *Leonard Weeks of Greenland, N. H., and Descendants, 1639-1888*. Albany, N. Y., 1889.

John Wentworth, *The Wentworth Genealogy, English and American*. Three volumes, Boston, Mass., 1878.

VERMONT GENEALOGY: A STUDY IN MIGRATION

Edward W. Hanson

Vermont is in many respects an historical anomaly and poses difficult problems for genealogists. Its history reflects the merging of tradition and transiency, as both the settled ways of the older New England colonies and the instability of the frontier were factors in its development. Although this mountainous region is the second largest state in New England, its population has never exceeded five hundred thousand. Permanent settlement began only in 1760, thus coinciding with signs of overpopulation in southern New England. Soon Massachusetts, New Hampshire, and New York were vying for the area, and their claims were further complicated when Vermonters declared themselves an independent republic in 1777. The territory retained this status until its admission to the Union in 1791.

In 1791, most of Vermont's population was Anglo-Saxon, having origins in Massachusetts or Connecticut.[1] The state was young demographically: in 1800, 51 percent of its inhabitants were under sixteen years of age, 67 percent were under twenty-six, and less than 10 percent were older than forty-five.[2] This population was geographically unstable, partly as the result of severe economic and climatic problems that affected the state. The Embargo of 1807, the floods of 1811, the War of 1812, and the Cold Season of 1816, coming one after the other, discouraged many young families and precipitated a large migration to the newer settlements in the West, particularly to the Great Lakes basin area. Many Vermonters continued to move westward so that an inordinate number of people living today at a great distance from New England can trace their ancestral roots to Vermont. The Green Mountain State has probably produced a higher per capita rate of eminent Americans than any other state.[3]

Vermont's pre-1760 history is largely one of exploration and military encampments rather than settlement. Samuel de Champlain visited the lakeshore area as early as 1609, but not until 1666 was the first French fortification, Fort Ste. Anne, built at Isle la Motte. Although this fort was destroyed when the regiment was withdrawn in 1670, others were later constructed around the shores of Lake Champlain. Farther south, the

1. In 1791, 95 percent of the population had English surnames, and 3 percent Scottish names. Lewis D. Stillwell, *Migration from Vermont* (Montpelier, 1948), 78.

2. *Ibid.*, 66, 86.

3. In 1935, *Who's Who in America* listed Vermont as having a higher percentage of natives listed in that publication than other states as compared with the population in 1930. See also Dorman B. E. Kent, *Vermonters* (Montpelier, 1937).

acting governor of Massachusetts, William Dummer, ordered a fort built above Northfield, Massachusetts, because of the growing Indian threat. Fort Dummer was erected on the present-day site of Brattleboro and was put under the command of Timothy Dwight, whose son Timothy, Jr., is reputed to have been the first white child born in Vermont. During the 1730s, Forts Sartwell and Bridgman were built on the site of Vernon, Vermont, and in 1736 the Massachusetts Bay Colony authorized the establishment of six numbered towns along the Connecticut River. Two of these lay to the west of the river, Fort Number 1 (now Westminster) and Fort Number 2 (now Rockingham), but none of these semi-military settlements ever prospered. The French also granted several large seigneuries between 1733 and 1737, but the actual number of settlers remained small.

During the French and Indian Wars, many New England soldiers trooped through the Green Mountains area and undoubtedly liked what they saw, for once the northern border with Canada was secured and the Indian threat laid to rest, they returned in large numbers, generating a complex series of territorial claims and counterclaims. Benning Wentworth, the governor of New Hampshire, asked New York authorities how they defined their eastern border. Receiving no immediate answer, Wentworth, on 3 January 1749, wrote a grant for the town of Bennington on the west bank of the Connecticut River. Though New York then proceeded to claim the Connecticut as its boundary, Massachusetts and the Colonial Office in London claimed that New York's frontier was a line twenty miles east of the Hudson and required New Hampshire to garrison and supply Fort Dummer. Wentworth soon adopted the latter view of sovereignty, and between January 1749 and June 1764 wrote grants for 129 towns and 6 military establishments in the Green Mountains area.[4] Settlers moved in, set up town governments, and cleared the land. However, in 1764 a change in government in England brought a new rule which declared New York's eastern "boundary to be the western banks of the River Connecticut." This phraseology quickly created two camps: while New Hampshire interpreted it as a boundary change beginning in 1764, New York claimed that it established its previous ownership and thus invalidated the New Hampshire grant. Immediately New York began writing its own grants to the same territory. In all, 107 town-size grants were written—24 going to families or individuals as in the New York patroon system, 20 confirming New Hampshire grants, and 5 creating

4. Hiram A. Huse, *The New Hampshire grants being transcripts of the Charters of townships and minor grants of land made by the Provincial government of New Hampshire, within the present boundaries of the State of Vermont, from 1749 to 1764. With an appendix containing the petitions to King George the Third, in 1766, by the Proprietors and settlers under the New Hampshire Grants, and lists of the subscribers; also historical and bibliographical notes relative to the towns in Vermont* (Concord, N. H., 1895). New Hampshire State Papers, vol. 26, contains notes on references to state and county histories gazetteers, Hemenway, state papers, etc.

original towns, while the remaining 58 existed mainly on paper.[5] A conflict was inevitable between the numerous holders of the New Hampshire grants and the few newcomers with New York authority. New York made itself particularly resented by insisting upon the operation of its county governments in the area, and the residents of the New Hampshire grants took matters into their own hands. A convention met in Dorset in 1776 "to take suitable measures to declare the New Hampshire Grants a free and independent district." On 17 January 1777, the continuing convention voted at Windsor to adopt a declaration of independence and the name of New Connecticut. The new name proved somewhat of an embarrassment when it was discovered that a district in Pennsylvania was already using it. Therefore, on 30 June 1777, the name Vermont was established for the new republic, in honor of its Green Mountains range.

As Vermont was not admitted to the Union until 1791, the records covering the independent period are of particular importance. *The Records of the Council of Safety and Governor and Council of the State of Vermont, 1775-1836* (edited by Eliakim Persons Walton. 8 vols. [Montpelier, 1873-1880]) contains important lists of local committee appointments and a number of biographical sketches from the period. The continuing story of new towns can be studied in *Charters granted by the State of Vermont: being Transcripts of Early Charters of Townships and Smaller Tracts of Land Granted by the State of Vermont; with an appendix containing . . . Historical and Bibliographical Notes Relative to Vermont Towns, Continued and Brought up to Date,* edited by Franklin H. Dewart ([Montpelier, 1922]. Vermont State Papers, vol. 2). Also on the statewide level is the series of General Petitions to the legislature published as part of the State Papers of Vermont (*General Petitions, 1778-1787, 1788-1792,* vols. 9 and 10, edited by Edward A. Hoyt [Montpelier, 1952-1955]. *General Petitions, 1793-1796, 1797-1799,* vols. 11 and 12, edited by Allen Soule. [Montpelier, 1958-1962]).

By the time of the Revolution approximately twenty thousand residents were in the area. They came largely from the state of Connecticut, traveling along the Connecticut River, and some forty town names in Vermont bear testimony to this Connecticut heritage. Those who settled east of the mountains originated mainly in Tolland and Windham counties and took up land on both sides of the Connecticut River. The western half of Vermont was generally settled from Litchfield County. Non-Connecticut emigrants were often closely allied—Rhode Islanders from border towns mixing with New Yorkers from Dutchess County (which was settled by Nutmeggers) and with Massachusetts natives from the central and eastern sections of their state. During the prosperous years, from the end

5. Mary Greene Nye, ed., *New York Land Patents 1688-1786 covering land now included in the state of Vermont (not including military patents)* (Montpelier, 1947). Vermont State Papers, vol. 7. Primary information on the grants territory, including lists of inhabitants for some of the towns involved, can be found in *The Documentary History of the State of New York* (Albany, N. Y., 1851), 4:529-1034.

of the Revolution to the Embargo of 1807, Vermont's population increased rapidly: to 30,000 in 1781; 85,000 in 1791; 154,000 in 1800; and 217,000 in 1810. Connecticut continued as the major source of immigrants, although New Hampshire began to play a greater role, and eastern as well as western Massachusetts also provided many more new settlers.

Many Vermonters did not remain long in their original settlements, but rather migrated north within the state. The town of Stowe, for example, was founded by Woodstockers. Some of this restless population spilled over into Lower Canada (today the Province of Québec), while many more moved into northern New York State. Numerous towns in Essex, Clinton, Franklin, St. Lawrence and Jefferson counties were first settled by Vermonters. It is often difficult to determine which families settled on which side of the Vermont-New York border and hence into which jurisdiction they fall. Accounts of these border families can be found in Theresa Hall Bristol's "Notes on some early Vermont-New York settlers" (*New York Genealogical and Biographical Record,* 44 [1913]: 285-289); "More notes on the ancestry of early Vermont-New York settlers" (*ibid.,* 44 [1913]: 334-338); and Merrett Clark Barden's *Vermont, Once no man's land* (Rutland, Vt., 1928). The latter source contains genealogical sketches of families along the New York border as well as scattered census and burial records. Regrettably, it is poorly indexed and gives no reference notes.

The best study of the peregrinations to and from the Green Mountain State is Lewis D. Stillwell's *Migration from Vermont* (Montpelier, 1948; first published as vol. 5, Growth of Vermont series). Both scholarly and very readable, Stillwell's work puts the migrations into historical context while also answering the oft-asked question: "Why did they leave?"[6] The first great out-migration of Vermonters consisted of Loyalists who left during the Revolution. Approximately five thousand left at this time for the "Eastern Townships" in Lower Canada. Others went to the northern shores of Lake Ontario and to the upper St. Lawrence. The size of the exodus as well as the relative wealth of the departing Tories enabled Vermont to meet the expenses of the Revolution for three years through the sale of Loyalist estates.[7]

Aside from this migration away from the state, Vermont continued until 1808 to receive settlers, mainly from Connecticut, Massachusetts and New Hampshire. Beginning in 1808, however, a series of political events and natural disasters nearly ended movement into Vermont. First the Embargo of 1807 severely crippled Vermont's economy. Second, the state was devastated by a series of disasters: the floods of 1811, the disruptions of the War of 1812, and the spotted fever epidemic of 1813, which claimed more than six thousand victims. Finally the "Cold Season" of 1816, which

6. Another, more general treatment is Stewart H. Holbrook's *The Yankee Exodus: An account of migration from New England* (New York, 1950).

7. Mary Greene Nye, ed., *Sequestration, confiscation and sale of estates; Loyalist material, 1777-1822* (Montpelier, 1941). State Papers of Vermont, vol. 5.

continued throughout the summer, destroyed a large percentage of the state's crops. With good inexpensive land still available in the West, there was little reason to remain in Vermont. By 1808, all but three of the thirty counties in central and western New York contained Vermont settlers. In 1812 and 1813, the opening of the St. Lawrence Turnpike made migration into New York even easier, and in 1816-1817 movement out of Vermont peaked, leaving the northernmost section of the state and the region west of the mountains severely depopulated. With most of the cheap land in northern New York taken by 1820, Vermonters continued westward, going primarily to Ohio. Three-quarters of these settlers were under thirty years of age and came from the four older counties in southern Vermont.

Migration during this period was seldom a once-in-a-lifetime event; rather it was ongoing. Such was the case of Nathan Wheeler, born in 1781 in Shrewsbury, Massachusetts. Residing in Shrewsbury until his marriage to Susanna Heard of Rutland, Massachusetts, in 1805, he and his wife in that year moved to Montague, Massachusetts. In 1807 they moved again to Bridport, Vermont, making the journey on foot with only one horse to carry their possessions. After several years in Bridport they went to nearby Shoreham, Vermont, and later to Middlebury, where Susanna died in 1832. All eight of the Wheeler children subsequently moved to Wisconsin and northern Illinois in 1836, and about 1840 Nathan himself migrated to the West, settling in Kewaskum, Washington County, Wisconsin, where he lived until his death in 1860.

In the 1820s, fully half of Vermont's emigrants crossed into New York State, clustering around established Vermont settlements. Others went to the eastern townships of Lower Canada, the northern counties of Pennsylvania, the Western Reserve, central Ohio, or to Jersey and Greene counties in Illinois. The movement of people westward continued during the 1830s and reached an all-time peak in 1836. More Vermonters emigrated in the 1840s and 1850s with New York, Ohio, southern Michigan, northern Illinois and southeastern Wisconsin remaining the prime areas of settlement. During this period also a few Vermont families went to Indiana, where they founded the towns of Montpelier and Orland, and others located themselves in Iowa, Missouri and throughout the South, where they served mainly as teachers. The first sizeable influx of Irish and French-Canadians into Vermont also occurred in these decades, a trend which partially offset the Yankee exodus from the state. The 1850 census shows 232,086 Vermonters living in their home state, while 52,599 resided in New York; 17,646 in Massachusetts; 14,320 in Ohio; 11,381 in Illinois; 11,266 in New Hampshire; 11,113 in Michigan; and 10,157 in Wisconsin. During this period 15,377 immigrants from Ireland and 14,470 from British America settled in Vermont.[8]

The times continued to draw away the native population. Because of

8. Eleanor Myers, comp., *A Migration study of the thirty-two states and four organized territories comprising the United States in 1850; based upon the Federal census of 1850* (Syracuse, N. Y., 1977), 30.

64   *Vermont Genealogy: A Study in Migration*

the Industrial Revolution, in 1846 alone, 1,200 Vermont girls went to work in the mills of Lowell, Massachusetts. By 1850, 1,100 Vermonters had arrived in California with the gold rush, not counting those who did not make it to the coast, but by the boom's end nearly one-third had returned home or to the Midwest. At the 1860 census, 42 percent of those people born in Vermont were living outside their native state, and this figure does not include a sizeable number who had gone to Canada.

Despite the great numbers of people leaving Vermont, their loyalty to the state was steadfast. Thus in 1878, almost three hundred members of the Sons of Vermont were active in Chicago; similar organizations were formed in other cities and towns.

The county and civic history of Vermont is as complex as the rest of its past. When New York claimed the territory west of the Connecticut River, it set up Cumberland County in 1768 to gain some control over the area. In 1770, the county of Gloucester was founded to the north of Cumberland, and in 1772 Charlotte County was created with Skenesboro (a New York patent town near Fair Haven) as its county seat. When Vermont's first General Assembly convened at Windsor in 1778, it divided the state into Bennington County to the west of the Green Mountains and Unity County to the east. The name Unity County proved unpopular and was changed four days later to Cumberland County. It was later subdivided into Windsor, Orange and Windham counties in 1781, at which time the name Cumberland disappeared (see Table I). A number of histories, directories and gazetteers were published in the 1880s covering most counties.

TABLE I
VERMONT COUNTIES

County	Established	Created from	Shire Town
Bennington	17 March 1778	Original County	Manchester
Windsor	22 February 1781	Cumberland County	Woodstock
Orange	"	"	Chelsea
Windham	"	"	Newfane
Rutland	"	Bennington County	Rutland
Addison	18 October 1785	Rutland County	Middlebury
Chittenden	22 October 1787	Addison County	Burlington
Caledonia	5 November 1792	Orange County	St. Johnsbury
Essex	"	"	Guildhall
Orleans	"	"	Newport
Franklin	"	Chittenden County	St. Albans
Grand Isle	9 November 1802	Franklin County	North Hero
Washington[1]	1 November 1810	Addison, Caledonia, Chittenden and Orange Counties	Montpelier
Lamoille	26 October 1835	Chittenden, Washington, Orleans and Franklin Counties	Hyde Park

1. Called Jefferson County until 8 November 1814.

At the local level, Vermont's civic subdivisions—cities, towns, gores, grants—number more than two hundred fifty and range in size from Vergennes City with 1,200 acres to Chittenden with 46,315. Each municipality is easily located on the standard map of the state produced by the National Survey, but the modern map reveals only a fraction of the local historical background necessary for genealogical research. Such familiar names as Bellows Falls and Ascutney do not appear on these maps as they are simply post-office names or village subdivisions that have never attained independent town status. Bellows Falls Village, for example, is part of Rockingham township which also contains the villages of Saxtons River, Cambridgeport, Bartonsville and Brockway. Some full municipalities are considerably more obscure, such as Warren Gore in Essex County, which never had any permanent inhabitants until one individual was listed in the 1970 census. The town of Somerset in Windham County had three hundred people living there in 1850; by 1916 it had grown so small that the post office was closed, and in 1937 the Vermont legislature disenfranchised Somerset, declaring it an official wilderness. The post office named Waite (Dummerston town) existed for only two years, from 1895 to 1897, and for only one person. It was established solely to accommodate Rudyard Kipling during his sojourn in the North; the office was closed following the novelist's return to England but remains among the numerous place-names associated with the state. A good guide through this confusion of localities is Esther Munroe Swift's *Vermont Place-Names: Footprints of History* (Brattleboro, 1977), which briefly and clearly describes the names and history associated with each county's subdivisions, including obsolete place-names. The book is well indexed and also contains valuable appendices on the New Hampshire, New York and Vermont grants.

For statewide local history, the foremost source is Abby M. Hemenway's *Vermont Historical Gazetteer* (5 vols., 1867-1891. Published at Burlington and other places). Miss Hemenway had originally intended to cover the entire state in a three-volume series of sketches on local history, but five volumes had been completed at the time of her death in 1890. She was already planning a sixth volume which was never published. As a result, the entire state is not covered. Some years later the state financed a comprehensive index which now stands as volume six of the series (*Index,* compiled under George W. Wing. [Rutland, Vt., 1923]). Miss Hemenway solicited original papers from local historians throughout the state and reprinted several other histories. Because much of her material was obtained by interviewing the early settlers themselves, the *Gazetteer* is not entirely accurate. Still, it provides information that would not otherwise be available, and, in general, the work is highly reliable. A number of towns count the *Gazetteer* as their only published history, and the researcher will find it contains biographical and genealogical information as well as details from original town records long since destroyed by fire or neglect.

For primary research on the local level, the work of the Vermont Historical Records Survey is invaluable. This organization, which was ad-

ministered by the Works Progress Administration, sent workers throughout the state in the 1930s to inventory all local records held by Vermont
towns. Although the project was still incomplete at its dissolution in 1943,
its last director, Henry H. Eddy, published a *Final Report and Inventory
of the Vermont Historical Records Survey* (Rutland, 1942), which describes the work accomplished and lists unpublished work sheets which
have since been transferred to the Public Records Division, State Administration Building, Montpelier. The following towns have had their records
inventory published in mimeo form:

Addison County	Bridport
Chittenden County	Bolton, Charlotte, Essex
Franklin County	Fairfax
Grand Isle County	all towns
Lamoille County	all towns
Orleans County	Albany, Coventry, Derby
Rutland County	Benson, Castleton, Clarendon, Danby, Hubbardton, Mt. Tabor, Shrewsbury, Tinmouth, Wallingford
Windham County	Brookline, Grafton, Jamaica
Windsor County	Cavendish, Plymouth

Vital records were not required to be kept by town clerks in Vermont
until 1840. Before that date only scattered records are available. In 1919,
a state law required all town clerks to make copies of the vital records in
their custody and return them on cards to the Office of the Secretary of
State. Today these records, along with incomplete cemetery records
through 1870, are filed in the Vermont Vital Records Collection in Montpelier's Pavilion Building, in several large time sequences. (Those of
1760-1870 and 1871-1908 are of the most interest to genealogists.) Like
similar projects in New Hampshire, many sets of vital records had already
been destroyed over the years and were no longer available by 1919. In
addition there have been fires since 1919 which have left the Montpelier
cards the only existent record. The completeness of the transcription
project depended upon the individual town clerk. Thus failure to locate
a record in Montpelier should not preclude a search in the locality. The
card file has been completely open to the public, but it is currently in the
process of being microfilmed by the state's Public Records Division, after
which the original cards will no longer be used. During an earlier microfilming project undertaken by the Genealogical Society of Utah in the
1950s, major errors were made in the 1760-1870 period. They are being
completely refilmed. The microfilm of the 1871-1908 period has only
minor errors which are also being corrected. When this project is completed, use of the vital records will remain unlimited only in regard to
the microfilm copies. All new vital records will be forwarded from the
Health Department to the Vital Records Division and will accumulate
for periods of five years before being microfilmed.

The microfilm copy is held by the Public Records Division, which also houses the individual town records (vital records, town meetings, cemetery and land records, deeds, proprietors' deeds), probate records and some church records. The individual town records are of particular importance in that they include the registry of deeds, so necessary in tracing a family's residency. The general cutoff date for these records is 1850, and that portion has been filmed by the Church of Latter-Day Saints. The Public Records Division has continued from that date, and a number of towns are now covered to the present day. A few towns have also had part of their vital records published, mainly in regional periodicals. Of these, the publication *Vermont Marriages* (Burlington, 1903) began to print the state's marriage records but only produced one unindexed volume containing records for Montpelier, Burlington and Berlin.[9] Among the other published vital records are births, marriages and deaths for Barton, Rockingham and Worcester; births for Fairlee, West Fairlee and Bradford (1768-1820); marriages in Pownal (through 1850); and death records for Jamaica (1832-1837) and Ludlow (1790-1901).[10]

Because of the scarcity of early vital records in Vermont, Bible records take on an added importance for this period. The Daughters of the American Revolution have played an important role in preserving these personal records in their typescript collections, which also include cemetery and church records, Revolutionary service records, wills and vital statistics. To date the DAR has compiled forty-five volumes in this set, and copies are located both in the Vermont Historical Society and the DAR Memorial Hall in Washington.

While some church records are available through the DAR, others have been microfilmed and are available in the Public Records Division, Montpelier. They include Congregational records for Bakersfield (1839-1908; 1913-1953), Burlington (1805-1967), Franklin (1822-1887), Peacham (1794-1956), Tinmouth (1804-1866), and West Glover (1807-1970); and Quaker records for the Danby meeting (formed 1795 from Easton, New York, meeting), Easton, New York, meeting (formed 1778 from Nine Partners), Ferrisburg meeting (formed 1801 from Danby), Granville, New York, meeting (formed 1795 from Easton, New York), Peru, New York, meeting (formed 1799 from Danby), and Starksboro, Vermont, meeting (formed 1813 from Ferrisburgh). Additional church records have been published in journals and include Fairfield Congregational records (*The American Genealogist,* 12 [1935]: 86-100); Benning-

9. Montpelier: Town Clerk's records, 1791-1852; Congregational records, through 1852; Christ Church Episcopal records, through 1852. Burlington: Town Clerk's records, 1789-1833; Unitarian records, 1822-1831. Berlin: Town Clerk's records, 1790-1876.

10. *DAR Historical Magazine,* 66:529; 67:244; *Rockingham Vital Records* (Boston, 1908); *A record of births, marriages and deaths, in Worcester, Vermont, from Oct., 1813 to June 18, 1858,* comp. by Simon C. Abbott (Montpelier, 1858); *Register,* 104 (1950): 21-26, 114-122, 262-269; *Berkshire Geneological (sic) notes,* no. 3; *Register,* 121 (1967): 91-94; Rufus S. Warner, comp., *Records of Deaths in the Town of Ludlow, from 1790 to 1901 inclusive* (Ludlow, 1902).

ton First Congregational admissions (*Early Settlers of New York State,* 2 [1936]: 147-148, 163-164, 179-180; 3 [1936]: 3-4, 19-20, 35-36, 51-52, 67-69); Poultney Baptist church records (*ibid.,* 7 [1941]: 101-102, 117-118, 133-134, 149-150, 165-166; 8 [1941]: 197-198, 213-214); records of the First Church of Rockingham (*Register,* 54 [1900]: 197-202, 289-300, 435-439; 55 [1901]: 58-65, 425-431; 56 [1902]: 248-260, 384-396); and New Haven Congregational records (*ibid.,* 123 [1969]: 45-53, 90-101, 222-227, 302-313).

Cemetery records for Vermont are available through a number of sources. The Vital Records Division at Montpelier has incomplete gravestone registration through 1870; the records by town are housed at the Public Records Division; and the DAR collection is maintained at the Vermont Historical Society. Also at the Vermont Historical Society is the Works Progress Administration's Veterans' Grave Registration file. This collection is alphabetically arranged in fourteen drawers and covers veterans from the Revolution through World War I with headstone information and other scattered details. Several towns have had their cemetery records published,[11] and others have appeared from time to time in journals.[12] In *Branches and Twigs,* the Vermont Society of Genealogists has printed some cemetery records, and it has encouraged cooperation with the Vermont Old Cemeteries Association in regard to cemetery data.

Estate probate in Vermont is handled on the district level rather than by county as in most New England states. Vermont's fourteen counties have been divided into twenty probate districts. (The larger counties have been divided into two probate districts.) Table II shows each of these districts, the location of the probate office, its area of jurisdiction, and the beginning date for its records. However, it must be remembered that records kept before the subdivision of the various counties remain with the parent county. The records themselves contain probated wills, estate administrations, guardianships, name changes, trusteeships, commitments, adoptions, some early birth records, and establishments and corrections of birth and marriage certificates. A few probate records have been published.[13]

Census reports for Vermont begin with the 1790 federal enumeration,

11. Mrs. Gordon W. Churchill, comp., *Cemeteries of Cavendish, Vermont* (Springfield, Vt., 1976); Ellen C. Hill, Bob and Lois Webster, *The Cemeteries of East Montpelier, Vermont, 1795-1971* (mimeo.); James M. Cutler, *The Village Cemetery, Essex Junction, Vermont* (typescript, 1970); Levi Henry Elwell, comp., *The Gravestone Inscriptions of Rupert, Bennington County, Vermont* (Amherst, Mass., 1913); and Fannie (Smith) Spurling, comp., *Evergreen Cemetery, Pittsford, Vermont. St. Alphonsus Cemetery, Pittsford, Vermont. Bump Cemetery, North Chittenden, Vermont* (Delavan, Wisc., 1946).

12. Bennington inscriptions (*Early Settlers of New York State,* 4 [1937]: 57-58, 74-75, 90-92, 106-108, 123-124, 138-139); Ferrisburgh inscriptions (*Register,* 95 [1941]: 202-203); Hubbardton inscriptions (*ibid.,* 122 [1968]: 108-113, 216-220, 286-290); Bakersfield (*ibid.,* 74 [1920]: 150-155, 167-178, 310-319; 75 [1921]: 12-28, 98-104); East Bakersfield inscriptions (*ibid.,* 73 [1919]: 186-188); and North Sheldon inscriptions (*ibid.,* 63 [1909]: 300).

13. "Abstracts from volume I, of the probate records of Orleans County, Vt.," *Register,* 65 (1911): 374-379; 66 (1912): 19-25.

which actually took place in 1791 when Vermont was admitted to the Union. Gilbert Doane, the noted genealogist and a native Vermonter, points out that because of this one-year discrepancy, one of his Soule ancestors was listed as a resident of Pawling, New York, in the 1790 census and also as living in Fairfield, Vermont, thus narrowing the time of his migration to within a year.[14] The 1790 census for Vermont was among those published by the Government Printing Office,[15] and the 1800 census was also published early by the Vermont Historical Society.[16] The 1810 censuses for Bennington and Rutland counties have been published but should be checked carefully for error.[17] This margin for error must also be allowed in the indexes for the 1810-1850 censuses published by Accelerated Index Service, Inc., a useful but not particularly reliable set. As with all federal censuses, those for 1790 through 1880 are readily available on microfilm, and that for 1900 has recently been released for public use.

Military records for the state of Vermont have been published for each major war since the Revolution. The *Rolls of the Soldiers in the Revolutionary War, 1775 to 1783* (compiled and edited by John E. Goodrich [Rutland, 1904]) contains mostly company lists and is indexed. Additional lists include "Soldiers of the Revolution Buried in Vermont" (compiled by Walter H. Crockett, *Proceedings of the Vermont Historical Society* [1903-1904], 93-106, 114-165, 189-203), which covers about six thousand names including many who served from other states and migrated after the war. Crockett analyzed the 1818 and 1832 pensioner enumerations and found that of the 3,196 soldiers named, 172 served from Vermont, 1,409 from Massachusetts, 701 from Connecticut, 444 from New Hampshire, 104 from Rhode Island, 75 from New York, and 291 others from various additional states or who served in the navy. The *Roster of Soldiers in the War of 1812-14* (prepared and published under the direction of Herbert T. Johnson, Adjutant General [St. Albans, 1933]) lists each soldier in alphabetical order giving his service record along with excellent additional information including pension numbers and widow certificate references, each of which aids searches through the National Archives records. A *List of Pensioners of the War of 1812,* edited by Byron N. Clark (Burlington, 1904; reprint ed. Baltimore, 1969), gives abstracts from some fifty claims for the War of 1812 pensions including marital data if applicable. It contains lists of 189 volunteers for the Plattsburgh Expedition, and the payrolls of a number of regiments stationed at

14. Gilbert H. Doane, "A stumbling block in Midwestern genealogy," *Indiana Magazine of History,* 34 (1938): 27.

15. *Heads of families at the first census of the United States taken in the year 1790: Vermont* (Washington, 1907).

16. *Heads of families at the second census of the United States taken in the year 1800: Vermont* (Montpelier, 1938; reprint ed. Baltimore, 1972).

17. Elisha Ellsworth Brownell, *Bennington County, Vermont, Genealogical Gleanings* (Philadelphia, 1941); *Rutland County, Vermont, Genealogical Gleanings* (Philadelphia, 1942). See also Jean Rumsey, "Some corrections in Brownell's readings of the 1810 census of Rutland County, Vermont," *The American Genealogist,* 45 (1969): 94-95.

TABLE II
VERMONT PROBATE DISTRICTS

District	District Town	Jurisdiction	Records from[1][2]
Addison	Middlebury	(all of Addison County until 1824 and again after 1962); Bridport, Cornwall, Goshen, Granville, Hancock, Leicester, Middlebury, Orwell, Ripton, Salisbury, Shoreham, Weybridge, Whiting	1800[2]
Bennington	Bennington	Bennington, Glastenbury, Pownal, Readsboro, Searsburg, Shaftsbury, Stamford, Woodford	1778
Bradford	Wells River	Bradford, Corinth, Fairlee, Newbury, Strafford, Thetford, Topsham, Vershire, West Fairlee	1781
Caledonia	St. Johnsbury	all of Caledonia County	1796
Chittenden	Burlington	all of Chittenden County	1795
Essex	Guildhall	all of Essex County	1791
Fair Haven	Fair Haven	Benson, Castleton, Fair Haven, Hubbardton, Pawlet, Poultney, Sudbury, Wells, West Haven	1797[3]
Franklin[4]	St. Albans	all of Franklin County	1796
Grand Isle[5]	North Hero	all of Grand Isle County	1796
Hartford	Woodstock	Barnard, Bethel, Bridgewater, Hartford, Hartland, Norwich, Pomfret, Rochester, Royalton, Sharon, Stockbridge, Woodstock	1783
Lamoille	Hyde Park	all of Lamoille County	1837
Manchester	Manchester	Arlington, Dorset, Landgrove, Manchester, Peru, Rupert, Sandgate, Sunderland, Winhall	1779
Marlboro	Brattleboro	Brattleboro, Dover, Dummerston, Guilford, Halifax, Marlboro, Newfane, Somerset, Stratton, Vernon, Wardsboro, Whitingham, Wilmington	1781

New Haven[6]	Vergennes	Addison, Bristol, Ferrisburg, Lincoln, Monkton, New Haven, Panton, Starksboro, Waltham, Vergennes	1824- ca. 1962
Orleans	Newport	all of Orleans County	1796
Randolph	Chelsea	Braintree, Brookfield, Chelsea, Orange, Randolph, Tunbridge, Washington, Williamstown	1792
Rutland	Rutland	Brandon, Chittenden, Clarendon, Danby, Ira, Mendon, Middletown Springs, Mount Holly, Mount Tabor, Pittsford, Proctor, Rutland, Rutland City, Sherburn, Shrewsbury, Tinmouth, Wallingford, West Rutland	1784
Washington	Montpelier	all of Washington County	1811
Westminster	Bellows Falls	Athens, Brookline, Grafton, Jamaica, Londonderry, Putney, Rockingham, Townshend, Westminster, Windham	1781
Windsor	Ludlow	Andover, Baltimore, Cavendish, Chester, Ludlow, Plymouth, Reading, Weathersfield, Weston, West Windsor, Windsor	1787[7]

1. Beginning dates are from the Public Records Division, Montpelier, and differ slightly from those given in "Vermont Probate Districts," by Grace W. W. Reed and Winifred Lovering Holman (*The American Genealogist*, 27 [1951]: 65-69).

2. All records and files were burned 25 Feb. 1852; salvaged material (mostly in poor condition) has been microfilmed by date rather than volume; not indexed.

3. Of twenty-two volumes (1797-1851), volumes 1, 2, 7, 9, 12-18 were missing when microfilmed; the first two volumes and part of volume 3, as well as the files from that period, were destroyed by fire.

4. Originally known as Georgia District.

5. At one time Grand Isle District included Alburgh District; Act of 23 Oct. 1790, to divide Chittenden County into three districts: Chittenden, Franklin and Alburgh; by Act of 2 Nov. 1805, Grand Isle District was formed.

6. Records for the New Haven District were filed separately from 1824 to about 1962, and since that date have been combined with Addison District probate, q.v.

7. Files burned 4 July 1850; books saved.

Burlington during the war. The lists are alphabetical, but there is no general index.

For the Civil War, there is a narrative history, *Vermont in the Civil War; A History of the Part Taken by the Vermont Soldiers and Sailors in the War for the Union 1861-1865,* by G. G. Benedict (2 vols. [Burlington, 1886]), as well as the *Revised Roster of Vermont Volunteers and Lists of Vermonters who Served in the Army and Navy of the United States During the War of the Rebellion, 1861-66,* compiled under the direction of Theodore S. Peck, Adjutant General (Montpelier, 1892). *Vermont in the Spanish-American War* (Montpelier, 1929) has also been published by the Adjutant General's Office. Although not of great use to genealogists because of their recentness, compendiums for both World Wars I and II are also available: *Roster of Vermont Men and Women in the Military and Naval Service of the United States and Allies in the World War 1917-1919* (prepared and published under the direction of Herbert T. Johnson, the Adjutant General [Montpelier, 1927]); and *Roster of Vermonters in Uniformed Service of the United States During the Second World War, 1941-1945* (assembled under the direction of Reginald M. Cram, the Adjutant General et al., 2 vols. [Montpelier, 1972]).

Researchers with a Vermont ancestry would find worthwhile a personal visit to Montpelier. Vermont's records, particularly those of the pre-1850 period, but also including many through the present day, are highly concentrated in a one-block area of the capital. The Pavilion Building, formerly the city's grand hotel, houses the Vermont Historical Society with its museum and extensive library of Vermontiana. Also in the same building is the important vital records collection and the state papers office, which has many state records indexed through 1890 (see *Vermont History News,* 29 [1978]: 67). Next door, in the Supreme Court Building, the State Library holds census records and microfilm of newspapers and town reports. Quite nearby, the Public Records Office houses the important microfilm collection of early town records, probate, cemetery, land and vital records.

Genealogists interested in Vermont basically divide into two groups—those with Vermont families who have resided in the state for more than a century and those whose ancestors were part of the westward movement. The former group is fortunate in that their ancestors may be found in the centralized records at Montpelier, the larger collection of vital records for the later period, and the growing number of town histories which include genealogical sections. Moreover, the "mug books" and collected genealogies that began appearing in the 1880s, while not very dependable as a class, remain an important source of clues on Vermont families. Among the more important of these works are the *Genealogical and Family History of the State of Vermont* (compiled under the supervision of Hiram Carleton. 2 vols. [New York, 1903]) and *The Vermont of Today; With its Historic Background, Attractions and People,* by Arthur F. Stone (4 vols., of which vols. 3 and 4 are biographical [New York, 1929]). A more detailed checklist for Vermontiana will be found in the forthcoming Vermont volume of the New England bibliography project.

For the second group of genealogists, particularly those concentrating on the Mid- and Far West, the period between 1760 and 1820 is the most significant. Unfortunately, this period is generally considered the most difficult for all New England genealogy, and Vermont's position on the frontier creates additional research problems. Sometimes published censuses and census indices for this period will narrow the search so that the problem can be attacked on a local level. For the period before 1790, the printed collection of state papers will often turn up leads as to the specific location of individuals. Because of the strong influence of the Connecticut River on the settlement of the Green Mountains region, many genealogists searching for pre-Vermont ancestry will find useful the index to pre-1850 Connecticut vital records at the Connecticut State Library, also known as the "Barbour Collection." The major Connecticut Valley genealogies like Donald Lines Jacobus's *Hale-House Genealogy* (Hartford, Conn., 1952) will provide additional clues. Genealogical sources in the other New England states will uncover the origins of a majority of the remaining settlers as few immigrants ever traveled directly to Vermont from overseas.

Generalizations are difficult to form concerning this state, which has proved troublesome to so many genealogists. An important fact for researchers to remember is that families often moved to and from Vermont as part of a larger settlement—a collection of extended family, former neighbors or friends—although lone migrations of single families happened frequently as well. Any successful genealogical search in Vermont will depend upon a sound understanding of the complex historical forces that have operated in this state.

GENEALOGIES IN SOME VERMONT TOWN HISTORIES

BARNARD

William Monroe Newton, *History of Barnard with family genealogies, 1761-1927.* Montpelier, 1928. 2 vols.

BARNET

Frederic Palmer Wells, *History of Barnet from the outbreak of the French and Indian War to present time; with genealogical records of many families.* Burlington, Vt., 1923.

BRADFORD

Rev. Silas McKeen, *A history of Bradford, containing some account of the places of its first settlement in 1765, and principal improvements made, and events which have occurred down to 1874 ... With various genealogical records, and biographical sketches of families. . . .* Montpelier, 1875.

BRAINTREE

H. Royce Bass, *The history of Braintree, including a memorial of families that have resided in town.* Rutland, Vt., 1883.

FAIR HAVEN

Andrew N. Adams, *A history of the town of Fair Haven.* Fair Haven, Vt., 1870. Pt. 3, biographical and family notices.

GUILDHALL

Everett Chamberlin Benton, *A history of Guildhall, containing some account of the place of its first settlement in 1764 ... With various genealogical records, and biographical sketches of families and individuals....* Waverley, Mass., 1886.

GUILFORD

Official history of Guilford, 1678-1961. With genealogies and biographical sketches. Guilford, Vt., 1961.

HARTFORD

William Howard Tucker, *History of Hartford, 1761-1889. The first town on the New Hampshire Grants chartered after the close of the French war.* Burlington, Vt., 1889. Genealogies, pp. 406-476.

LONDONDERRY

Addison E. Cudworth, *The history with genealogical sketches of Londonderry.* Montpelier, 1936.

MARLBORO

Rev. Ephraim H. Newton, *The history of Marlborough, Windham County, Vermont.* Montpelier, 1930.

MARSHFIELD

Ozias C. Pitkin and Fred E. Pitkin, *History of Marshfield.* North Andover, Mass., 1941. "Family histories of settlers and residents of Marshfield," pp. 95-308.

NEWBURY

Frederick Palmer Wells, *History of Newbury from the discovery of Coos County to present time. With genealogical records of many families.* St. Johnsbury, Vt., 1902.

NEWFANE

Centennial proceedings and other historical facts and incidents relating to Newfane, the county seat of Windham County, Vermont. Brattleboro, 1877. Family genealogies, pp. 155-176.

PAWLET

Hiel Hollister, *Pawlet for one hundred years.* Albany, 1867. Family sketches, pp. 155-267.

PEACHAM

Jennie Chamberlain Watts and Elsie A. Choate, *People of Peacham.* Montpelier, 1965.

PITTSFORD

History of the town of Pittsford, with biographical sketches and family records. Rutland, Vt., 1872.

PLYMOUTH

Blanche Brown Bryant and Gertrude Elaine Baker, *Genealogical records of the founders and early settlers of Plymouth, Vermont.* DeLand, Fla., 1967.

POMFRET

Henry Hobart Vail, *Pomfret, Vermont.* Boston, 1930. 2 vols. Vol. 2, genealogical records.

POULTNEY

A history of the town of Poultney from its settlement to the year 1875, with family and biographical sketches and incidents. Poultney, 1875.

ROCKINGHAM

Lyman Simpson Hayes, *History of the town of Rockingham, including the villages of Bellows Falls, Saxtons River, Rockingham, Cambridgeport and Bartonsville, 1753-1907, with family genealogies.* Bellows Falls, Vt., 1907.

Frances Stockwell Lovell and Leverett C. Lovell, *History of the town of Rockingham, including the villages of Bellows Falls, Saxtons River, Rockingham, Cambridgeport and Bartonsville, 1907-1957, with family genealogies.* Bellows Falls, 1958.

ROYALTON

Evelyn M. Wood Lovejoy, *History of Royalton with family generalogies, 1769-1911.* Burlington, Vt., 1911.

SPRINGFIELD

C. Horace Hubbard and Justus Dartt. *History of the town of Springfield, with a genealogical record, 1752-1895.* Boston, 1895.

WAITSFIELD

Matt Bushnell Jones, *History of the town of Waitsfield, 1782-1908, with family genealogies.* Boston, 1909.

WELLS

Grace Esther Pember Wood, *A history of the town of Wells from its settlement with family and biographical sketches and incidents.* Wells, Vt., 1955.

WILMINGTON

Barbara H. Look, *Wilmington Reunions, 1890-1970 and family genealogies* by Margaret C. Greene. Bennington, Vt., 1970.

Edward W. Hanson resides in Boston. He is currently compiling a complete genealogy of the descendants of Luke[1] Heard of Ipswich, Massachusetts.

GENEALOGICAL RESEARCH IN MASSACHUSETTS: A SURVEY AND BIBLIOGRAPHICAL GUIDE

*Edward W. Hanson and Homer Vincent Rutherford**

Few areas in this country or the British Isles equal the Commonwealth of Massachusetts for the quantity and quality of its historical records. Interest in preserving written accounts of families and localities began in the first settlements of the Bay Colony. A legacy from the English forebears of the earliest immigrants, this long tradition of recordkeeping has proved to be of immense benefit to the family researcher, who today has access to primary sources that run without interruption from the third or fourth decade of the seventeenth century to the present. During the past hundred years several major collections of the state's primary records have appeared in print. Complementing its unparalleled holdings of local materials is the Commonwealth's splendid collection of town and family histories. It is estimated that 70 to 80 percent of the state's pre-nineteenth-century population can be located in these printed sources, as compared with sometimes only 30 percent for other states. Much basic research may be accomplished here easily — Essex County, in fact, is said to be the best documented locality in the country. But for many more complex problems, especially regarding families in the western part of the state, genealogists must learn to use a wide variety of materials. This article is designed to familiarize researchers with the full range of available data. Both primary and secondary materials will be considered, but special emphasis will be placed upon secondary sources that lead to primary records.[1] Because the history of Massachusetts is too lengthy and complex to repeat here even in summary sketch, only events directly relating to the records being discussed will be noted. Readers seeking a better continuum are referred to Benjamin W. Labaree, *Colonial Massachusetts: A History* (Millwood, N.Y., 1979); the classic of Governor Thomas Hutchinson, *History of the Colony and Province of Massachusetts Bay,* edited by Lawrence Shaw Mayo (Cambridge, Mass., 1936); and for a study through the present century, Albert Bushnell Hart, ed., *Commonwealth History of Massachusetts: Colony, Province and State,* 5 vols. (N.Y., 1927-1930).

The earliest genealogical sources in the Commonwealth were not Massachusetts records *per se* but were produced by the settlement of Plymouth in 1620. Plymouth Colony existed as a distinct entity until 1691, and the chronicling of *Mayflower* families is a special case relative

*The authors would like to thank the following people for their assistance in preparing this article: Ralph J. Crandall and David C. Dearborn of the Society; Denis J. Lesieur of the Berkshire Athenaeum; and especially Gary Boyd Roberts of Boston, for both initial outlines listing many sources and extensive comments on early drafts of this essay.
1. For a detailed introduction to record types and research considerations, see Val D. Greenwood, *The Researcher's Guide to American Genealogy* (Baltimore, 1973).

to local history. Because of the unique nature of the *Mayflower* voyage more interest has been shown in establishing descent from its passengers than from those of any other ship; and a vast amount of research has been undertaken on Plymouth Colony descendants. The vital records, court orders, judicial acts, laws and deeds (for the period 1620-1651) of Plymouth Colony all appear in Nathaniel B. Shurtleff and David Pulsifer, eds., *Records of the Colony of New Plymouth in New England,* 12 vols. (Boston, 1855-1861). The vital data from volume 8 are reprinted in Nathaniel B. Shurtleff, ed., *Records of Plymouth Colony: Births, Deaths, Marriages, and Burials, and other Records, 1633-1689,* (Baltimore, 1976). A multivolume set of the Plymouth Colony probate records is being prepared for publication by Anne Yentsch of Brown University. The index to this set, which cross indexes women by maiden and married surnames, contains more than 10,000 entries.

Secondary sources on the Pilgrims are numerous. The best, superseding all previous work, is the new series sponsored by the General Society of Mayflower Descendants, *Mayflower Families Through Five Generations: Descendants of the Pilgrims Who Landed at Plymouth Massachusetts, December, 1620,* 3 vols. to date (Plymouth, Mass., 1975-1980). Five generations, or in effect the colonial progeny, of seven passengers have been treated so far.[2] Later volumes will cover the remaining sixteen Pilgrims who left descendants. Until the completion of this series, however, researchers should use Hubert K. Shaw, *Families of the Pilgrims* (Boston, 1956), which covers the known children and grandchildren of *Mayflower* passengers, and the Algernon A. Aspinwall manuscript collection at NEHGS. This last includes an early tracing of the progeny for six generations of each of these sixteen remaining Pilgrims except Peter Brown; carefully compiled in the first decades of this century, it is undocumented, however, and contains many gaps. Additionally, lists of husbands of daughters, granddaughters, great-granddaughters, and great-great-granddaughters for each of the twenty-three Pilgrims except Edward Doty and Degory Priest have appeared in the *Mayflower Quarterly* over the past fifteen years, and those published through 1977 are themselves listed in the November issue of that year (43 [1977]: 115). Among individual families note the Bradford, Brewster, Fuller, and Howland genealogies among major single family works listed in the Appendix and *Register* articles on the early Alden, Allerton, Hopkins, Standish, and Warren descendants (beginning in volumes 51, 54, 102, 87 and 55 respectively).

For *Mayflower* families in Plymouth itself, or on Cape Cod, see William T. Davis, *Genealogical Register of Plymouth Families* (Baltimore, 1975), originally Part II of *Ancient Landmarks of Plymouth* (Boston, 1883), and the manuscript collection of Lydia Brownson, Grace Held, and Doris Norton, "Genealogical Notes of Cape Cod Families," at

2. Vol. 1: Francis Eaton, Samuel Fuller, and William White; vol. 2: James Chilton, Richard More, and Thomas Rogers; vol. 3: George Soule.

the Sturgis Library in Barnstable and widely available elsewhere on microfilm. For abstracts of primary sources, especially vital and probate records, concerning early *Mayflower* families see *The Mayflower Descendant: A Quarterly Magazine of Pilgrim Genealogy and History,* 34 vols. (Boston, 1899-1936), published by the Massachusetts Society of Mayflower Descendants and indexed in *The Mayflower Descendant: Index of Persons,* 2 vols. (Boston, 1959). Many of this journal's best articles were reprinted in George E. Bowman, *The Mayflower Reader: A Selection of Articles From The Mayflower Descendant* (Baltimore, 1978). A successor journal, *The Mayflower Quarterly,* has been published by the General Society since 1935, and a recent periodical of *Mayflower* interest, *The Plymouth Colony Genealogical Helper,* continued briefly as *The Plymouth Colony Genealogist,* was published by the Augustan Society. Finally, all accepted lineages of members of the General Society through the 1950s were outlined — without dates or documentation, however, and with some errors — as an alphabetized list of ancestors, in Lewis E. Neff, *The Mayflower Index,* 3 vols. in 2 (Boston, 1960). An updating and revision of this last is currently underway.

Strictly speaking, Massachusetts records begin with the Great Migration to New England which started about 1630 and ended in 1642 with the calling of Parliament and beginning of civil war. Although a limited number of emigrants came afterwards, nearly all people who lived in Massachusetts at the time of the American Revolution could trace their families to the 30,000 or fewer people who crossed the Atlantic during that twelve-year period (unless their background was in Plymouth Colony). Despite the homogeneity of the Great Migration, some ethnic differentiation occurred quite soon in the Bay Colony. As early as 1690 a few Irish merchants and sea captains were living in the coastal towns. A number of French Huguenots came after the revocation of the Edict of Nantes in 1685 and formed communities in Boston and Oxford. Some Channel Islanders settled in the Salem area.[3] In 1650 and 1651, several hundred Scots who had been taken prisoner during the border wars were sent as laborers to the Saugus and Braintree ironworks. Although these operations failed, the Scots remained and were absorbed into the population. It should be noted that nearly all these latecomers were Protestants who were readily assimilated into the colony.

Comprehensive attempts at listing and compiling genealogies of the early immigrants have appeared in the form of directories and published passenger lists. The two standard directories are John Farmer, *A Genealogical Register of the First Settlers of New England* (Lancaster, Mass., 1829; reprint ed., Baltimore, 1976) and James Savage, *A Genealogical Dictionary of the First Settlers of New England, Showing*

3. See David T. Koning, "A New Look at the Essex 'French': Ethnic Frictions and Community Tensions in Seventeenth-Century Essex County, Massachusetts," *Essex Institute Historical Collections,* 110 (1974): 167-180.

Three Generations of Those Who Came before May 1692, 4 vols. (Boston, 1860-1862; reprint ed., Baltimore, 1965). The most complete lists of immigrants appear in Charles Edward Banks, *The Planters of the Commonwealth: A Study of the Emigrants and Emigration in Colonial Times; To Which are Added Lists of Passengers, the Ships which Brought Them, Their English Homes* . . . (Boston, 1930; reprint ed., Baltimore, 1972) and *The Winthrop Fleet of 1630* (Boston, 1930; reprint ed., Baltimore, 1980). Caution must be used in consulting Banks's other list of immigrants, *A Topographical Dictionary of 2885 English Emigrants to New England, 1620-1650,* ed. Elijah Ellsworth Brownell (Philadelphia, 1937; reprint ed., Baltimore, 1957). Although Banks himself was a most careful genealogist, when his work was edited posthumously many qualifying phrases were dropped from his notes, and uncertainties were published as facts. Most of the original Banks manuscripts are now in the Library of Congress.[4] Besides Banks, Charles Henry Pope, *The Pioneers of Massachusetts, a Descriptive List, Drawn from the Records of the Colonies, Towns and Churches and from Other Contemporaneous Documents* (Boston, 1900; reprint ed., Baltimore, 1977) should be consulted for the earliest immigrants as well.

Original passenger lists that have survived can be located through two bibliographies: P. William Filby with Mary K. Meyer, ed., *Passenger and Immigration Lists Index: First Edition,* 3 vols. (Detroit, 1981) and Harold Lancour, *A Bibliography of Ship Passenger Lists, 1538-1825* (New York, 1963). Two major compilations of actual lists have also been published recently: Carl Boyer, ed., *Ship Passenger Lists: National and New England (1600-1852)* (Newhall, Calif., 1977), which contains all Massachusetts lists mentioned in Lancour; and Michael Tepper, ed., *Passengers to America: A Consolidation of Ship Passenger Lists from the New England Historical and Genealogical Register* (Baltimore, 1977).

Although transatlantic research is not the primary purpose of this article, two studies establish the identity of numerous families who were part of the Great Migration to the Bay Colony. These are Henry F. Waters, *Genealogical Gleanings in England,* 2 vols. (Boston, 1885-1889; reprint ed., Baltimore, 1969) and C. E. Banks, *The English Ancestry and Homes of the Pilgrim Fathers* (New York, 1929; reprint ed., Baltimore, 1962).

Compared to the seventeenth and the nineteenth centuries, few immigration records survive for the eighteenth century. Only a scattering of passenger lists have been published. Among these are William H. Whitmore, comp., *Port Arrivals and Immigrants to the City of Boston, 1715-1716 and 1762-1769* (Boston, 1900; reprint ed., Baltimore, 1973) and Mrs. Georgie A. Hill, "Passenger Arrivals at Salem and Beverly, Mass., 1798-1800," *Register,* 106 (1952): 203-209. The above-mentioned bibliographies and compilations also include immigrants from this period.

4. Additional Banks manuscripts are located in the Society (his notes on Martha's Vineyard families), the Bangor Public Library, and the Old Gaol Museum in York, Maine.

For the nineteenth century, immigration resources become stronger and reflect the increasing heterogeneity of the population. By mid-century, the 1850 census shows how diverse and diffuse the Massachusetts population had become. It lists 695,236 natives living in their home state, and 199,592 more resided in other states. In addition, 164,448 foreign-born individuals, including 115,917 Irish, had settled in the Commonwealth.[5] To locate the foreign-born, note that the National Archives has customs passenger lists for a number of entry ports.[6] Also, naturalization records have been maintained by a series of Massachusetts courts. In the State Archives are abstracts of naturalization returns from 1885 to 1931 for state and municipal courts; these abstracts will allow the researcher to locate the proper court if name and date of naturalization are known. From 1790 to 1906 naturalization records were kept by state and municipal courts; the actual documents remain in the court of origin, although duplicates are in the National Archives along with accompanying Soundex name indexes. The papers of individuals who were naturalized through United States district and circuit courts between 1790 and 1906 are located in the regional branch of the National Archives in Waltham, Massachusetts, again with accompanying name indexes. Duplicates of naturalization records for all courts after 26 September 1906 can be found at the Immigration and Naturalization Service in Washington.

The earliest Massachusetts towns have been the subject of much academic study during the past two decades. Besides illustrating the usefulness of genealogy to history, and vice versa, these studies reinforce the notion that all Massachusetts towns spread from the seacoast to the Connecticut Valley to the Berkshire Mountains.[7] Eventually all towns abutted, and today there is no unincorporated land in the Commonwealth. Larger and older communities often split into smaller units as economic and political conditions changed. In fact, two-thirds of all

5. For a complete breakdown, see Eleanor Myers, *A Migration Study of the Thirty-Two States and Four Organized Territories Comprising the United States in 1850 Based Upon the Federal Census of 1850* (Syracuse, N.Y., 1977).
6. Barnstable, 1820-1826; Boston and Charlestown, 1820-1874, 1883-1899, with immigration passenger lists, 1 August 1891-December 1943; Dighton, 1820-1836; Edgartown, 1820-1870; Fall River, 1837-1865; Gloucester, 1820, 1832-1839, 1867-1870, with immigration passenger lists, October 1906-June 1923, 1 February 1930-December 1943; Hingham, 1852; Marblehead, 1820-1852; Nantucket, 1820-1862; New Bedford, 1823-1899, with immigration passenger lists, 1 July 1902-July 1942; Newburyport, 1821-1839; Plymouth, 1821-1843; Salem and Beverly, 1865-1866. The Boston Public Library has microfilm copies of these lists. The State Archives has original passenger lists for the Port of Boston, 1848-1891 with a WPA-produced index. The index can also be found on microfilm at the Boston Public Library.
7. See Philip J. Greven, *Four Generations: Population, Land, and Family in Colonial Andover, Massachusetts* (Ithaca, N.Y., 1970); Michael Zuckerman, *Peaceable Kingdoms: New England Towns in the Eighteenth Century* (N.Y., 1970); John Demos, *A Little Commonwealth: Family Life in Plymouth Colony* (N.Y., 1970); Darrett B. Rutman, *Winthrop's Boston: A Portrait of a Puritan Town, 1630-1649* (Chapel Hill, N.C., 1965); Edward M. Cook, *The Fathers of the Towns: Leadership and Community Structure in Eighteenth-Century New England* (Baltimore, 1976); and Kenneth A. Lockridge, *A New England Town: The First Hundred Years* (N.Y., 1970).

towns incorporated after 1700 were subdivisions of earlier communities. An excellent guide through all these municipal complexities is a booklet published by the Secretary of the Commonwealth, *Historical Data Relating to Counties, Cities and Towns in Massachusetts* (Boston, 1948, et passim). Although gazetteers, such as Elias Nason, *A Gazetteer of the State of Massachusetts* (Boston, 1874; revised and enlarged edition compiled by George J. Varney, Boston, 1890), are helpful, the state still lacks a good directory of all place names within incorporated towns; but *Historical Data* includes a section on "extinct places," which lists name changes, annexations, and a few very unusual developments. For example, four central Massachusetts towns, Greenwich, Enfield, Prescott, and Dana, were disestablished in 1938 when their territory was flooded to create the new Quabbin Reservoir as a state water supply. Small parcels of land not affected by the flooding were annexed to neighboring towns. The records of these four extinct towns are now in the office of the Metropolitan District Commission at the dam in Belchertown.

In Massachusetts, the most direct contact between individuals and government was local. Most local records remain in offices of town clerks, although some have passed into private hands. During the 1930s the Historical Records Survey of the Works Progress Administration began a massive inventory of town and city archives across the state. Unfortunately, the project terminated before more than a handful of inventories were created.[8] Many of the records themselves have been published in journals or separately. Excellent examples of this genre are the series of town meeting records for Plymouth and Lynn.[9] The WPA also transcribed the town records of several communities, such as Reading and Scituate. These are generally available only at local libraries.

Because of the large number of published sources on local history for Massachusetts, only a few representative titles will be mentioned here. For a more complete bibliography, see John D. Haskell, ed., *Massachusetts: A Bibliography of Its History* (Boston, 1976), which is excellent for local histories but contains few genealogical citations. Family sources, including journal articles and some manuscripts, are listed in Charles A. Flagg, *A Guide to Massachusetts Local History* (Salem, Mass., 1907). See also the George Fingold Library, Boston, *General Index Of and Articles On, Massachusetts People and Places, to be Found in Certain Massachusetts-Imprint Periodicals* (Boston, 1964).

Among the several types of local sources, the most useful are vital records.[10] Although extremely dated, the premier guide to these records

---

8. The existing ones are Ashfield, Athol, Auburn, Avon, Ayer, Barre, Bellingham, Berlin, Bernardston, Boston (partial), Brookline, Buckland, Chicopee, Holbrook, and Maynard.
9. *Records of the Town of Plymouth, 1636-1783*, 3 vols. (Plymouth, Mass., 1889-1903); and *Records of Ye Towne Meetings of Lynn* (Lynn, Mass., 1949-1971), covering 1691-1783.
10. Boston was first established as a town in 1630 but not incorporated as a city until 23 February 1822, when it became the first city in the state. For simplicity, all municipalities will be referred to as towns.

is still Carroll D. Wright, *Report on the Custody and Condition of the Public Records of Parishes, Towns, and Counties* (Boston, 1885). This excellent volume carefully details which records were then extant and describes their location and condition.[11] Another useful volume, Richard LeBaron Bowen, *Massachusetts Records: A Handbook for Genealogists, Historians, Lawyers and Other Researchers* (Rehoboth, Mass., 1957), gives background on the various counties with lists of towns and dates of incorporation.

In 1902, a Massachusetts law went into effect to promote the publication of town vital records. It provided that the state would purchase the first five hundred copies of all printed volumes for free distribution to libraries, public offices, and historical societies across the Commonwealth, and for certain libraries out of state. This incentive prompted three major organizations — the Society, the Essex Institute, and the Systematic History Fund of Worcester — as well as several smaller institutions, to publish vital records of 149 towns between 1902 and 1918. A few volumes had already been printed at the expense of private individuals, societies, or towns. These earlier works generally do not follow the "official" format of separating vital records into births, marriages, and deaths, and then alphabetizing the lists; instead, they reproduce the chronological sequence in the originals and include a separate index. This latter format, although more cumbersome to use, retains data as first recorded and actually proves to be more valuable to historians and genealogists. Unfortunately, the Commonwealth repealed the Vital Records Act in 1918 as a war economy, and, although the legislature voted a similar act in 1920, the program never recovered its earlier strength.[12] The published volumes thus generated are not limited to civil records but usually include church, cemetery, Bible, and other private sources. Vital records have been published as monographs for most of the towns in eastern Massachusetts, while some for Cape Cod communities appear mainly in *The Mayflower Descendant*. Births, deaths, and marriages for much of western Massachusetts and the Connecticut Valley remain in manuscript form and are available only in town clerks' offices. Table II attempts to list all available vital records, including several volumes published in the last decade. It is limited, however, to civil records and does not include separately printed church registers or private sources.[13] Also, this list applies only to towns incorporated before 1841. The records of towns incorporated later will be found with those of the parent community.

11. A helpfully annotated copy of this work is in the Society's Library.
12. See "The Publication of Vital Records in Massachusetts Towns," *Register,* 73 (1919): 52-62; and Florence Conant Howes, "Vital Records," *Register,* 103 (1949): 202-207.
13. This list is based in part upon Kenneth Richard Brown, "A List of the Massachusetts Published Vital Records," *National Genealogical Society Quarterly,* 45 (1957): 137-143; Winifred Lovering Holman, "Unpublished Records of Massachusetts Cities and Towns Incorporated Ante 1850," *ibid.,* 199-202; and Norman E. Wright, *Genealogy in America* (Salt Lake City, 1968), 1:75-85.

Through the late eighteenth century, the courts of general sessions kept by town for each county lists of marriages, and occasionally births and deaths. Some of these have been published, and generally they are also included in the printed vital records series.[14] Existing vital records are listed in Wright's *Report on the Custody and Condition of the Public Records,* pages 333-363.[15] For unrecorded seventeenth-century marriages, the best source is Clarence Almon Torrey's *New England Marriages Prior to 1700,* published in a microfilm edition of seven reels by the Society in 1979; it indexes pre-1960 secondary source material in its library and includes probably 99 percent of these early unions. See Gary Boyd Roberts, "New Sources for Seventeenth-Century New England and the Pioneer Population of 1750 to 1850: A Review Essay," *Register,* 135 (1981): 57-68.

In 1841, a new state law required all town and city clerks to submit annual copies of all vital records to the Secretary of the Commonwealth. For the first few years, this statute met with varying success. Early volumes, often somewhat sketchy, include letters of complaint from the clerks and reports submitted on a variety of paper sizes. However, by 1850 standard forms were employed, and the quality of the returns greatly improved. The records from 1841 to the present time are kept by the Registrar of Vital Statistics in Boston. Except for the first ten-year period, which is treated separately, the index to this collection is divided into five-year segments which cover the entire state in a single alphabetical listing. These are open to the public, although births and marriages must first be checked by a staff member to ensure privacy in cases of illegitimacy or adoption.

Data supplementing vital records can often be found in newspapers. The Boston Public Library has microfilm copies of most of the state's nineteenth- and twentieth-century newspapers; public libraries outside the capital often maintain files as well. Printed aids to newspaper research include the American Antiquarian Society's "Index of Marriages in the *Massachusetts Centinel* and *Columbian Centinel,* 1784-1840," 8 vols., typescript (Worcester, 1952?), and "Index of Deaths in *Massachusetts Centinel* and *Columbian Centinel,* 1784-1840," 12 vols., typescript (Worcester, 1952), which abstract these notices alphabetically, and the Boston Athenaeum's *Index of Obituaries in Boston Newspapers, 1704-1800,* 3 vols. (Boston, 1968). The American Antiquarian Society also prepared "Index to Obituary Notices in the *Boston Transcript,*

14. Frederick William Bailey, ed., *Early Massachusetts Marriages Prior to 1800,* 3 vols. (Cambridge, Mass., 1898-1900; reprint ed., Baltimore, 1979), includes records from Berkshire, Bristol, Hampshire, Middlesex, Plymouth, and Worcester counties.
15. Generally they are Berkshire County marriages, 1788-1795; Bristol County marriages, 1783-1795; Dukes County marriages, 1761-1768, 1773-1795; Essex County births, marriages, and deaths, 1654-1691, and marriages, 1681-1795; Hampshire County marriages, 1786-1790; Middlesex County births, marriages, and deaths, 1632-1745, and marriages, 1733-1793; Nantucket County marriages, 1766-1790; Norfolk County marriages, 1793-1795; Old Norfolk County births, marriages, and deaths, 1641-1671; Plymouth County marriages, 1724-1788.

1875-1899," 2 vols., typescript (Worcester, 1938), and "Index to Obituary Notices in the *Boston Typescript,* 1900-1930," 3 vols., typescript (Worcester, 1940). Other unpublished newspaper indexes include one for the *Hampshire Gazette,* 1786 to the present, deposited at the Forbes Library in Northampton; several for Springfield newspapers kept at the Springfield City Library; and a number for twentieth-century Boston newspapers available at the Boston Public Library. For further indexes see New England Library Association Bibliography Committee, *A Guide to Newspaper Indexes in New England* (Lynnfield, Mass., 1978).

Tax lists, another type of record found at the local level, are available from the town clerk or treasurer of each municipality. The State Archives has tax valuation returns for 1768 and 1771, and the State Library maintains those for 1780, 1783, 1784, 1791, 1792, 1793, 1800, 1801, 1810, and 1811. The valuation for 1771 has been published in Bettye Hobbs Pruit, ed., *The Massachusetts Tax Valuation List of 1771* (Boston, 1978). A microfilm compilation of some lists has been prepared by Ruth Crandall, *Tax and Valuation Lists of Massachusetts before 1776* (Cambridge, Mass., 1971).[16]

Published histories exist for most Massachusetts Towns. These are valuable for describing the lives and activities of early residents. Many also include genealogical sections or "family registers" which organize large amounts of data based upon nineteenth-century recollections that might otherwise have gone unrecorded. These sections should be used with caution, as much of the material is unverified. A select bibliography appears as an appendix to this article.

More trustworthy as a secondary source are the many periodicals published in the state. The oldest is the *Register,* published continuously since 1847, which contains much of interest both to historians and genealogists.[17] From 1859 the *Essex Institute Historical Collections* included much genealogical data, as did the *Essex Antiquarian: A Quarterly Magazine Devoted to the Biography, Genealogy, History, and Antiquities of Essex County, Massachusetts,* 13 vols. (Salem, Mass., 1897-1909). Other local societies have also published useful journals. Among the best are *The Historical Collections of the Danvers Historical Society,* 43 vols. (Danvers, Mass., 1913-1967); *The Dedham Historical*

16. The towns included in this work are: Woburn, 1673-1728, miscellaneous, 1735-1758, 1729-1776; Reading, 1663-1705, 1773-1793, miscellaneous, 1815-1852; Medford, 1675-1781; Danvers, 1752-1774; Topsfield, 1744-1779; Boxford, 1760-1775; Salem, 1689-1763, 1764-1773, miscellaneous, 1751-1831; Beverly, 1739-1779; Wenham, 1731-1777; Marblehead, 1757, 1767-1776; 1734-1735, 1749; Chelmsford, 1727-1736, 1740-1770, 1770-1779; Middleton, 1728-1799, 1862-1863; Westford, 1745-1783; Lunenburg, 1761-1770; Needham, 1711-1731; Wrentham, 1736-1776; Milton, 1668-1792; Walpole, 1724-1777; Stoughton, 1727-1776; Dedham, 1636-1706, miscellaneous, 1711-1801, 1707-1773; Waltham, 1738-1820.
17. The two major indexes to the *Register* are *New England Historical and Genealogical Register: Index of Persons, Subjects, and Places* (volumes 1-50), 4 vols. (Boston, 1906-1911; reprint ed., Baltimore, 1972); and Margaret Wellington Parsons, comp., *Index (Abridged) to the New England Historical and Genealogical Register, Volumes 51 through 112 (1897-1958)* (Marlborough, Mass., 1959).

Register, 14 vols. (Dedham, Mass., 1890-1903); *The Medford Historical Register,* 43 vols. (Medford, Mass., 1898-1940); and *The Historical Collections of the Topsfield Historical Society,* 31 vols. (Topsfield, Mass., 1895-1951). Not to be overlooked as well are the publications of the Massachusetts Historical Society and the Colonial Society of Massachusetts. Both organizations have printed a great variety of documentary and secondary materials pertaining to family and local history.

The next set of records to examine on the local level are church and burial registers. Often baptismal, marriage, and burial entries in the former provide the only surviving clue to individuals who do not appear in the civil records. Important, too, are records for admissions and dismissals from any given parish, as they often suggest migration patterns among towns. For Congregational church registers consult Harold Field Worthley, *Inventory of the Records of the Particular (Congregational) Churches of Massachusetts Gathered 1620-1805,* Harvard Theological Study, vol. 26 (Cambridge, Mass., 1970). Also useful are several of the *Reports of the Commissioner of Public Records,* 32 vols. (Boston, 1885-1919) which describe church records by denomination, town, and parish.[18] Other denominational bibliographies include *A Description of the Manuscript Collections in the Massachusetts Diocesan (Episcopal) Library* (Boston, 1939); and *Inventory of Church Archives of Massachusetts: Protestant Episcopal Church; An Inventory of Universalist Archives in Massachusetts* (Boston, 1942). Major Boston-area repositories for unpublished church records no longer maintained at the originating parish are the Congregational Library for Congregational records; the Diocesan House for Episcopal records; Boston University Theological School Library for Methodist records; and the Harvard Divinity School Library in Cambridge for Unitarian and Universalist records. Quaker records for all of New England can be found in the Rhode Island Historical Society Library in Providence; and some synagogue records are available at the American Jewish Historical Society. By the mid-nineteenth century, records of the Roman Catholic Church are of increasing importance for Massachusetts genealogy. Many of the parish registers of this period are now located at the new Chancery Archives for the Archdiocese in Brighton. These are generally from parishes in greater Boston, but several are from parishes outside the immediate metropolitan area. The dioceses of Springfield, Worcester, and Fall River have not centralized their parish records, which generally remain with the individual parish. For further discussion of Catholic records see James M. O'Toole, "Catholic Church Records: A Genealogical and Historical Resource," *Register,* 132 (1978): 251-263.

Many church registers of the Commonwealth have been published. They appear in journals like the *Register* and as separate publications.

18. *Report* (1885), 9-79; *10th Report* (1897), 1-189; "Additional Church Records," *12th Report* (1900), 10; *15th Report* (1902), 14-16.

The best of these latter are "Plymouth Church Records, 1620-1859," "Records of the First Church in Boston, 1630-1868," and the "Records of Trinity Church, Boston, 1728-1830" — all part of the *Publications of the Colonial Society of Massachusetts;*[19] and Richard D. Pierce, ed., *The Records of the First Church in Salem, Massachusetts, 1629-1736* (Salem, Mass., 1974).

Cemetery records, like church registers, are often difficult to locate. Until the early 1800s burial grounds were often near particular churches and burials were entered in church records. Beginning in the 1830s, private cemeteries and later municipal cemeteries came into vogue. In the former case, records are usually retained in an office within the cemetery itself, while municipal cemeteries usually maintain an office in the town or city hall. The City of Boston assumed administration of a number of cemeteries in 1897, principally those of towns annexed by Boston. These records are maintained by the Cemetery Division, Parks and Recreation Department, Boston, at Mount Hope Cemetery. Administrative offices of the several Catholic cemeteries in the Boston Archdiocese are located at Holy Cross Cemetery in Malden.

Unlike burial records, gravestone inscriptions in the Commonwealth have been frequently transcribed, by local chapters of the Daughters of the American Revolution especially. Regrettably, Massachusetts, unlike other New England states, lacks a central depository for such records; often they have been given to local libraries. A large collection of individual transcripts are available at the Society, and transcripts of various western cemeteries are in the Rollin G. Cooke Collection at the Berkshire Athenaeum in Pittsfield. Others have been published as monographs or in major journals, notably the *Register*. For those towns covered by the Systematic Fund, gravestone records are included in the published vital records series.

A discussion of county records must begin with a brief review of the history of these localities. County divisions in Massachusetts date from 1643, when the Bay Colony was split into Essex, Middlesex, Suffolk, and Norfolk counties. "Old" Norfolk County consisted of the towns of Dover, Exeter, Portsmouth, and Hampton, and what is now Essex County north of the Merrimac River, reminding us that New Hampshire was under Massachusetts jurisdiction from 1641/2 until 1679.[20] In 1680, Old Norfolk became extinct when New Hampshire was reestablished as a separate colony, and the area now comprising the towns of Amesbury, Merrimac, Salisbury, Haverhill, Methuen, and the northern region of Lawrence was set off to Essex County. In 1692, as a result of its new pro-

19. They are found in vols. 22, 23; 39-41; and 55, 56 respectively. Vols. 55 and 56 for Trinity Church will be published in 1981-1982.
20. See David C. Dearborn, "New Hampshire Genealogy: A Perspective," *Register*, 130 (1976): 244-258. Maine, including the counties of Cumberland, Hancock, Kennebec, Lincoln, Oxford, Penobscot, Somerset, Washington, and York, was also part of Masschusetts from 1652 to 1820. See John Eldridge Frost, "Maine Genealogy: Some Distinctive Aspects," *ibid.*, 131 (1977): 243-266.

vincial charter, Massachusetts acquired the islands of Martha's Vineyard
and Nantucket, as well as the old colony of Plymouth. The islands,
which formerly belonged to the colony of New York, were added as
Dukes County, while Plymouth was administered as Barnstable, Bristol,
and Plymouth counties — divisions created in 1685 by Plymouth Colony
itself.[21] Later, in 1746, a Royal Commission settled a boundary dispute
between Rhode Island and Massachusetts by awarding to Rhode Island
the Bristol County towns of Barrington (with parts of Swansea and
Rehoboth), Bristol, Tiverton, Little Compton, and Cumberland.[22]
Westward expansion produced several more counties: Hampshire (1662),
Worcester (1731), Berkshire (1761), Franklin (1811), and Hampden
(1812).

Published histories exist for every county in the Commonwealth.
Among the first such works produced in the United States was Peter
Whitney, *The History of the County of Worcester* (Worcester, Mass.,
1793). Its mid-nineteenth-century successors were often multi-volume
"mugbooks" of varying quality. For a complete listing, consult the
Haskell and Flagg bibliographies cited above.

In addition to vital and church records, files concerning court cases are
of much genealogical value, particularly those maintained at the county
level. A simple division into county or quarterly courts, and an appellate
system headed by the Court of Assistants, was reorganized by the
legislature in 1692. The new system established a Superior Court of
Judicature to oversee the entire colony, and county courts of general sessions and common pleas for criminal and civil cases respectively. Probate
courts were formalized to handle wills, estate administrations, and guardianships. With frequent minor adjustments, most notably the creation
of the Supreme Judicial Court in 1780 and countywide superior courts in
1859, this system has prevailed to the present day.[23]

Of these various courts, the probate court and its sibling, the Registry
of Deeds, are of the greatest interest to genealogists.[24] The use of probate
and deeds is generally straightforward. Each series is in the custody of a
registrar with county-wide jurisdiction, although the territory of some
large counties is divided for the sake of convenience (see Table I). The
location and extent of these records appear on the Table, but the reader
should note, too, a few exceptions to the usual pattern. When "Old" Norfolk County was dissolved in 1680, its deeds and estates from 1649 were

21. Hingham which is currently in Plymouth County was, however, always part of the
Massachusetts Bay Colony.
22. A number of deeds and some wills from this adjacent portion of Massachusetts are
among the Rhode Island Colony Deeds in the Secretary of State's Office, State House, Providence.
23. A good description is in Winifred Lovering Holman, "Massachusetts," *Genealogical
Research: Methods and Sources,* ed. Milton Rubincam (Washington, D.C., 1960), 113-124.
24. Since 1922 probate courts also include divorce records, which were previously kept by
county in the superior courts. These records are often restricted. Additionally, name
changes and adoptions are now registered with the Probate Court. See *List of Persons
Whose Names Have Been Changed in Massachusetts, 1780-1892* (Boston, 1893; reprint ed.,
Baltimore, 1972).

supposedly suspended, yet transfers were recorded as late as 1714. Also in Essex County, a quarterly court was established in Ipswich covering Newbury and later Rowley, which recorded deeds from 1640 to 1694. These irregular early items, as well as the subsequent records for the entire county, are now in the Essex Courthouse in Salem. Additionally, during the administration of Governor Edmund Andros (1686-1689), any estate valued at fifty pounds or more had to be probated in Boston. Thus the files of Suffolk County Probate Office contain records from as far away as New York, Connecticut, Rhode Island, and even Antigua and Barbados.[25] Estates of mariners who left from the port of Boston were also probated in Suffolk County. Other idiosyncrasies in the court records include deeds for Hopkinton (1743-1783) and Upton pertaining to land once owned by Harvard College, which are filed in a separate series in the Middlesex Courthouse; and Rochester probates, originally in Barnstable County, which were transferred when that town was added to Plymouth County in 1707. This last fortuitous circumstance saved these records from the disastrous Barnstable Courthouse fire of 1827, which destroyed nearly all other Barnstable county documents.

The transfer of Barnstable's records was an exception to the general practice of allowing parent counties to keep their towns' court records through the date of transfer. For example, Charlestown's files until 1874, when it was annexed to Boston, are in the Middlesex Courthouse; records since that date are at the Suffolk Courthouse in Boston. The distribution of court documents for Dorchester and Roxbury is more complex. Those through 1793 are located in the Suffolk Courthouse; for the period 1793-1874 for Dorchester and 1793-1867 for Roxbury, they are in the Norfolk County Courthouse in Dedham; and those after 1869 or 1867, when these communities were incorporated into Boston, are once more in the Suffolk Courthouse. Likewise, in western Massachusetts, if a family settled in Montague before the Revolution and descendants lived there a century later, probate records through 1811 are located in Northampton and deeds through about 1788 in Springfield; all later documents are in Greenfield.[26]

Probates and deeds have been published for a few counties in the Commonwealth. The best of these sets are *The Probate Records of Essex County, Massachusetts* [1635-1681], 3 vols. (Salem, Mass., 1916-1920); and *Suffolk Deeds* [1640-1697], 14 vols. (Boston, 1880-1906).[27] Printed probate indexes for Middlesex, Norfolk, Suffolk, and Worcester coun-

25. See Winifred Lovering Holman and Mary Lovering Holman, "Suffolk County Probate (1686-1692)," *The American Genealogist,* 12 (1936): 175-184, 222-234; 13 (1936): 989-106; 14 (1937): 34, 35.
26. Claude W. Barlow, *Sources for Genealogical Searching in Connecticut and Massachusetts* (Syracuse, N.Y., 1973), 21.
27. Some probates are available on microfilm at the Boston Public Library — those for Suffolk County 1636-1852; Middlesex County, 1648-1871; and part of Hampshire County 1660-1820. These are the copybooks only and do not include individual files. Berkshire County probates, 1761-1865, are on microfilm at the Berkshire Athenaeum, Pittsfield.

ties are available in various libraries, including the Society; and many Barnstable County probates are abstracted in the *Mayflower Descendant.*

Because Massachusetts settlers were highly litigious, many of them appear in civil court records. These along with criminal records are also maintained locally. Some seventeenth-century quarterly court files for Suffolk and Essex counties are published. See "Records of the Suffolk County Court, 1671-1680," 2 vols., in *Publications of the Colonial Society of Massachusetts,* vols. 29 and 30; and *Records and Files of the Quarterly Courts of Essex County, Massachusetts, 1636-1686,* 9 vols. (Salem, Mass., 1911-1975). The introduction to the Suffolk volumes provides an excellent description of the types of cases frequently heard. Access to the civil and criminal records of other counties, often unindexed, is much more difficult. Without prior knowledge of individual cases, extracting information from these files requires considerable effort. One helpful aid, however, is Michael S. Hindus, *The Records of the Massachusetts Superior Court and its Predecessors; An Inventory and Guide* (Boston, 1977). Available on microfilm at the Boston Public Library are the records of the Suffolk County Court of Common Pleas, 1701-1855.

Among these court records, "warnings out" may be of particular interest to genealogists. The practice of warning out, dating from the mid-seventeenth century, was used by towns to prevent nonresidents from becoming public charges. Towns employed this system to minimize the costs of charity and to ensure that the poor would be maintained as a rightful responsibility in their native place. Originally an "inhabitancy" could be gained by simply living in a town for several months and paying taxes, but in 1739 provincial law required consent of the town meeting or selectmen. Eventually any new resident regardless of profession or social standing was officially warned out of town in order to avoid later claims of pauperism or illness. In most cases, this legal step did not necessarily mean that the person warned out was actually physically removed from the community. This practice continued into the 1790s. Warnings out, which document many in-state migrations throughout this period, remain largely unpublished, but see *Worcester County, Massachusetts, Warnings, 1737-1788* (Worcester, Mass., 1899).

In addition to county records, several classes of records survey the entire population of Massachusetts. The earliest censuses for the years 1764 and 1765 consist of statistical totals only and are deposited in the State Archives. After the federal census of 1790, which was published by the government printing office in 1908, the next available population survey is the Massachusetts and Maine Direct Tax Census of 1798. This valuable document lists all owners of property and renters. Its schedules were literally saved from the flames by William Henry Montague when he discovered a janitor in the Boston Customs House using the old papers as kindling. In 1848 the surviving schedules were transferred to the Society, which published a microfilm edition of them in 1979.[28] Also available are the federal censuses of Massachusetts through 1880. Microfilm copies of these can be used at the regional branch of the National Archives in Waltham and at the Boston Public Library. Name indexes to the federal censuses have been completed through 1850.[29] Note that the 1800 returns for Hull and Cohasset are incomplete, and those for Boston and Chelsea are missing altogether (see Elizabeth Petty Bentley, *Index to the 1800 Census of Massachusetts* [Baltimore, 1978]). A partial replacement of the 1890 census, which was destroyed by fire in 1924, is the veterans' census of that year, listing all Union soldiers or their widows. Three other state censuses are available only at the State Archives. Like the 1850 and later federal censuses, those for 1855 and 1865 list individuals; the 1875 census, however, is statistical only. The State Archives also has the originals of the Commonwealth's 1850, 1860, and 1870 federal censuses.

Legislative records, particularly of the colonial and early national periods, contain much family data, especially in private bills and suits. See John Noble and John F. Cronin, eds., *Records of the Court of Assistants of the Colony of the Massachusetts Bay, 1630-1692 . . .,* 3 vols. (Boston, 1901-1928); Nathaniel B. Shurtleff, ed., *Records of the Governor and Company of the Massachusetts Bay in New England,* 5 vols. in 6 (Boston, 1853-1854); *Journals of the House of Representatives of Massachusetts . . .,* 49 vols. in 55 to date (Boston, 1919-); *The Acts and Resolves, Public and Private, of the Province of the Massachusetts Bay . . .,* 21 vols. (Boston, 1869-1922); and for Plymouth Colony, Nathaniel B. Shurtleff and David Pulsifer, eds., *Records of the Colony of New Plymouth, in New England,* 12 vols. (Boston, 1855-1861).

Military records of the state are well preserved, and many, from the earliest colonial wars through the Civil War, have been published. Muster rolls for service between 1643 and 1783 are kept in the State Archives; later records through World War I are maintained in the Adjutant General's Office in Boston. Printed military records appear mainly as regimental lists. A still important reference for the seventeenth century is George M. Bodge, *Soldiers in King Philip's War* (Leominster, Mass., 1896; reprint ed., Baltimore, 1967). Several lists have recently been sponsored by the Society of Colonial Wars in the Commonwealth of Massachusetts, and the Society. To date the series includes: Mary E. Donahue, ed., *Massachusetts Officers and Soldiers, 1702-1722: Queen Anne's War to Dummer's War* (Boston, 1980); Myron O. Stachiw, ed., *Massachusetts Officers and Soldiers, 1723-1743: Dummer's War to the*

28. The schedules for parts of Norfolk and Suffolk counties, Massachusetts, as well as parts of Washington, Hancock, and Lincoln counties, Maine, were destroyed. See Michael H. Gorn, ed., *An Index and Guide to the Microfilm Edition of the Massachusetts and Maine Direct Tax Census of 1798* (Boston, 1979).
29. Laraine Welch, comp., *Massachusetts 1800 Census* (Provo, Utah, 1973); *Massachusetts 1810 Census Index* (Bountiful, Utah, 1976); *Massachusetts 1820 Census Index* (Bountiful, Utah, 1976); *Massachusetts 1830 Census Index* (Bountiful, Utah, 1976); *Massachusetts 1840 Census Index* (Bountiful, Utah, 1978); *Massachusetts 1850 Census Index* (Bountiful, Utah, 1978).

War of Jenkins' Ear (Boston, 1980); Robert E. MacKay, ed., *Massachusetts Soldiers in the French and Indian Wars, 1744-1755* (Boston, 1978); and Nancy S. Voye, ed., *Massachusetts Officers in the French and Indian Wars, 1748-1763* (Boston, 1975). A sixth volume, to be published in 1982, will name Massachusetts officers and soldiers who fought in the colonial wars of the seventeenth century. For the Revolution see *Massachusetts Soldiers and Sailors of the Revolutionary War,* 17 vols. (Boston, 1896-1908), an alphabetized list of all Massachusetts participants with a summary of their service records. Soldiers who fought in the first battles of the war are listed in Charles E. Hambrick-Stowe and Donna D. Smerlas, eds., *Massachusetts Militia Companies and Officers in the Lexington Alarm* (Boston, 1976). Massachusetts chapters of the DAR have compiled a valuable card file, "Grave Locations of Massachusetts Men who Served in the Revolutionary War, 1775-1783, with Service Records, A-Z, as Reported to the National Society for Publication by the Smithsonian Institute in the Senate Reports for 1898-1955." This file, available at NEHGS, much supplements the *DAR Patriot Index,* 2 vols (Washington, D.C., 1967-1980); *Lineage Books, National Society of the DAR,* 166 vols. (Washington, D.C., 1890-1921), with an *Index to the Rolls of Honor [Ancestor's Index],* 4 vols. (Washington, D.C., 1916-1940; reprint ed., Baltimore, 1972); and *Index of Revolutionary War Pension Applications in the National Archives,* National Genealogical Society, special publication no. 40 (Washington, 1976), for some discussion of which see the *Register* 135 (1981): 65-66. For Massachusetts revolutionary officers and many of their descendants see Bradford Adams Whittemore, *Memorials of the Massachusetts Society of the Cincinnati* (Boston, 1964).

Several biographical studies also exist for Loyalists. Tory sentiment, by no means confined only to the social elite of the seaports, was spread throughout the Commonwealth. A recent work, David E. Maas, comp. and ed., *Divided Hearts: Massachusetts Loyalists, 1765-1790, A Biographical Directory* (Boston, 1980) offers the most authoritative listing to date. It often corrects the earlier major work in this field — E. Alfred Jones, *The Loyalists of Massachusetts: Their Memorials, Petitions and Claims* (London, 1930), which includes many individual biographies. Valuable but less comprehensive are James H. Stark, *The Loyalists of Massachusetts, and the Other Side of the American Revolution* (Boston, 1907; reprint ed., Clifton, N.H., 1972); and Lorenzo Sabine, *Biographical Sketches of Loyalists of the American Revolution with an Historical Essay* (Boston, 1864; reprint ed., Port Washington, N.Y., 1966).

Definitive lists of Commonwealth soldiers in the War of 1812 and the Civil War are readily available in print. For the former see *Records of the Massachusetts Volunteer Militia Called Out by the Governor of Massachusetts to Suppress a Threatened Invasion during the War of 1812-14* (Boston, 1913); for the Civil War see *Massachusetts in the Army and*

Navy during the War of 1861-65, 8 vols. (Boston, 1896-1935). To locate soldiers in this last set consult *Index to Army Records* (Boston, 1937). Navy and Marine entries are arranged alphabetically in volumes 7 and 8. Records of Massachusetts participants in later wars, notably World War I, have been compiled on the local level by the WPA and others, and are generally deposited in town libraries.

The Commonwealth's military records are most valuable when used in conjunction with pension and service files in the National Archives. A useful aid, already mentioned, is the *Index of Revolutionary War Pension Applications in the National Archives;* and a general guide to military biographical material is Mary Ellen Baker, *Bibliography of Lists of New England Soldiers* (Boston, 1911; revised ed., Boston, 1977). Perhaps of more social than military importance is the Massachusetts Ancient and Honorable Artillery Company, the oldest military organization in the country. Biographical sketches of all members appear in Oliver Ayer Roberts, *History of the Military Company of the Massachusetts Now Called the Ancient and Honorable Artillery of Massachusetts, 1637-1888,* 4 vols. (Boston, 1895-1901).

Genealogical research in Massachusetts is at once enormously facilitated and made much more difficult by the state's unparalleled volume of primary and published sources. Successful results require expert use of guides and indexes, and a thorough knowledge of the holdings of numerous libraries and depositories. In summary we might list again the major institutions serving family history in Massachusetts. In Boston, the Society owns an extraordinary collection of Massachusetts family and local histories, as well as the largest collection of genealogical manuscripts in the country.[30] In the Bureau of Vital Statistics are the Commonwealth's birth, marriage, and death records since 1840, the earliest centralized and most comprehensive in the nation. The State Archives and State Library have the bulk of the state's unequalled public documents.[31] In addition, the Boston Public Library and the Massachusetts Historical Society also have large collections of both primary and printed sources[32]. Much material of interest is also at the regional branch of the National Archives in Waltham, the American Antiquarian Society in Worcester, and the Berkshire Athenaeum in Pittsfield. For further information regarding the holdings of these and many other Massachusetts libraries and archives, see New England Library Association Bibliography Committee, *A Genealogist's Handbook for New England Research* (Lynnfield, Mass., 1980).

Although often frustrating, with some insurmountable gaps, Massa-

---

30. See Gary Boyd Roberts's list of thirty major manuscript collections at the Society in "The Most Needed Genealogical Reference Publications of 1966: An Update and General Review," *The Detroit Society for Genealogical Research Magazine,* 41 (1978): 139, 140.
31. See Kenneth E. Flower, *A Guide to Massachusetts Genealogical Material in the State Library of Massachusetts* (Boston, 1978).
32. See *Catalog of Manuscripts of the Massachusetts Historical Society,* 7 vols. (Boston, 1969).

chusetts research can also be exhilarating. The oldest of the New England states, with the longest series of primary records and the most extensive corpus of published data as well, the Commonwealth frequently offers genealogists the rare satisfaction of tracing almost all forebears to 1630 of any ancestor migrating from this region.

Edward W. Hanson is an archivist at the Boston National Historical Park, Boston, and the author of "Vermont Genealogy: A Study in Migration," *Register,* 133 (1979): 3-19; Homer Vincent Rutherford is Professor of History at the University of Winnipeg, Winnipeg, Canada R3B 2E9.

TABLE I

MASSACHUSETTS COUNTIES: PROBATES AND DEEDS

BARNSTABLE COUNTY, established 2 June 1685, from Plymouth Colony
County Seat: Barnstable
Probate: from 19 July 1686. Volumes xxix, said to have an index, and xliv, miscellaneous papers, 1821-1825, were destroyed by fire, 22 October 1827; files are complete after that date but previous ones were destroyed. There was also an earlier fire in 1701. The Hinckley papers at the Society contain 9 volumes of copies of records relating to Barnstable.

Deeds: from 24 October 1827. Ninety-three of the 94 volumes were destroyed in the fire of 22 October 1827. Thirty-two of the present volumes contain re-registered deeds.

BERKSHIRE COUNTY, established 21 April 1761, from Hampshire County
County seat: Pittsfield
Probate: from 30 July 1761. Prior to 1761, all wills were registered in Northampton, Hampshire County
Deeds: 30 June 1761-18 June 1788, at Pittsfield; earlier deeds at Springfield. Three separate deeds registries were established on 18 June 1788: Northern District, with registry at Adams, covering Adams, Cheshire, Clarksburg, Florida, Hancock, Lanesborough, New Ashford, North Adams, Savoy, Williamstown and Windsor; Middle District, with registry at Pittsfield, covering Becket, Dalton, Hinsdale, Lee, Lenox, Otis, Peru, Pittsfield, Richmond, Stockbridge, Tyringham and Washington; Southern District, with registry at Great Barrington, covering Alford, Egremont, Great Barrington, Monterey, Mount Washington, New Marlborough, Sandisfield, Sheffield and West Stockbridge.

BRISTOL COUNTY, established 2 June 1685, from Plymouth Colony
County seat: Taunton. Bristol, Rhode Island (then Massachusetts), was the seat until 13 November 1746.
Probate: from 1686.
Deeds: 2 June 1685-1 July 1837. At the latter date, two separate deeds registries were established: Northern District, with registry at Taunton, covering Fall River, Taunton, Attleborough, Berkley, Dighton, Easton, Freetown, Mansfield, Norton, Raynham, Rehoboth, Seekonk, Somerset, Swansea. Additional records: Fall River, R.I. (3 vols.), copies of Proprietors of Taunton (6 vols.), and copies of Tiverton, R.I., now in Fall River (8 vols.); Southern District, with registry at New Bedford, covering New Bedford, Acushnet, Dartmouth, Fairhaven and Westport; additional records: 2 vols. of copies of Dartmouth Land Records.

DUKES COUNTY, established 1 November 1683 by New York, 22 June 1695 by Massachusetts
County seat: Edgartown
Probate: from 14 July 1697
Deeds: from 1686

ESSEX COUNTY, established 10 May 1643 (Original County)
County seat: Salem
Probate: from 1635
Deeds: prior to 1869 all deeds are at Salem. In that year two separate registries were established: Northern District, with registry at Lawrence covering Lawrence, Andover, Methuen, and North Andover; Southern District, with registry at Salem, covering Gloucester, Haverhill, Lynn, Newburyport, Salem, Amesbury, Beverly, Boxford, Bradford, Danvers, Essex, Georgetown, Groveland, Hamilton, Ipswich, Lynnfield, Manchester, Marblehead, Merrimac, Middleton, Nahant, Newbury, Peabody, Rockport, Rowley, Salisbury, Saugus, Swampscott, Topsfield, Wenham and West Newbury; additional records: Ipswich series, 1640-1694; "Old" Norfolk County series, 1637-1714.

FRANKLIN COUNTY, established 24 June 1811, from Hampshire County
County seat: Greenfield
Probate: from 7 April 1812. Prior records are at the Hampshire County Courthouse in Northampton, but copies of earlier records relating to towns placed in Franklin County are available in Greenfield.
Deeds: registry established 2 December 1811. (See note *sub* Hampshire County.)

HAMPDEN COUNTY, established 25 February 1812, from Hampshire County
County Seat: Springfield
Probate: from 11 August 1812. Prior to 1812 records are at the Hampshire registry in Northampton, with some probate records in the registry of deeds.
Deeds: registry established 1 August 1812. (See note *sub* Hampshire County.) The registry at Springfield was registry for the original county of Hampshire, which comprised the present county of Berkshire until 1761, the present county of Franklin until 1811, the present county of Hampden until 1812, certain towns later in present-day Worcester County, and the towns of Somers and Suffield, now in Connecticut.

HAMPSHIRE COUNTY, established 7 May 1662, from Middlesex County
County Seat: Northampton
Probate: from 27 March 1660
Deeds: Northampton registry established 1 March 1787. On that date three registries were established in Hampshire County: one at Northampton for twenty-one towns, which are named in the Act; one at Deerfield "for towns north of the above," and one at Springfield "for towns south of the above." The towns covered by the Northampton registry were: Amherst, Belchertown, Chester, Chesterfield, Cummington, Easthampton, Goshen, Granby, Greenwich, Hadley, Hatfield, Middlefield, Northampton, Norwich (now Huntington), Pelham, Plainfield, Southampton, South Hadley, Ware, Westhampton, and Williamsburg; covered by the Deerfield registry, but transferred to the Greenfield registry in 1812 were: Ashfield, Bernardston, Buckland, Charlemont, Colrain, Conway, Deerfield, Greenfield, Heath, Leverett, Leyden, Montague, New Salem, Northfield, Orange, Rowe, Shelburne, Shutesbury, Sunderland, Warwick, Wendell and Whately; the registry at Springfield covered Blandford, Brimfield, Granville, Holland, Longmeadow, Ludlow, Monson, Montgomery, Palmer, South Brimfield (now Wales), Southwick, Springfield, Tolland, Westfield, West Springfield and Wilbraham.

MIDDLESEX COUNTY, established 10 May 1643 (Original County)
County Seat: Cambridge
Probate: from 14 May 1654. One volume was lost about 1849 when files were removed during repairs to the Courthouse, but the files are substantially complete. The second volume, relating to births, marriages, and deaths, 1678-1745, is bound at

the end of the first volume relating to wills and inventories; a copy is with the clerk of courts.

Deeds: 14 June 1649-1855. On 1 July 1855, the county was divided into two registries. The Northern District, with registry at Lowell, covers Lowell, Billerica, Carlisle, Chelmsford, Dracut, Dunstable, Tewksbury, Tyngsborough, Westford, Wilmington. The Southern District with its registry at Cambridge, covers Cambridge, Malden, Newton, Somerville, Waltham, Acton, Arlington, Ashby, Ashland, Ayer, Bedford, Belmont, Boxborough, Burlington, Concord, Everett, Framingham, Groton, Holliston, Hopkinton, Hudson, Lexington, Lincoln, Littleton (from 1 June 1856 to 1 June 1860 in the Middlesex Northern District), Marlborough, Maynard, Medford, Melrose, Natick, North Reading, Pepperell, Reading, Sherborn, Shirley, Stoneham, Stow, Sudbury, Townsend, Wakefield, Watertown, Wayland, Weston, Winchester and Woburn. Additional records: there is a 16-volume series of "Deeds of Hopkinton and Upton"; and one volume of "Littleton Records," a copy of records in Middlesex Northern District on Littleton.

NANTUCKET COUNTY, established 22 June 1695, from Dukes County
County Seat: Nantucket
Probate: from 27 September 1706
Deeds: from February 1659. Additional records: 6 vols. of "Records of Proprietors of the Common and Undivided Lands, 1716-1885."

NORFOLK COUNTY, "OLD," established 10 May 1643, disestablished 4 February 1680
Probate and Deeds: 1637-1714 are in the Essex County Courthouse in Salem.

NORFOLK COUNTY, established 26 March 1793, from Suffolk County
County Seat: Dedham
Probate: from 22 August 1793
Deeds: from 24 September 1793. Additional records: "Records of the Common & Undivided Lands of the Townships of Dorchester and Stoughton, 1713-1793."

PLYMOUTH COUNTY, established 2 June 1685, from Plymouth Colony
County Seat: Plymouth
Probate: from 14 May 1686. Records of Estates of deceased persons prior to 1685 are in the Plymouth Colony Records, in the County Commissioner's Office, Plymouth.
Deeds: Plymouth Colony records from 3 July 1630, Plymouth County records from 20 July 1700. Additional records: Commissioner of the United Colonies (2 vols.), court actions (1 vol.), court orders (6 vols.) and wills (6 vols.).

SUFFOLK COUNTY, established 10 May 1643 (Original County)
County Seat: Boston
Probate: from 1636. In the earlier volumes there are records of estates of residents of Salem, mixed with the records of resident estates for this county. Numerous papers belonging to the files are lost. About 1854 many papers were placed in the cellar of the probate court building, without any regard to order, and various of these papers were carried away.
Deeds: from 1639. Volumes cxii, covering January-July 1768, and cxiv, covering January-March 1769, were lost, probably in moving the records to Dedham, as authorised by the General Court, 8 February 1776, to avoid their capture by the British.

WORCESTER COUNTY, established 2 April 1731, from Middlesex, Suffolk and Hampshire counties
County Seat: Worcester
Probate: from 12 July 1731
Deeds: through 1 August 1884. On that date the county was divided into two registry districts. Worcester District includes Worcester, Athol, Auburn, Barre, Berlin, Blackstone, Bolton, Boylston, Brookfield, Charlton, Clinton, Dana, Douglas, Dudley, Gardner, Grafton, Hardwick, Harvard, Holden, Hubbardston, Lancaster, Leicester, Mendon, Milford, Millbury, New Braintree, Northborough, Northbridge, North Brookfield, Oakham, Oxford, Paxton, Petersham,

Phillipston, Princeton, Royalston, Rutland, Shrewsbury, Southborough, Southbridge, Spencer, Sterling, Sturbridge, Sutton, Templeton, Upton, Uxbridge, Warren, Webster, Westborough, West Boylston, West Brookfield, Winchendon; the Worcester Northern District, with registry at Fitchburg covers Fitchburg, Ashburnham, Leominster, Lunenburg, and Westminster. A copy of those records relating to towns in the Northern District between 1 August 1864 and 1 August 1884 is at the Fitchburg registry.

TABLE II
MASSACHUSETTS VITAL RECORDS

The following bibliography is for published and unpublished vital records of Massachusetts towns incorporated before 1841, the year when centralized statewide registration began. Most of the titles in the state-sponsored series read: *Vital Records of _____, Massachusetts, to the year 1849,* and so only publication data, not titles, are repeated here. For towns with full separate volumes other references are omitted. Manuscript items are noted by an asterisk (*) with the location of the collection. The date of incorporation follows each town name.

Abington (1712) — Boston, NEHGS, 1912. 2 vols.

Acton (1735) — Boston, NEHGS, 1923. 311 pp.

Adams (1778) — * Marriages and marriage intentions through 1850, in the Rollin H. Cooke Collection, Berkshire Athenaeum, Pittsfield (hereafter referred to as the Cooke Collection).

Alford (1773) — Boston, NEHGS, 1902. 32 pp.

Amesbury (1668) — Topsfield, Mass., Topsfield Historical Society, 1913. 600 pp.

Amherst (1759) — * 1747-1855, from the town books, in the Corbin Collection, NEHGS (hereafter referred to as the Corbin Collection); * Boltwood Collection, Jones Library, Amherst.

Andover (1646) — Topsfield, Mass., Topsfield Historical Society, 1912. 2 vols.

Arlington (1867; established as West Cambridge, 1807) — Boston, NEHGS, 1904. 162 pp.

Ashburnham (1765) — Worcester, F. P. Rice, 1909.

Ashby (1767) — * Births, marriages and deaths, 1754-1859, at the NEHGS.

Ashfield (1765) — Boston, NEHGS, 1942. 273 pp.

Athol (1762) — Worcester, Mass., F. P. Rice, 1910. 230 pp.

Attleboro (1694) — Salem, Mass., Essex Institute, 1934. 745 pp.

Auburn (1837; established as Ward, 1778) — Worcester, Mass., F. P. Rice, 1900. 142 pp.

Barnstable (1638) — *Mayflower Descendant,* 2(1900):212-15; 3 (1901):51-54, 71-73, 149-52; 4(1902):120-22, 221-27; 5(1903):72-75, 171; 6(1904):97-99, 135-40, 236-39; 10(1908):249-50; 11(1909):95-100, 130-32, 153-56; 12(1910):153-56; 14(1912):86-89, 225-27; 19 (1917):77-83, 125-28, 154-56; 20(1918):41-43; 23 (1921):125-29; 25(1923):129-33, 147-50; 27 (1925):5-10; 31(1933):6-15, 81-87, 139-42, 147-52; 32(1934):51-60, 148-56; 33(1935):23-29, 116-28,

162-71; 34(1936):17-21, 115-19. Index published by Leonard H. Smith Clearwater, Fla., 1975.

Barre (1776, established as Hutchinson, 1774; as District of Rutland, 1753)

Worcester, Mass., F. P. Rice, 1903. 276 pp.

Becket (1765)

Bedford (1729)

Belchertown (1761)

Bellingham (1719)

Berkley (1735)

Berlin (1784)

Boston, NEHGS, 1903. 98 pp.

Boston, NEHGS, 1903. 142 pp.

* 1734-1843 from town books, in Corbin Collection.

Boston, NEHGS, 1904. 222 pp.

* Marriages, 1776-1791, typescript in NEHGS.

To the end of 1899. Compiled by Francis L. Eaton, edited by Martha F. Duren Eaton. Marlboro, Mass., 1935. 380 pp.

Bernardston (1762)

* 1738-1905, from various sources, in Corbin Collection.

Beverly (1668)

Topsfield, Topsfield Historical Society, 1906-1907. 2 vols.

Billerica (1655)

Blandford (1741)

Boston, NEHGS, 1908. 405 pp.

* 1740-1834 from town records, typescript at NEHGS; * 1740-1775 from various sources, in Corbin Collection.

Bolton (1738)

Boston (1630)

Worcester, F. P. Rice, 1910. 232 pp.

Births, 1630-1699, *Report of the Record Commissioners,* vol. 9 (1883); births, 1700-1800, *ibid.,* vol. 24 (1894); marriages, 1695-1697, 1700-1751, *ibid.,* vol. 28 (1898); marriages, 1752-1809, *ibid.,* vol. 30 (1903); *Index to the Vital Records of Boston (1630-1699),* by Sanford Charles Gladden. Boulder, Colo., 1969. Note: the two volumes of births have been reprinted together (Baltimore, 1978), as have the two volumes of marriages (Baltimore, 1977).

Boxborough (1783)

Compiled by Thomas W. Baldwin. Boston, Wright & Potter Printing Co., 1915. 78 pp.

Boxford (1694)

Topsfield, Topsfield Historical Society, 1905. 274 pp.

Boylston (1786)

Bradford (1675; annexed to Haverhill, 1897)

Braintree (1640)

Worcester, F. P. Rice, 1900. 124 pp.

Topsfield, Mass., Topsfield Historical Society, 1907. 373 pp.

Records of the Town of Braintree, 1640-1793, edited by Samuel A. Bates. Randolph, Mass., 1886. 940 pp.

Brewster (1803)

Boston, Massachusetts Society of Mayflower Descendants, 1904. 281 pp.

Bridgewater (1656)

Boston, NEHGS, 1916. 2 vols.

Brighton (1817; annexed to Boston, 1874)

Brimfield (1714)

Brockton (1874; established as North Bridgewater, 1821)

Boston, NEHGS, 1931. 336 pp.

Boston, NEHGS, 1911. 371 pp.

Brookfield (1673)

Brookline (1705)

Buckland (1779)

Worcester, Mass., F. P. Rice, 1909.

Salem, Mass., Essex Institute, 1929. 244 pp.

Salem, Mass., Essex Institute, 1934. 214 pp. Bound with Colrain and Montague.

Burlington (1799)

Compiled by Thomas W. Baldwin. Boston, Wright & Potter, 1915. 100 pp.

Cambridge (1636)

Compiled by Thomas W. Baldwin. Boston, Wright & Potter, 1914. 2 vols.

Canton (1797)

Carlisle (1780)
Carver (1790)
Charlemont (1765)
Charlestown (1630; annexed
  to Boston, 1874)

Charlton (1754)
Chatham (1712)

Chelmsford (1655)
Chelsea (1739)

Cheshire (1793)
Chester (1783; established
  as Murrayfield, 1765)
Chesterfield (1762)
Chilmark (1694)
Clarksburg (1798)
Cohasset (1770)

Colrain (1761)

Concord (1635)
Conway (1767)
Cummington (1779)

Dalton (1784)
Dana (1801; annexed to
  Petersham, 1938)
Danvers (1752)
Dartmouth (1652)
Dedham (1636)

Deerfield (1677)

Dennis (1793)

Dighton (1712)

Dorchester (1630; annexed
  to Boston, 1870)

Edited by Frederic Endicott. Canton, Mass., W. Bense, 1896. 317 pp.
Salem, Mass., Essex Institute, 1918. 100 pp.
Boston, NEHGS, 1911. 179 pp.
Boston, NEHGS, 1917. 166 pp.
Abstracted in *The Genealogies and Estates of Charlestown in the County of Middlesex and Commonwealth of Massachusetts, 1629-1818*, by Thomas Bellows Wyman. Boston, David Clapp & Son, 1879. 2 vols. A forthcoming volume from the NEHGS will cover vital records through 1840.
Worcester, Mass., F. P. Rice, 1905. 268 pp.
Mayflower Descendant, 4(1902):182-85, 198-202; 5 (1903):120-22, 141-43; 7(1905):137-43; 9 (1907):33-36, 179-82, 221; 10(1908):194-98; 11 (1909):39-42, 119-21; 12(1910):171-76, 215-18; 13 (1911):27-31; 15(1913):130-35; 16(1914):212-17; 17 (1915):87-99; 24(1922):64-68, 101-03.
Salem, Mass., Essex Institute, 1914. 460 pp.
Compiled by Thomas W. Baldwin. Boston, Wright & Potter, 1916. 558 pp.
————
Boston, NEHGS, 1911. 256 pp.

* 1765-1839 from town books, in Corbin Collection.
Boston, NEHGS, 1904. 96 pp.
————
Compiled by Thomas W. Baldwin. Boston, Wright & Potter, 1916.
Salem, Mass., Essex Institute, 1934. 209 pp. Bound with Buckland and Montague.
Concord, Mass., by the town, 1891. 496 pp.
Boston, NEHGS, 1943. 276 pp.
Compiled by William W. Streeter, Daphne H. Morris. Cummington, Mass., Streeter, 1979. 415 pp.
Boston, NEHGS, 1906. 82 pp.
Compiled by Thomas W. Baldwin. Boston, Burr Printing Co., 1925. 66 pp.
Salem, Mass., Essex Institute, 1909-1910. 2 vols.
Boston, NEHGS, 1929-1930. 3 vols.
Edited by Don Gleason Hill. Births, deaths and marriages, 1635-1890. Dedham, Mass., Dedham Transcript Press, 1886, 1894, 1896. 3 vols.
Compiled by Thomas W. Baldwin. Boston, Wright & Potter, 1920. 328 pp.
Mayflower Descendant, 6 (1904):2-6, 91-95, 165-69, 251-54; 7 (1905):3-5, 66-72, 159-62; 8 (1906):50-54; 10 (1908):36-38, 116-18, 209-13; 11 (1909):211-14; 12 (1910):40-44; 13 (1911):14-18; 120-26, 254-56. Indexed by Leonard H. Smith. Clearwater, Fla., 1976.
* 1714-1868, births, marriages and deaths, in NEHGS; 1714-1868, from various sources, in Corbin Collection.
1630-1825, Boston, *Report of the Record Commissioners*, vol. 21(1891); 1826-50, *ibid.*, vol. 36; (1905).

Douglas (established as
District of New Sherburn,
1742; name changed 1746;
established as town, 1775)

Worcester, F. P. Rice, 1906. 192 pp.

Dover (1784)   Boston, NEHGS, 1908. 107 pp.
Dracut (1702)   Boston, NEHGS, 1907. 302 pp.
Dudley (1732)   Worcester, Mass., F. P. Rice, 1908. 288 pp.
Dunstable (1673)   Salem, Mass., Essex Institute, 1913. 238 pp.
Duxbury (1637)   Boston, NEHGS, 1917. 446 pp.
East Bridgewater (1823) Boston, NEHGS, 1917. 406 pp.

Eastham (1651; established   *Mayflower Descendant* (published with Orleans),
as Nawsett, 1646)   8(1906):243-47; 9(1907):7-14; 15(1913):52-58, 67-76,
                              140-45, 227-34; 16(1914):26-34, 68-76, 141-48,
                              195-205; 17(1915):29-37, 79-82, 140-50; 19
                              (1917):100-05, 185-86; 20(1918):94-96, 155-58; 24
                              (1922):86-91, 138-41, 189-92; 25(1923):40-42; 27
                              (1925):102-08, 186-88; 28(1930):7-16, 75-83, 108-17,
                              171-82; 29(1931):10-17; 31(1933):172-78; 32
                              (1934):39-44, 61-70, 111-15, 171-77; 33(1935): 11-18,
                              80-89, 132-36, 181-90; 34(1936):58-63, 134-37,
                              183-90. Index by Leonard H. Smith. Clearwater,
                              Fla., 1976.

Easthampton (1785)   * 1785-1844, from various sources, in Corbin Collec-
                              tion.

Easton (1725)   * Marriages, 1725-1802, typescript in NEHGS; *
                              Deaths, 1753-1844, typescript in NEHGS.

Edgartown (1671)   Boston, NEHGS, 1906. 276 pp.

Egremont (1760 as district;   ————
established as town, 1775)

Enfield (1816; annexed 1938   * 1816-1844 from various sources, in Corbin
to Belchertown, New Salem,   Collection.
Pelham and Ware)

Erving (1838)   ————
Essex (1819)   Salem, Mass., Essex Institute, 1908. 86 pp.
Fairhaven (1812)   ————
Fall River (1803; called   * Marriages and births, vols. 1 and 2, in the
Troy, 1804-1834)   DAR Library.
Falmouth (1694)   Compiled by Oliver B. Brown. Warwick, R.I. Socie-
                              ty of Mayflower Descendants, 1976. 262 pp.
Fitchburg (1764)   To 1860. Printed in vols. 2, 3 and 8 of the town
                              records. Fitchburg, 1899, 1900, 1913.
Florida (1805)   ————
Foxborough (1778)   Boston, NEHGS, 1911. 249 pp.
Framingham (1675)   Compiled by Thomas W. Baldwin. Boston, Wright
                              & Potter, 1911. 474 pp.
Franklin (1778)   1778-1872. Edited by Orestes T. Doe. Franklin,
                              Franklin Sentinel Office, 1898. 232 pp.
Freetown (1683)   *Genealogical Advertiser,* 4 (1901):33-37; 1686-1844,
                              births, *Plymouth Colony Genealogical Helper,*
                              1974, no. 1 pp. 9 ff; 1975, no. 2 pp. 25 ff; no. 3 pp.
                              43 ff; no. 4 pp. 52 ff; additions, *Plymouth Colony
                              Genealogist* (1976) no. 5, pp. 8-9; marriages,
                              1686-1844, compiled by Mary Phillips Herbert.
                              Glendale, Calif., 1934; * births, marriage intentions
                              and deaths, 1686-1793, at NEHGS.
Gardner (1785)   Worcester, F. P. Rice, 1907. 136 pp.

Georgetown (1838)

Salem, Mass., Essex Institute, 1928. 90 pp.

Gill (1793)

Boston, NEHGS, 1904. 97 pp.

Gloucester (1642)

Topsfield, Mass., Topsfield Historical Society, 1917-24. 3 vols.

Goshen (1781)

* 1766-1856 from various sources, in Corbin Collection.

Grafton (1735)

Worcester, Mass., F. P. Rice, 1906. 377 pp.

Granby (1768)

* 1763-1852, from various sources, in Corbin Collection.

Granville (1754)

Boston, NEHGS, 1914. 236 pp.

Great Barrington (1761)

Boston, NEHGS, 1904. 89 pp.

Greenfield (1753)

Boston, NEHGS, 1915. 299 pp.

Greenwich (1754; annexed 1938 to Hardwick, New Salem, Petersham and Ware)

* Typescript by Mary Mattoon Chapter, DAR. Amherst, Mass., 1963. Copy in NEHGS.

Groton (1655)

Salem, Mass., Essex Institute, 1926-1927. 2 vols.

Hadley (1661)

* Births, 1651-1687, marriages 1661-1688, deaths 1660-1686, typescript by Stuart G. Waite. Springfield, Mass., 1976. Copy in NEHGS; 1730-1845, from various sources, in Corbin Collection; Boltwood Collection, Jones Library, Amherst.

Halifax (1734)

Boston, Massachusetts Society of Mayflower Descendants, 1905. 211 pp.

Hamilton (1793)

Salem, Mass., Essex Institute, 1908. 112 pp.

Hancock (1776)

* 1770-1825, from various sources, in Corbin Collection.

Hanover (1727)

1727-1857. Rockland, Mass., Press of the Rockland Standard, 1898. 319 pp.

Hanson (1820)

Boston, NEHGS, 1911. 110 pp.

Hardwick (1739)

Compiled by Thomas W. Baldwin. Boston, Wright & Potter, 1917. 336 pp.

Harvard (1732)

Compiled by Thomas W. Baldwin. Boston, Wright & Potter, 1917. 326 pp.

Harwich (1694)

Mayflower Descendant, 3(1901):174-76; 4 (1902):175-79, 207-10; 5(1903):86-90, 202-04; 6 (1904):54-56, 82-85; 7(1905):194-98; 8 (1906):159-64, 217-20; 11(1909):173-76, 248-49; 13 (1911):55-60, 66-72, 147-49; 19(1917):55-60, 116-19; 20(1918):24-27; 23(1921):55-61, 117-22; 24 (1922):110-14, 150-54; 25(1923):60-64, 100-01; 33 (1935):60-73, 146-52; 34(1936):24-28, 67-73, 102-11. Index by Leonard H. Smith. Clearwater, Fla., 1976 (with Chatham).

Hatfield (1670)

* Births, 1722-1762, deaths, 1670-1843, marriages, 1670-1792, in NEHGS; 1661-1780, from various sources in Corbin Collection.

Haverhill (1641)

Topsfield, Mass., Topsfield Historical Society, 1910-1911. 2 vols.

Hawley (1792)

* 1770-1887, from various sources, in Corbin Collection.

Heath (1785)

Boston, NEHGS, 1915. 142 pp.

Hingham (1635)

* 1645-1844, manuscript in NEHGS.

Hinsdale (1804)

Boston, NEHGS, 1902. 98 pp.

Holden (1741)

Worcester, Mass., F. P. Rice, 1904. 236 pp.

Holland (1783)

———

Holliston (1724)

Boston, NEHGS, 1908. 358 pp.

Hopkinton (1715)   Boston, NEHGS, 1911. 462 pp.
Hubbardston (1767)   Worcester, Mass., F. P. Rice, 1907. 226 pp.
Hull (1644)   Compiled by Thomas W. Baldwin. Boston, 1911. 75 pp.

Huntington (1855; established   _____
as Norwich, 1773)
Ipswich (1634)   Salem, Mass., Essex Institute, 1910-1919. 3 vols.
Kingston (1726)   Boston, NEHGS, 1911. 396 pp.
Lancaster (1653)   Edited by Henry S. Nourse. Lancaster, W. J. Coulter, printer, 1890. 508 pp.

Lanesborough (1765)   1775-1886, in *History of the Town of Lanesborough,* by Charles Palmer, pp. 84-121; * 1756-1881, from town records, 1732-1842 from various sources, in Corbin Collection.

Lawrence (1847)   Salem, Mass., Essex Institute, 1926. 125 pp.
Lee (1777)   Boston, NEHGS, 1903. 239 pp.
Leicester (1714)   Worcester, Mass., F. P. Rice, 1903. 284 pp.
Lenox (1767)   * Marriages, 1771-1832, 1774-1848, Cooke Collection.

Leominster (1740)   Worcester, Mass., F. P. Rice, 1911. 369 pp.
Leverett (1774)   * 1732-1843, including church and town records, Corbin Collection.

Lexington (1713)   To 1898. Boston, 1898. 484 pp.

Leyden (1784)   _____
Lincoln (1754)   Boston, NEHGS, 1908. 179 pp.
Littleton (1715)   Littleton, Concord Patriot Press, 1900. 542 pp.
Longmeadow (1783)   Extracted in the *Register,* 31 (1877):318-20, 417-20; 32(1878): 67-70, 175-78, 302-05, 400-03; 33 (1879): 68-70, 202-04, 319-22, 416-19; 34 (1880): 31-34, 187-90, 264-67, 386-89; 35 (1881): 25-27, 159-63, 236-39, 356-59; 36 (1882): 75-77, 165-67, 313-15; 37 (1883): 358-61; 38 (1884): 46-49, 157-59.

Lowell (1826)   Salem, Mass., Essex Institute, 1930. 4 vols.
Ludlow (1774)   * Photostats of originals, 1774-1843, at NEHGS.
Lunenburg (1728)   Births, 1707-1764, marriage intentions, 1732-1764, marriages, 1727-1764, deaths, 1707-1764, in *Early Records of the Town of Lunenburg, Mass.,* (1896), pp. 223-350.

Lynn (1637)   Salem, Mass., Essex Institute, 1905-1906. 2 vols.
Lynnfield (1782 as district;   Salem, Mass., Essex Institute, 1907. 98 pp.
1814 as town)
Malden (1649)   Compiled by Deloraine P. Corey. Cambridge, University Press, 1903. 393 pp.

Manchester (1645)   Salem, Mass., Essex Institute, 1903. 296 pp.
Mansfield (1770)   Salem, Mass., Essex Institute, 1933. 230 pp.
Marblehead (1633; established   Salem, Mass., Essex Institute, 1903-1908. 3 vols.
1649)
Marlborough (1660)   Worcester, Mass., F. P. Rice, 1908. 404 pp.
Marshfield (1640)   Compiled by Robert M. and Ruth Wilder Sherman, Providence, R.I. Society of Mayflower Descendants, 1970.

Mashpee (1763)   _____
Medfield (1650)   Boston, NEHGS, 1903. 243 pp.
Medford (1630)   Boston, NEHGS, 1907. 469 pp.
Medway (1713)   Boston, NEHGS, 1905. 345 pp.

Mendon (1667)	Compiled by Thomas W. Baldwin. Boston, Wright & Potter, 1920. 518 pp.
Methuen (1725)	Topsfield, Mass., Topsfield Historical Society, 1909. 345 pp.
Middleborough (1669)	*Mayflower Descendant,* 1 (1899):219-24; 2 (1900): 41-43, 103-07, 157-60, 201-03; 3(1901): 83-86, 232-36; 4(1902): 67-75; 5(1903): 37-40; 6 (1904): 179-80, 226-29; 7(1905): 239-43; 8 (1906): 28-30, 248-50; 9(1907): 46-49; 12 (1910): 130-32, 230-33; 13(1911): 3-7, 249-53; 14 (1912): 243-46; 15(1913): 24, 120-22, 217-23; 16 (1914): 13-20, 106-09, 132-38, 244-48; 17 (1915): 19-22; 18(1916): 77-85, 151-58; 19 (1917): 46-48, 141-43, 173-76; 20(1918): 34-38; 22 (1920): 146-53; 23(1921): 43-48, 69-71; 24 (1922): 38-41, 55-58, 131-33, 185-86; 25(1923): 87-89, 104-09; 26(1924): 24-31; 27(1925): 131-34; 29 (1931): 183-90; 30(1932): 6-15; 31(1933): 133-39, 188-90; 32(1934): 3-12, 85-89, 135-41, 162-64; 33 (1935): 39-46, 75-78, 155-59; 34(1936): 123-30, 155-61. Index by Leonard H. Smith. Clearwater, Fla., 1974.
Middlefield (1783)	Boston, NEHGS, 1907. 138 pp.
Middleton (1728)	Topsfield, Mass., Topsfield Historical Society, 1904. 143 pp.
Milford (1780)	Compiled by Thomas W. Baldwin. Boston, Wright & Potter, 1917. 378 pp.
Millbury (1813)	Worcester, F. P. Rice, 1903. 158 pp.; 1850-1899, included in *Centennial History of the Town of Millbury, Massachusetts.* Millbury, by the Town, 1915.
Milton (1662)	Boston, A. Mudge & Son, 1900. 258 pp.
Monroe (1822)	
Monson (1760 as district; 1775 as town)	* 1750-1945, from various sources, in Corbin Collection.
Montague (1754; made town 1775)	Salem, Mass., Essex Institute, 1934. 167 pp. Bound with Buckland and Colrain.
Montgomery (1780)	Boston, NEHGS, 1902. 66 pp.
Mount Washington (1779)	
Nantucket (1795; mentioned as Sherburn 1687)	Boston, NEHGS, 1925-1928. 5 vols.
Natick (1650)	Compiled by Thomas W. Baldwin. Boston, Stanhope Press, 1910. 249 pp.
Needham (1711)	* Births to 1845, marriages and deaths to 1850, DAR typescript in NEHGS; births, 1749-1762, in the *Register,* 56(1902):141-49; marriages, 1720-1798, *ibid.,* 56 (1902):30-39; deaths, 1749-1762, *ibid.,* 56 (1902):265-70.
New Ashford (1781; made town 1835)	Boston, NEHGS, 1916. 43 pp.
New Bedford (1787)	Boston, NEHGS, 1932-1941. 3 vols.
New Braintree (1751; as town 1775)	Boston, NEHGS, 1904. 163 pp.
New Marlborough (1759; as town 1775)	* Cooke Collection
New Salem (1753; as town 1775)	Salem, Mass., Essex Institute, 1927. 283 pp.
Newbury (1635)	Salem, Mass., Essex Institute, 1911. 2 vols.
Newburyport (1764)	Salem, Mass., Essex Institute, 1911. 2 vols.

Newton (1691)

North Brookfield (1812)

Northampton (1656)

Boston, NEHGS, 1905. 521 pp.

––––––

* 1655-1844 from town records, through 1950 from various sources, in Corbin Collection; * Boltwood Collection, Jones Library, Amherst.

Northborough (1766; as town 1775)

Worcester, Mass., F. P. Rice, 1901. 153 pp.

Northbridge (1772; as town 1775)

Compiled by Thomas W. Baldwin. Boston, Wright & Potter, 1916. 202 pp.

Northfield (1714)

* 1715-1842 from town records, in Corbin Collection; * Judd manuscript, Forbes Library, Northampton.

Norton (1710; established 1711)

Boston, NEHGS, 1906. 405 pp.

Oakham (1762; made town 1775)

Worcester, F. P. Rice, 1905. 133 pp.

Orange (1783; incorporated 1810)

––––––

Orleans (1797)

Published with Eastham, q.v.

Otis (1810; established as Loudon, 1773)

Boston, NEHGS, 1941. 150 pp.

Oxford (1693)

Worcester, Mass., F. P. Rice, 1905. 315 pp.

Palmer (1752; as town 1775)

Boston, NEHGS, 1905. 242 pp.

Paxton (1765; as town 1775)

* 1749-1852, from town records, Corbin Collection.

Pelham (1743)

Boston, NEHGS, 1902. 177 pp.

Pembroke (1712)

Boston, NEHGS, 1911. 465 pp.

Pepperell (1753; as town 1775)

* Births, deaths, marriages, 1739-1767, DAR typescript at NEHGS.

Peru (1806; established as Partridgefield, 1771)

Boston, NEHGS, 1902. 112 pp.

Petersham (1754)

Worcester, Mass., F. P. Rice, 1904. 193 pp.

Phillipston (1814; incorporated as Gerry, 1786)

Worcester, Mass., F. P. Rice, 1906. 121 pp.

Pittsfield (1761)

Abstracted in "Pittsfield Families," manuscript by Rollin G. Cooke at NEHGS.

Plainfield (1785; incorporated as town, 1807)

* Marriages, Corbin Collection.

Plymouth (1620)

Records of Plymouth Colony: Births, Marriages, Deaths, Burials and Other Records, 1633-1689, edited by Nathaniel B. Shurtleff (Baltimore, 1979); *Mayflower Descendant,* 1 (1899):139-48, 206-12; 2 (1900):17-21, 77-81, 163-66, 224-27; 3(1901): 12-15, 121-24; 4(1902): 110-14; 5(1903): 53-56, 99-100; 7 (1905): 176-79, 208-10; 12(1910): 10-13, 84-87, 222-26; 13(1911): 32-36, 111-16, 165-75, 199-208; 14 (1912): 34-40, 70-76, 156-61, 239-43; 15(1913): 38-44, 110-15, 159-64, 209-14; 16(1914): 62-64, 84-90, 164-72, 254-55; 17(1915): 3-9, 123-24, 131-38; 18 (1916): 28-32, 117-25, 139-46, 211-16; 19(1917): 5-9, 90-93, 149-52; 20(1918): 70-73; 21(1919): 19-23, 94-95, 162-66; 22(1920): 31-36, 105-08, 178-84; 23 (1921): 8-12, 186-88; 24(1922): 14-19; 25 (1923): 51-54, 139-41, 187-89; 26(1924): 39-44, 84-87, 139-41, 189-90; 27(1925): 44-46, 175-78; 28 (1930): 34-35, 70-71; 29(1931): 90; 30(1932): 73-78, 115-19, 188-90; 31(1933): 2-4, 109-15, 182-84; 32 (1934): 21-24, 129-33; 33(1935): 33-35, 140-41, 179-80; 34(1936): 7-9.

Plympton (1707) — Boston, NEHGS, 1923. 540 pp.

Prescott (1822; annexed 1938 to Petersham and New Salem) — * Typescript, compiled by Mary Mattoon Chapter, DAR. Amherst, Mass., 1970. Copy at NEHGS.

Princeton (1759; as town 1771) — Worcester, Mass., F. P. Rice, 1902. 195 pp.

Provincetown (1727) — *Mayflower Descendant,* 9(1907): 100-03; 11 (1909): 47-49, 187-88, 216-19; 12(1910): 21-26, 76-80; 14(1912): 146-50; 15(1913): 149-53; 22 (1920): 101-04; 23(1921): 92-96, 141-44, 168-71; 26 (1924): 112-14, 123-28; 27(1925): 123-28.

Quincy (1792) — * 1792-1843, in the Waldo C. Sprague Collection, NEHGS; microfilm copy in Quincy Historical Society.

Randolph (1793) — * 1843-1850, in the Waldo C. Sprague Collection, NEHGS.

Raynham (1731) — *Register,* 51(1897): 437-40; 52 (1898): 295-96; 53 (1899): 58-60, 434-39; 54(1900): 15-20; 55 (1901): 41-47.

Reading (1644) — Compiled by Thomas W. Baldwin. Boston, Wright & Potter, 1912. 586 pp.

Rehoboth (1645) — 1642-1896; by James M. Arnold. Providence, Narragansett Historical Publishing Co., 1897. 926 pp.

Richmond (1785; incorporated as Richmont, 1765) — Boston, NEHGS, 1913. 113 pp.

Rochester (1686) — Boston, NEHGS, 1914. 2 vols.

Rockport (1840) — Salem, Mass., Essex Institute, 1924. 120 pp.

Rowe (1785) — * 1773-1852, from town books, in Corbin Collection

Rowley (1639) — Salem, Mass., Essex Institute, 1928. 2 vols.

Roxbury (1630; annexed to Boston, 1868) — Salem, Mass., Essex Institute, 1925-1926. 2 vols.

Royalston (1765) — Worcester, Mass., F. P. Rice, 1906. 196 pp.

Russell (1792) — * 1776-1836 from town books, in Corbin Collection

Rutland (1714) — Worcester, Mass., F. P. Rice, 1905. 255 pp.

Salem (1630) — Salem, Mass., Essex Institute, 1916-1925. 6 vols.

Salisbury (1640; called Colechester, 1639) — Topsfield, Mass., Topsfield Historical Society, 1915. 636 pp.

Sandisfield (1762) — Compiled by Capt. Elizur Yale Smith. Rutland, Vt., Tuttle, 1936. 111 pp.

Sandwich (1638) — *Mayflower Descendant,* 14 (1912):106-12, 166-74; 29 (1931):21-33, 68-75; 30 (1932):58, 99. Index to April 1775, by Leonard H. Smith. Clearwater, Fla., 1975 (with Wareham); *Genealogical Advertiser,* 3 (1900):33-36, 73-77; 4 (1901):9-14, 99-103.

Saugus (1815) — Salem, Mass., Essex Institute, 1907. 81 pp.

Savoy (1797) — * Marriages, 1797-1865, Corbin Collection; Cooke Collection.

Scituate (1633) — Boston, NEHGS, 1909. 2 vols.

Seekonk (1812) — *Vital Records of Rhode Island, 1636-1850,* by James M. Arnold. Providence, R.I., 1897. Vol. 9, pp. 1-295.

Sharon (1783; incorporated as Stoughtonham 1765; made town 1775) — Compiled by Thomas W. Baldwin. Boston, Stanhope Press, 1909.

Sheffield (1773) — *National Genealogical Society Quarterly,* deaths 1734-1813, 27 (1939):45-47; marriages, 1731-1786, 27 (1939):42-45; * typescript through 1783, by Joseph M. Kellogg, in NEHGS; * Cooke Collection.

Shelburne (1768; made town 1775)

Sherborne (1674)

Salem, Mass., Essex Institute, 1931. 190 pp.

Compiled by Thomas W. Baldwin. Boston, Stanhope Press, 1911. 229 pp.

Shirley (1753; made town 1775)

Boston, NEHGS, 1918. 211 pp.

Shrewsbury (1720; established 1727)

Worcester, Mass., F. P. Rice, 1904. 282 pp.

Shutesbury (1761)

* Index only in Corbin Collection.

Somerset (1790)

_____

South Hadley (1753; as town 1775)

* 1731-1843 from town records, in Corbin Collection.

Southampton (1753; made town 1775)

* 1728-1847 from town records, in Corbin Collection.

Southborough (1727)

Worcester, Mass., F. P. Rice, 1903. 187 pp.

Southbridge (1816)

_____

Southwick (1770; as town 1775)

_____

Spencer (1753; as town 1775)

Worcester, Mass., F. P. Rice, 1909. 276 pp.

Springfield (1641)

Births, 1640-1681, *Register,* 18 (1864): 82-86, 142-47; 19(1865): 61-64, 249-52; * 1639-1747 from town records, in Corbin Collection; * 1636-1800's, in Springfield City Library.

Sterling (1781)

Compiled by Frances Pratt Tapley. Sterling, Historical Commission, 1976. 134 pp.

Stockbridge (1739)

* Marriages 1739-1835, births from 1777, typescript in NEHGS.

Stoneham (1725)

Salem, Mass., Essex Institute, 1918. 191 pp.

Stoughton (1726)

1727-1800, edited by Frederic Endicott. Canton, Mass., W. Bense, 1896. 317 pp.

Stow (1683)

Boston, NEHGS, 1911. 270 pp.

Sturbridge (1738)

Boston, NEHGS, 1906. 393 pp.

Sudbury (1639)

Boston, NEHGS, 1903. 332 pp.

Sunderland (1718; established as Swampfield, 1714)

* 1716-1844 from town records in Corbin Collection; * Judd Manuscript, Forbes Library, Northampton.

Sutton (1714)

Worcester, Mass., F. P. Rice, 1907. 478 pp.

Swansea (1668; established as Wannamoisett, 1667)

1662-1705, edited by Alverdo Hayward Mason. East Braintree, Mass., A. H. Mason, 1900; 1702-1800, edited by Marion P. Carter, 1930.

Taunton (1639)

Boston, NEHGS, 1928-1929. 3 vols.

Templeton (1762)

Worcester, Mass., F. P. Rice, 1907. 212 pp.

Tewksbury (1734)

Salem, Mass., Essex Institute, 1912. 246 pp.

Tisbury (1671)

Boston, NEHGS, 1910. 244 pp.

Tolland (1810)

_____

Topsfield (1648; established 1650)

To 1850, Topsfield, Mass., Topsfield Historical Society, 1903. 258 pp.; 1850-1899, Topsfield Historical Society, 1916.

Townsend (1732)

_____

Truro (1709)

Boston, Massachusetts Society of Mayflower Descendants, 1933. 480 pp.

Tyngsborough (1789; as town 1809)

Salem, Mass., Essex Institute, 1912. 119 pp.

Tyringham (1762)

Boston, NEHGS, 1903. 108 pp.

Upton (1735)

Worcester, Mass., F. P. Rice, 1904. 190 pp.

Uxbridge (1727) — Compiled by Thomas W. Baldwin. Boston, Wright & Potter, 1916. 420 pp.

Wakefield (1868; incorporated as South Reading, 1812) — Compiled by Thomas W. Baldwin. Boston, Wright & Potter, 1912. 341 pp.

Wales (1828; incorporated as South Brimfield, 1812) — * 1751-1860 from town records, in Corbin Collection.

Walpole (1724) — Boston, NEHGS, 1902. 216 pp.

Waltham (1738) — Boston, NEHGS, 1904. 298 pp.

Ware (1761; as town 1775) — * 1732-1905 from town records, in Corbin Collection.

Wareham (1739) — *Mayflower Descendant,* 31 (1933):125-32, 153-58; 32 (1934):179-90. Index by Leonard H. Smith. Clearwater, Fla., 1975. (with Sandwich).

Warren (1834; established as Western, 1742) — Worcester, Mass., F. P. Rice, 1910. 196 pp.

Warwick (1763) — ———

Washington (1777) — Boston, NEHGS, 1904. 57 pp.

Watertown (1630) — Through 1822, in *Watertown Records,* prepared by the Historical Society. Watertown, 1894-1906, vols. 1-3.

Wayland (1835; incorporated as East Sudbury, 1780) — Boston, NEHGS, 1910. 160 pp.

Webster (1832) — ———

Wellfleet (1763; as town 1775) — * 1800-1849, manuscript in NEHGS.

Wendell (1781) — ———

Wenham (1643) — Salem, Mass., Essex Institute, 1904. 227 pp.

West Boylston (1808) — Worcester, Mass., F. P. Rice, 1911. 153 pp.

West Bridgewater (1822) — Boston, NEHGS, 1911. 222 pp.

West Newbury (1820; incorporated as Parsons, 1819) — Salem, Mass., Essex Institute, 1918. 122 pp.

West Springfield (1774) — Boston, NEHGS, 1944. 237 pp.

West Stockbridge (1774; as town 1775) — Boston, NEHGS, 1907. 115 pp.

Westborough (1717) — Worcester, Mass., F. P. Rice, 1903. 258 pp.

Westfield (1669) — * 1672-1864 from various sources, in Corbin Collection; *Boltwood Collection, Jones Library, Amherst.

Westford (1729) — Salem, Mass., Essex Institute, 1915. 325 pp.

Westhampton (1778) — * 1770-1844 from various sources, in Corbin Collection.

Westminster (1759; incorporated 1770) — Worcester, Mass., F. P. Rice, 1908. 258 pp.

Weston (1713) — Boston, McIndoe Brothers, printers, 1901. 649 pp.

Westport (1787) — Boston, NEHGS, 1918. 296 pp.

Weymouth (1635) — Boston, NEHGS, 1910. 2 vols.

Whately (1771) — Abstracted in *Whately 1771-1971: A New England Portrait,* by Ena M. Crane. Family records compiled by Paul F. Field. Northampton, Mass., 1972.

Wilbraham (1763) — * 1732-1849, from various sources, in Corbin Collection; * in DAR Library; * through 1850 in Springfield City Library.

Williamsburg (1771; as town, 1775.) — * 1749-1850, from various sources, in Corbin Collection.

Wilmington (1730) — To 1898. Compiled by James E. Kelley. Lowell, Mass., 1898. 255 pp.

Winchendon (1764)	Worcester, F. P. Rice, 1909. 223 pp.
Windsor (1778; established as Gageborough, 1771)	Boston, NEHGS, 1917. 153 pp.
Woburn (1642)	To 1901. 9 parts. Woburn, Andrew Cutler & Co., 1890-1918.
Worcester (1684)	Compiled by F. P. Rice. Worcester, Mass., Society of Antiquity, 1894. 527 pp.
Worthington (1768)	Boston, NEHGS, 1911. 159 pp.
Wrentham (1673)	Compiled by Thomas W. Baldwin. 2 vols. Boston, Stanhope Press, 1910.
Yarmouth (1639)	Compiled by Robert M. Sherman and Ruth Wilder Sherman. 2 vols. Providence, R.I. Society of Mayflower Descendants, 1975.

APPENDIX

Town Histories

The following is a highly selective list of a few histories of eastern towns whose genealogical sections cover virtually all, or very many, seventeenth- and eighteenth-century residents. Many other histories of Massachusetts towns contain less definitive genealogies of town inhabitants.

Barnstable: Amos Otis, *Genealogical Notes of Barnstable Families*. . . . 2 vols. in 1. Barnstable, 1888-1890, reprint ed., Baltimore, 1979.

Cambridge: Lucius R. Paige. *History of Cambridge, Massachusetts, 1630-1877*. Boston, 1877. Mary Isabella Gozzardi. *Supplement and Index* . . . . Cambridge, 1930.

Charlestown: Thomas B. Wyman. *The Genealogies and Estates of Charlestown . . . 1629-1818*. 2 vols. Boston, 1879.

Cohasset: George Lyman Davenport and Elizabeth Osgood Davenport. *The Genealogies of the Families of Cohasset, Massachusetts*. Cohasset, 1909.

Hanover: Jedediah Dwelley and John F. Simmons. *History of the Town of Hanover, Massachusetts with Family Genealogies*. Hanover, 1910.

Hingham: George Lincoln. *History of the Town of Hingham, Massachusetts*. 3 vols. in 4. Hingham, 1893.

Lexington: Charles Hudson. *History of the Town of Lexington From its First Settlement to 1868*. 2 vols. Boston, 1913.

Martha's Vineyard: Charles Edward Banks. *The History of Martha's Vineyard*. 3 vols. Boston, 1911-1925.

Nantucket: Alexander Starbuck. *The History of Nantucket* . . . . Boston, 1924; reprint ed., Rutland, Vt., 1969.

Plymouth: William T. Davis. *Ancient Landmarks of Plymouth*. Boston, 1883 2d. ed., 1899. Part II was reprinted as *Genealogical Register of Plymouth Families*. Baltimore, 1975.

Rehoboth: Richard leBaron Bowen. *Early Rehoboth: Documented Historical Studies of Families and Events in this Plymouth Colony Township*. 4 vols. Rehoboth, 1945-1950.

Rowley: George Brainard Blodgette, compiler, and Amos Everett Jewett, editor. *Early Settlers of Rowley*. Rowley, 1933.

Salem: Sidney Perley. *The History of Salem, Masschusetts*. 3 vols. Salem, 1924-1928.

Salisbury and Amesbury: David W. Hoyt. *The Old Families of Salisbury and Amesbury*. 4 vols. Providence, R.I., 1897-1919.

Watertown: Henry Bond. *Genealogies of the Families and Descendants of the Early Settlers of Watertown, including Waltham and Weston*. 2 vols. in 1. Boston, 1860; reprint ed., Boston, 1978.

Weymouth: George W. Chamberlain. *History of Weymouth, Massachusetts.* 4 vols. Boston, 1923.

Other towns are genealogically well covered by manuscripts at the Society. The following is again a highly selective list.

Andover: Charlotte Helen Abbott Collection.

Belchertown, Hancock, Northampton, Pittsfield (a copy of Rollin H. Cook's "Notes on Pittsfield Families," manuscript, 8 vols.), Southampton, Wales, and Ware: Walter E. Corbin Collection.

Braintree and vicinity: Waldo C. Sprague Collection.

Scituate and vicinity: Hamilton W. Welch Collection.

Springfield: Thomas B. Warren, "Springfield, Massachusetts Families," typescript. 4 vols. Springfield, 1934-1935.

SINGLE FAMILY GENEALOGIES

The number of genealogies which concentrate upon a single Massachusetts family or the descendants of a particular immigrant is very large; the following, therefore, cover only a few families well known in American history.

Adams: Andrew M. Adams. *A Genealogical History of Henry Adams of Braintree, Massachusetts and His Descendantsand also John Adams of Cambridge, Massachusetts, 1632-1897.* Rutland, Vt., 1898.

Ames: Winthrop Ames. *Ames Family of Easton, Massachusetts.* North Easton, Mass., 1938.

Bowditch: Harold Bowditch. "The Bowditch Family of Braintree, Mass.," *Register,* 79 (1925): 175-185, 268-286.

Bradford: Ruth G. Hall. *Descendants of Governor William Bradford.* N.p., 1951.

Brewster: Emma C. Brewster Jones. *The Brewster Genealogy 1566-1907.* 2 vols. New York, 1908.

Bulkeley: Donald Lines Jacobus, *The Bulkeley Genealogy: Rev. Peter Bulkeley.* New Haven, Conn., 1933.

Cabot: Lloyd V. Briggs. *History and Genealogy of the Cabot Family, 1475-1927.* 2 vols. Boston, 1927.

Choate: Ephraim O. Jameson. *The Choates in America, 1643-1896.* Boston, 1896.

Coolidge: Emma Downing Coolidge. *Descendants of John and Mary Coolidge of Watertown, Massachusetts, 1630.* Boston, 1930.

Crowninshield: G. Andrews Moriarty. "The Family of Clifford Crowninshield of Salem, Mass.," *Register,* 104 (1950): 285-290.

Cushing: James G. Cushing. *Cushing Family.* Montreal. 1905. Allston T. Cushing. *The Genealogy of the Cushing Family, 1905-1969.* Kansas City, Mo., 1969.

Dudley: Dean Dudley. *The History of the Dudley Family.* 2 vols. Wakefield, Mass., 1894.

Dwight: Benjamin W. Dwight. *Descendants of John Dwight of Dedham, Massachusetts.* 2 vols. N.Y., 1874.

Fuller: William H. Fuller. *Genealogy of Some Descendants of Edward Fuller of the Mayflower.* 3 vols. Palmer, Mass., 1908-1914.

Hale-House: Donald L. Jacobus. *Hale, House, and Related Families, Mainly of the Connecticut River Valley.* Hartford, Conn., 1952.

Howland: Mrs. Curtis W. Hunter. *The Family of John Howland, Mayflower Passenger.* Indianapolis?, 1970.

Lawrence: John Lawrence. *Family of John Lawrence . . . 1636-1869.* Boston, 1869.

Lowell: Delmar R. Lowell. *Historic Genealogy of the Lowells of America, 1636-1899.* Rutland, Vt., 1899.

Otis: William A. Otis. *Genealogical and Historical Memoir of the Otis Family in America.* Chicago, 1924.

Parkman: Arthur W. Hodgman. "Elias Parkman of Dorchester." Lowell, Mass., 1929. Typescript at the Society.

Phillips: Albert M. Phillips. *Phillips Genealogies Including the Family of George Phillips, First Minister of Watertown.* Auburn, Mass., 1885.

Pickering: Harris Ellery and Charles P. Bowditch. *Pickering Genealogy, An Account of the First Three Generations and the Descendants of John and Sarah (Burrill) Pickering of the Third Generation.* 3 vols. Cambridge, Mass., 1897. Six manuscript volumes of charts outlining the ancestry of all spouses of John Pickering descendants were deposited at the Society.

Saltonstall: Leverett Saltonstall. *Ancestry and Descendants of Sir Richard Saltonstall . . . .* N.Y., 1897; Robert E. Moody, "The Saltonstall Papers 1607-1815," *Massachusetts Historical Society Collections,* 80 (1972): 549-557.

Sargent: Emma W. and Charles S. Sargent. *Epes Sargent of Gloucester and his Descendants.* Boston, 1923.

Sedgwick: H. M. Sedgwick. *A Sedgwick Genealogy: Descendants of Deacon Benjamin Sedgwick.* New Haven, Conn., 1961.

Sears: Samuel P. May, "Richard Sears of Yarmouth and his Descendants," 2 vols. Newton, Mass., 1913. Typescript at the Society.

Strong: Benjamin W. Dwight. *The History of the Descendants of Elder John Strong of Northampton, Mass.* 2 vols. Albany, N.Y., 1871.

Thatcher: John R. Totten. *Thacher-Thatcher Genealogy.* 3 vols. N.Y., 1910.

Winslow: David P. Holton and Mrs. F. K. Holton. *Family Records of the Winslows and their Descendants in America.* 2 vols. N.Y., 1877.

Winthrop: Lawrence S. Mayo. *The Winthrop Family in America.* Boston, 1948. Ellery Kirke Taylor. *The Lion and the Hare.* Ann Arbor, Mich., 1939.

SEVENTY MULTI-ANCESTOR GENEALOGIES

This list was compiled by Gary Boyd Roberts as a supplement to the sixty similar works listed by Donald Lines Jacobus in "My Own Index," an appendix to his *Index to Genealogical Periodicals,* vol. 3 (1947-1952) (New Haven, 1953). The first three volumes of Seversmith's compendium (see below), and the ten additional multi-ancestor works by W.G. Davis were listed by Jacobus, and all of the pre-1960 works in both lists are indexed for married seventeenth-century New Englanders in Clarence Almon Torrey's *New England Marriages Prior to 1700.* This list, like Jacobus's, is limited to works concerning largely New Englanders (most of Massachusetts Bay) and residents of Long Island. Deliberately excluded as not quite of the standard set by the works below, but certainly worth pursuing, are the several multi-ancestor volumes compiled by Mrs. Josephine C. Frost.

Allaben, Frank. *The Ancestry of Leander Howard Crall.* N.Y., 1908.

Backus Mary E.N. *The New England Ancestry of Dana Converse Backus.* Salem, Mass., 1949.

Bartlett, Genevieve W. *Forefathers and Descendants of Willard and Genevieve Wilson Bartlett.* St. Louis, 1952.

Bassette, Buel B. *One Bassett Family in America.* Springfield, Mass., 1926.

Bates, George E. *A Bates-Breed Ancestry.* Boston, 1975.

Blake, Frances E. *Edgecombe, Yates and Allied Lines.* Kalamazoo, Mich., 1968.

Boyer, Carl. *Slade-Babcock Genealogy: Ancestors and Descendants of Benjamin and*

Angeline (Babcock) Slade of Renssalaer and Saratoga Counties, New York. Newhall, Calif., 1970; *Ancestral Lines: 144 Families in England, Germany, New England, New Jersey, and Pennsylvania.* Newhall, Calif., 1975.

Bunce, Julia L.F. *Some of the Ancestors of the Reverend John Selby Frame and his wife, Clara Winchester Dana.* Minneapolis, 1948.

Coe, Levi E. *Coe-Ward Memorial and Immigrant Ancestors.* Meriden, Conn., 1897.

Davis, Betsey W. *The Warren, Jackson, and Allied Families, being the Ancestry of Jesse Warren and Betsey Jackson.* Philadelphia, 1903.

Davis, Walter G. *The Ancestry of Charity Haley* . . . . Boston, 1916; *The Ancestry of Nicholas Davis* . . . . Portland, Me., 1956; *The Ancestry of Sarah Hildreth* . . . . Portland, Me., 1958; *The Ancestry of Dudley Wildes* . . . . Portland, Me., 1959; *The Ancestry of Sarah Johnson* . . . . Portland, Me., 1960; *The Ancestry of Abel Lunt* . . . . Portland, Me., 1963.

Deforest, Louis E. *Ballard and Allied Families.* N.Y., 1924; *Ludington-Saltus Records.* New Haven, 1925; *Babcock and Allied Families.* N.Y., 1928; *Jelke and Frazier and Allied Families.* N.Y., 1931; *James Cox Brady and His Ancestry.* N.Y., 1933; *Ancestry of William Seaman Bainbridge.* Oxford, 1950.

Delafield, John R. *Delafield: The Family History.* 2 vols. N.Y., 1945.

Elston, James S. *Descent from 79 (now 92) Early Immigrant Heads of Families.* 2 vols. Middleboro, Mass., 1962-1971; *Ancestors of Francis Walker and Sarah Effie Vinton Kelley.* Burlington, Vt., 1964.

Emery, William M. *Newell Ancestry: The Story of the Antecedent of William Stark Newell.* Boston, 1944.

Fish, Stuyvesant. *Ancestors of Hamilton Fish and Julia Ursin Niemcewicz Kean, his Wife.* N.Y., 1929.

Hickok, Charles N. *The Hickok Genealogy.* Rutland, Vt., 1938.

Holman, Alfred L. *A Register of the Ancestors of Dorr Eugene Felt and Agnes (McNulty) Felt.* Chicago, 1921.

Hook, James William. *Lt. Samuel Smith: His Children and One Line of Descendants and Related Families.* New Haven, 1953; *Smith, Grant, and Irons Families of New Jersey's Shore Counties, Including the Related Families of Willets and Birdsall.* New Haven, 1955.

Johnson, Miles Beardsley. *Ancestral Sketches.* North Hollywood, 1968.

King, Charles D. *An Interim Tracing of the Ancestry of Valerie Daly King.* Richmond, Va., 1956.

Leach, Josiah G. *Memoranda Relating to the Ancestry and Family of Hon. Levi Parsons Morton, Vice President of the United States (1889-1893).* Cambridge, Mass., 1894.

Lowell, D.O.S. *A Munsey-Hopkins Genealogy: Being the Ancestry of Andrew Chauncey Munsey and Mary Jane Merrett Hopkins, The Parents of Frank A. Munsey, His Brothers and Sisters.* Boston, 1920.

Massey, George, V. *The Mitchells and Days of Philadelphia.* N.Y., 1968.

McArthur, Selim Walker. *McArthur-Barnes Ancestral Lines.* Portland, Me., 1964.

McCormick, Robert H. III, and Elizabeth D. *McCormick-Hamiton-Lord-Day Ancestral Lines.* Chicago, 1957.

Morse, William I. *Genealogiae, or Data Concerning the Families of Morse, Chipman, Phinney, Ensign and Whiting.* Boston, 1925.

Norris, D.W. and H.A. Feldman, *The Wells Family.* Milwaukee, 1942.

Noyes, Charles P. *Noyes-Gilman Ancestry.* St. Paul, 1907.

Paine, Sarah C. *Paine Ancestry: The Family of Robert Treat Paine, Signer of the Declaration of Independence, Including Maternal Lines.* Edited by Charles H. Pope. Boston, 1912.

Parke, Nathan G. II. *The Ancestry of Rev. Nathan Grier Parke and His Wife, Ann Gildersleeve.* Edited by D.L. Jacobus. Woodstock, Vt., 1959; *The Ancestry of Lorenzo Ackley and His Wife, Emma Arabella Bosworth.* Edited by D.L. Jacobus. Woodstock, Vt., 1960; *The Ancestry and Descendants of Frederick Tracy Camp and His Wife, Marion Fee.* Edited by D.L. Jacobus. Woodstock, Vt., 1961.

Paul, Edward Joy. *The Ancestry of Katherine Choate Paul, Now Mrs. William J. Young, Jr.* Milwaukee, 1914.

Pitman, Harold M. *Snyder-Brown Ancestry.* Bronxville, N.Y., 1958; *Comstock-Thomas Ancestry of Richmond Wilmot Comstock.* Bronxville, N.Y., 1964; *Ancestry of William Stingler Mitchell, Cornelius Von Erden Mitchell, John Van Beuren Mitchell.* ?, 1967; *Boyd-Patterson Ancestry.* ?, 1967.

Preston, Belle. *Bassett-Preston Ancestors.* New Haven, 1930.

Prindle, Paul W. *Ancestry of Elizabeth Barrett Gillepsie (Mrs. William Sperry Beinecke).* New Orleans, La., 1976.

Rideout, Mrs. Grant. *Ancestors and Descendants of Sarah Eleanor Ladue.* Chicago, 1930.

Rutherford, William K. and Anna C. (Zimmerman) Rutherford. *Genealogical History of Our Ancestors.* ?, 1970, rev. ed., Marcelline, Mo., 1977.

Salisbury, Edward E. *Family Memorials: A Series of Genealogical and Biographical Monographs on the Families of Salisbury, Aldworth-Elbridge, Sewall, Pyldren-Dummer, Walley, Quincy, Gookin, Wendell, Breese, Chevalier-Anderson, and Phillips.* New Haven, 1885.

Salisbury, Edward E., and Evelyn M. *Family Histories and Genealogies: A Series of Genealogical and Biographical Monographs on the Families of MacCurdy, Mitchell, Lord, Lynde, Digby, Newdigate, Hoo, Willoughby, Griswold, Diodati, Lee, and Marvin, and Notes on the Families of Buchanan, Parmellee, Boardman, Lay, Locke, Cole, DeWolf, Drake, Bond, and Swayne, Dunbar and Clarke.* New Haven, 1892.

Seversmith, Herbert F. *Colonial Families of Long Island, New York, and Connecticut, Being the Ancestry and Kindred of Herbert Furman Seversmith.* Vol. 4. Washington, D.C., 1953.

Snow, Nora D. *The Snow-Estes Ancestry.* 2 vols. Hilburn, N.Y. 1939.

Stryker-Rodda, Harriet M. *Ancestors and Descendants of Frank Lusk Babbott, Jr., M.D., and His Wife Elizabeth Bassett French.* Princeton, 1974.

Sumner, Edith B. *Ancestry of Edward Wales Blake and Clarissa Matilda Glidden with 90 Allied Families.* Los Angeles, 1948; *Ancestry and Descendants of Samuel Bartlett and Lucy Jenkins.* Los Angeles, 1951; *Ancestry and Descendants of Amaziah Hall and Betsey Baldwin.* Los Angeles, 1954; *Ancestry and Descendants of James Hensman Coltman and Betsey Tobey.* Los Angeles, 1957; *Descendants of Thomas Farr of Harpswell, Maine and 90 Allied Families.* Los Angeles, 1959.

Talcott, S.V. *Genealogical Notes of New York and New England Families.* Albany, 1883; reprint ed., Baltimore, 1973.

Watson, Estell C. *Loyalist Clarks, Badgleys and Allied Families.* Rutland, Vt., 1954.

Weis, Frederick L. *One Thousand New England Ancestors of Frank Chester Harrington and Leora (Leighton) Harrington.* Worcester, Mass., 1958.

Williams, Cornelia B. *Ancestry of Lawrence Williams.* Chicago, 1915.

Woolson, Lula May (Fenno) and Charles A. *The Woolson Fenno Ancestry and Allied Lines with Biographical Sketches.* Springfield, Vt., 1907.

ADDITIONS AND CORRECTIONS

Page 91

Two recent additions to the guides for religious archives are: James M. O'Toole, *Guide to the Archives of the Archdiocese of Boston* (New York, 1982); and Mary Frederica Rhinelander Morgan, "Manuscript Collections of The Congregational Library at Boston: A Survey" (M.A. thesis, University of Massachusetts, Boston, 1982), available at the Society.

Vital Records

In addition to those published volumes listed on pages 97-108, many towns continue to publish vital records in their annual town reports. These can be found either at the town level or at the State Library in Boston. Addenda to the previous list include:

Barnstable (1638)	*Vital Records of Southeastern Massachusetts,* Vol. III. 280 p. Reprint from *Mayflower Descendant* with new index by Leonard H. Smith. Clearwater, Fla., Owl Books, 1982.
Eastham (1651)	*Vital Records of Southeastern Massachusetts.* Vol. I. 269 p. Reprint from *Mayflower Descendant* with new index by Leonard H. Smith. Clearwater, Fla., 1980.
Harwich (1694)	Harwich, Harwich Historical Society, 1982. 603 p.
Middleborough (1669)	*Vital Records of Southeastern Massachusetts.* Vol. II. 288 p. Reprint from *Mayflower Descendant* with new index by Leonard H. Smith. Clearwater, Fla., Owl Books, 1981.
Orleans (1797)	Published with Eastham, see above.
Sandwich (1638)	Published with Barnstable, see above.
Southbridge (1816)	Oxford, Mass., Holbrook Research Institute, 1981. 292 p.
Topsfield (1648)	1900-1950 published in vol. 33, *Historical Collections of the Topsfield Historical Society.* Topsfield, 1982.
Truro (1709)	*Marriages, 1850-1899. Compiled by Mrs. W. Alden Burrell for Lexington Chapter, DAR, 1950. Copy at NEHGS.

Wareham (1739)   Published with Middleborough, see above.

Webster (1832)   Oxford, Mass., Holbrook Research Institute, 1980. 321 p.

Williamstown (1765)   Boston, NEGHS. 1907. 173 p.

Page 78, line 39
For 54 *substitute* 44 (the *Register* volume containing an Isaac Allerton article).

Page 111, line 2
For the second Carl Boyer entry *substitute Ancestral Lines Revised: 190 Families in England, Wales, Germany, New England, New York, New Jersey, and Pennsylvania,* Newhall, Calif., 1981.

Page 111, line 14
For Deforest *substitute* deForest.

Page 112, line 23
For Snow, Nora D. *substitute* Snow, Nora E.

CONNECTICUT GENEALOGICAL RESEARCH: SOURCES AND SUGGESTIONS

Elizabeth Abbe

Connecticut may look small geographically, but genealogists and historians should not be deceived by its size. Its historical and genealogical resources are superior to most other states, and genealogists fortunate in tracing their families to Connecticut will find an abundance of records and a high degree of centralization. The purpose of this article is to provide a detailed observation of important primary sources not in print.[1] There is a progression to those sources, but the researcher must first be aware of the standard secondary and printed primary sources available to him.

General guides to the earliest settlers of Connecticut include Nathaniel Goodwin, *Genealogical Notes or Contributions to the Family History of Some of the First Settlers of Connecticut* (Hartford, 1856). It contains sketches of a selective number of early settlers and their connected lines. Also, Royal Hinman, *Catalogue of the Names of the First Puritan Settlers of the Colony of Connecticut with the Time of their Arrival in the Colony* (Hartford, 1846) has information collected from state and town records. A second, more detailed edition appeared in 1852 but only covers surnames through Danielson. Starting in the 1800s, biographical publications became popular and sketches of prominent citizens included genealogical data. Directories of special groups of people, college alumni publications, and books on Connecticut craftsmen all contain references to specific individuals as well. These sources are generally available and, in combination with printed family genealogies and general indexes (such as the multivolumed Freemont Rider, ed., *The American Genealogical-Bio-*

---

1. Other articles written on Connecticut's genealogical sources and the vast resources of the Connecticut State Library include: Margery Case, "Connecticut Resources for Genealogical Research," *National Genealogical Society Quarterly*, 36 (1948): 2-4; Robert Claus, *Guide to Archives in the Connecticut State Library*, 2nd ed. (Hartford, 1978). This is a concise guide, compiled by the state archivist, to the record groups in the State Library; Robert E. Schnare, Jr., *Local Historical Resources in Connecticut: A Guide to Their Use* (Darien, Conn., 1975). This source is particularly helpful to people compiling town histories; Robert E. Schnare, Jr., "The Genealogical Resources of the Connecticut State Library," *Bulletin of the Stamford Genealogical Society*, 14 (1971): 5-9; Sylvie Turner, "The Connecticut Archives," *Connecticut Historical Society Bulletin*, 33 (1968): 81-89. The "Connecticut Archives" are the records of the General Assembly through 1820 which are arranged by topic. Several projects on genealogical research in Connecticut are ongoing. David Palmquist (Head, Historical Collections at the Bridgeport Public Library) in cooperation with Thomas Kemp (local history and genealogy librarian at the Ferguson Library in Stamford) and a staff of volunteers are updating and expanding an earlier publication, *Guide to the Genealogical Resources in Southwestern Fairfield County* (Stamford, Conn., 1959).

graphical Index [Middletown, Conn., 1952-   ]), serve as a place to begin the search for a Connecticut ancestor.

I

Once the search has begun, the genealogist is inevitably led to the primary sources, originating in the historical period with which they are concerned. Some have been printed from the original manuscripts which detracts little from their accuracy and increases their availability. The primary sources cited in this section may be found in major public, university, and several special libraries. Others may be borrowed via interlibrary loan, and a few will necessitate a visit to or correspondence with Connecticut's repositories of historical records.

Perhaps the most widely used of these sources are the census records, which can be the most consistent and periodic source of information on individuals and families. The colonial Connecticut censuses were merely statistical compilations taken in 1756, 1762, and 1775. A helpful *Connecticut 1670 Census* (Oxford, Mass., 1977) has been reconstructed by Jay Holbrook who compiled data from household, estate, tax, landowner, church, and freeman lists. This census is significant because it lists household heads and freemen by surname. Some Connecticut town lists and town censuses are cited in John D. Stemmons, *The United States Census Compendium* (Logan, Utah, 1973). The earliest town list for Connecticut was a grain inventory for Hartford, Wethersfield, and Windsor taken in 1669/70, giving the name of the household head and number of persons in each family. It has been printed in "The Wyllys Papers," Vol. 21 in *Collections of The Connecticut Historical Society* ([Hartford, 1924], 190-199). Special state industrial, agricultural, and social censuses were conducted in the nineteenth century and may be consulted at the Connecticut State Library (231 Capitol Ave., Hartford, Conn. 06115).

The federal census for Connecticut has been taken decennially since 1790. From these records one can not only determine the composition of a specific household, but also trace family relocations within the state and the migration routes of Connecticut people. The National Archives and Records Service Administration published the 1790 census in hardbound copies with an alphabetical index. All other open census schedules, with the exception of 1890, are available on microfilm. A special index to the Connecticut federal census records from 1790 to 1850 is housed at the Connecticut State Library. Connecticut censuses have also been indexed by Accelerated Indexing Systems from 1800 through 1850. The 1880 and 1900 schedules are indexed using the Soundex system.

Military records are often consulted by people seeking membership in patriotic societies. Connecticut's lists of servicemen are extensive and accessible in most major libraries. Connecticut men who served in colonial wars may be located in: Madison Bodge, *Soldiers in King Philip's War* (Leominster, Mass., 1896); "Rolls of Connecticut Men in the French and Indian War," Vol. 10 in *Collections of The Connecticut Historical Society*

(Hartford, 1905); Donald Lines Jacobus, *List of Officials Civil, Military and Ecclesiastical of Connecticut Colony . . . and of New Haven Colony* (New Haven, 1935); *Roll and Journal of Connecticut Service in Queen Anne's War, 1710-1711* (New Haven, 1916); The Society of Colonial Wars in the State of Connecticut, *Register of Pedigrees and Services of Ancestors* (Hartford, 1941); and James Shepard, *Connecticut Soldiers in the Pequot War* (Meriden, Conn., 1913).

The standard work on Connecticut men in the Revolution is Adjutant General, comp., *Record of Service of Connecticut Men in the War of the Revolution, War of 1812, Mexican War* (Hartford, 1889). It is supplemented by "Rolls and Lists of Connecticut Men in the Revolution," Vols. 8 and 12 in *Collections of The Connecticut Historical Society* (Hartford, Conn., 1901, 1909). For Revolutionary soldiers or their widows who received annual stipends or land grants for their service, the researcher should examine The United States Pension Bureau, *Pension Records of the Revolutionary Soldiers of Connecticut* (Washington, D. C., 1919). A complete record of all Connecticut Loyalists does not exist. However, two helpful works are Wilbur H. Siebert, "The Refugee Loyalists of Connecticut," Vol. 3, *Proceedings and Transactions of the Royal Society of Canada* (third series, 1916), and John W. Tyler, *Connecticut Loyalist Land Confiscated in Greenwich, Stamford and Norwich* (New Orleans, 1977). Publications by the Ontario Department of Archives should be consulted as well.

The Adjutant General's office also compiled the *Record of Service of Connecticut Men in the Army and Navy of the United States during the War of the Rebellion* (Hartford, 1889), and like its companion volume for the Revolution, this is the first source to consult for the record of one's Connecticut Civil War ancestor. Soldiers who received annuities for their service are named in The Adjutant General, comp., *Pension Records for Connecticut Men in the Civil War* (Hartford, 1918). Spanish-American War records will be found in The Adjutant General, comp., *Roster of Connecticut Volunteers who Served in the War between the United States and Spain 1898 and 1899* (Hartford, 1899).

The Connecticut State Library houses the largest official military collection of manuscripts and documents in the state. It consists of original muster rolls, lists, orderly books, journals, and the personal correspondence of military and governmental figures. The State Library also maintains a card file on all reported veterans' deaths for each war which gives names, death dates, burial places, and service records for each veteran.

Newspapers contain a variety of useful family information, yet they are sometimes overlooked. The earliest Connecticut newspapers give notices of probate court proceedings, merchants' advertisements, and news stories concerning notable figures. Deaths and marriage lists were introduced later. Eventually the papers gave birth records, port arrivals, letters left at the post office, and items of social interest. *The Connecticut Courant* is the oldest continually published newspaper in Connecticut and probably the most important newspaper source for statewide birth, marriage, and death statistics. Besides the *Courant,* the researcher should consult general newspaper bibliographies; particularly helpful is Donald Gustafson, *A Preliminary Checklist of Connecticut Newspapers 1755-1975,* 2 vols. (Hartford, 1978).

Without the aid of indexes, locating individuals in newspapers is tedious and time-consuming. Fortunately the New England Library Association Bibliography Committee has recently issued *A Guide to Newspaper Indexes in New England* (Holden, Mass., 1978). The major newspaper indexes in Connecticut are Doris Cook's index to the *Connecticut Courant* from 1764 to 1820, deposited at The Connecticut Historical Society (1 Elizabeth St., Hartford, Conn. 06105), and the Charles R. Hale index of marriages and deaths from the first ninety Connecticut newspapers, available at the Connecticut State Library and on microfilm. Scrapbooks and clipping files have also been kept by some libraries. The most significant of these is Mary P. Morris's scrapbook collection at The Connecticut Historical Society. She clipped obituaries and items of social interest from four area newspapers from 1877 to 1923. Between 1910 and 1967 the *Hartford Times* featured a genealogical answer-query column, and those printed from 1957 have been indexed and reproduced on microfilm by the Godfrey Memorial Library (134 Newfield St., Middletown, Conn. 06457).

City directories were intended as a kind of nineteenth-century "yellow pages," and are another important printed primary source. City directories have been issued for virtually every major metropolitan area in Connecticut. The earliest of these are cited in Dorothea Spear, *Bibliography of American Directories through 1860* (Worcester, Mass., 1961). The majority of those issued between 1860 and 1910 are included in Diana McCain, "An Annotated Bibliography and Checklist of Connecticut City, County, and Business Directories . . ." (Master's thesis, Southern Connecticut State College, 1979), available at The Connecticut Historical Society.

The Hartford city directories have the longest history of publication in the state and could well serve as a model for city directories. In them, merchants and professional people were listed along with city and town officers, ministers, members of the militia, banks and insurance companies, social organizations, and schools. Besides the town leaders, the Hartford directories provide an alphabetical list of all residents with their occupations, place of work, and home address. This latter section is particularly useful because it makes it possible to trace a person's life, occupations, and relocations within the city by checking the city directories for a span of years. In the 1880s the publisher of the Hartford city directories introduced an alphabetized list of births, marriages, divorces, and deaths that occurred the previous year, in addition to removals from the city which indicated where a person resettled if it was known. These sections were discontinued in 1914. Complete sets of Hartford city directories and runs for other cities are located at the Connecticut State Library, The Connecticut Historical Society, and the Hartford Public Library. Hartford and New Haven directories from the 1800s to 1901 are available on microfiche from Research Publications (New Haven).

Like the Connecticut city directories, the *State Register and Manual* is a primary source seldom consulted. Yet, these small books contain information difficult to locate anywhere else. This publication has appeared annually, with few exceptions, since 1785. Even the earliest *Register*s are indexed and give the names of state officials, town officeholders, naval and militia officers, college students, professors, and ministers. By the 1800s practicing attorneys, physicians, and postmasters in the state were recorded. Lists of societies and their members, insurance companies and their executives, and schools with their administrators make it possible to identify Connecticut's prominent eighteenth- and nineteenth-century citizens and the corporations they ran or societies to which they belonged. Today, the *Connecticut State Register and Manual* has evolved into a handy reference guide to state and town information. Town clerks and registrars of vital statistics are listed here, along with their addresses and phone numbers.

Prior to 1850, few county or town maps were issued for Connecticut, but in the 1860s these maps became popular and profitable. They contain details helpful in determining just where an ancestor lived, how far his home was from where he worked, and what the town was like where he resided. Details included street names, locations of buildings and factories, and most significantly, private residences with the owner's name. County atlases for each Connecticut county were produced after the 1860s and contain town maps of considerable detail. Used in conjunction with land deeds, census records, and city directories, these atlases will yield a clear picture of an ancestor's exact house location, property ownership, and years of residence. For homes and other buildings still in existence or built after the 1860s, photographs may be found in some Connecticut libraries which help complete the visual context of an ancestor's life.

Sometimes a genealogist is faced with the name of a place on a death or probate record which cannot be readily located on old or modern maps. Two sources are particularly useful in solving this problem, as well as providing background on the origin of a specific town, its general history, and location. Florence S. Marcy Crofut compiled a *Guide to the History and the Historic Sites of Connecticut,* 2 vols. (New Haven, 1937), and Arthur H. Hughes with Morse S. Allen collaborated on *Connecticut Place Names* (Hartford, 1976).

II

Any serious researcher with Connecticut lines should plan a trip to the major repositories in Connecticut. Some of the most important primary sources, while generally centralized, have not been made available in print. Few descriptive studies of these collections have been done and therefore the greater portion of this article will be devoted to pointing out their value to the genealogist. Wherever possible, locations will be given as well as the existence of microforms and what may be accomplished via correspondence.

Vital Records

As early as 1640, the Connecticut Court of Election ordered all magistrates to record the marriages they performed. In 1644, the registration of births and marriages became the responsibility of town clerks and registrars; death records were added to their duties in 1650.[2] The new husband, father, or widower was required to register the event within a month and pay a fee, or suffer a fine. In many towns these vital records are full and complete as a result of the conscientiousness shown by the town clerk in fulfilling his duties. In other towns the records are meager and few. The vital records from 1660 until the close of the Revolutionary War are generally well recorded. Then for a period of about two generations until the mid-nineteenth century, the recording of vital statistics declines noticeably in some towns. However in the 1870s the State Board of Health saw the registration of births, marriages, and deaths as a means of monitoring public health and efforts were made to improve their registration. In these town vital records the genealogist may discover relationships to other family members, spouses' maiden names, parents' names, burial places, and occupations.

Students of Connecticut families are fortunate in having the Barbour Collection, which centralized vital records up to 1850 at the Connecticut State Library. Lucius Barnes Barbour was the Connecticut Examiner of Public Records and in that capacity directed a project in which the vital records kept by the towns up to about 1850 were copied and abstracted. These abstracts are in book form by town and on slips of paper, alphabetically by surname. The library staff will check the Barbour Collection for a specific name or two for a correspondent.[3] Microfilm copies have also been made of the Barbour Collection, making it accessible to residents outside of Connecticut.[4]

Connecticut births, marriages, and deaths up to 1850 can therefore be consulted both in the towns themselves or in the Barbour Collection. From 1850 to 1 July 1897, vital records were kept only in the towns. After 1897 and to the present they are recorded by the town clerks and also centralized at the State Department of Health (79 Elm Street, Hartford, Conn.

2. J. Hammond Trumbull, ed., *The Public Records of the Colony of Connecticut 1636-May, 1665* (Hartford, 1850), 1:48, 105, 106; see also Edwin S. Welles, *Births, Marriages and Deaths Returned from Hartford, Windsor and Fairfield* (Hartford, 1898), preface.

3. Mr. Barbour hired people who had considerable experience copying old records, such as James Arnold, compiler of the *Rhode Island Vital Records*, so that Barbour's collection has a high degree of accuracy. The Collection of Vital Records at the State Library also includes those births, marriages, and deaths copied by private individuals and patriotic societies. The seal of the State of Connecticut may be added to copies of entries in the Barbour Collection for a fee.

4. Microfilm copies of the Barbour Collection are available for purchase by institutions from: Genealogical Department, Library of the Church of Jesus Christ of Latter-Day Saints, 50 East North Temple, Salt Lake City, Ut. 84150.

06105). By Connecticut law any person may have access to Connecticut vital records by proving that the records are being consulted for genealogical purposes or by showing a Superior Court summons.[5]

Some vital records have been printed in Connecticut town histories, genealogical periodicals, and a few as separate monographs. The earliest vital records in print are Edwin Stanley Welles, *Births, Marriages and Deaths Returned from Hartford, Windsor and Fairfield* (Hartford, 1898). This covers the dates from 1640 to 1691 when records kept by town clerks were annually submitted to the secretary of the court and inscribed in the land records.

Church Records

Connecticut church records not only supplement the town vital records but may rival them in accuracy and detail, or contain information not recorded by the town clerk. Baptisms, marriages, deaths, admissions, dismissals, and lists of members were faithfully recorded by the minister or his clerk. Although some have long since been lost or destroyed, a surprising number of church records have survived and are most important primary sources.

The Congregational church was the established religious order in Connecticut through the early 1800s. Each town had its church and parish. When the population increased to the extent that another parish was needed, an "ecclesiastical society" was formed to handle the additional religious, business, and secular matters. In some cases, the ecclesiastical society was the forerunner to a new town. Its records, now found with church records, contain therefore the earliest town votes and town vital records. Baptist and Episcopal churches began to appear in Connecticut in the early eighteenth century, followed by Methodist, Presbyterian, Universalist, Unitarian, Quaker, and Catholic churches in the 1820s.[6]

A Guide to Vital Statistics in the Church Records of Connecticut was prepared by the Connecticut Historical Records Survey (New Haven, 1942).[7] It lists each church in the state alphabetically by town along with the location of extant records and the dates they covered. Although incomplete, this survey is useful for further research—especially for those who have an idea of the towns where their ancestors may have lived and the churches they attended.

In the 1930s the Connecticut State Library made a concerted effort to

5. *Connecticut Statutes 1979 Revision* (Hartford, 1979), 530- Sec. 7-41a. "All records of vital statistics including births, marriages and deaths in the custody of any registrar of vital statistics of the department of health services shall be open for research to any member of a legally incorporated genealogy society and such societies shall be permitted to incorporate statistics derived therefrom in their publications."

6. Richard J. Purcell, *Connecticut in Transition 1775-1818* (Middletown, Conn., 1968), 61. The Jews of Connecticut had no formal organization, nor is it probable that there were more than a few families this early in the state's history.

7. A useful series of publications by the Historical Records Survey, includes: *Inventories of the Church Archives of Connecticut: Baptist, Episcopal, Lutheran, Methodism, Presbyterians, and Universalism* (New Haven, 1940-1941).

preserve the state's church records. They asked all churches to deposit their old record books in the state archives for safekeeping. In return, the churches received photostats of the original records. This procedure was quite successful, and to date the Connecticut State Library has either the originals or copies of over six hundred church registers. Others may still be in the possession of the churches themselves, individual members, or local historical societies. *A List of Church Records in the Connecticut State Library* is available upon request from the State Library. It shows the church records they house, alphabetically by town, and the dates covered. Approximately one-fourth of the church records at the State Library have been indexed, and the index consists of the vital records contained in the older Congregational churches. The records are indexed, like the Barbour Collection, in book form by church and on slips of paper, alphabetically by surname. This index, known as the Church Record Abstract File, was drawn from baptism, marriage, death, dismissal, and member lists. The library staff will check the index briefly. Microfilm copies of some of the State Library's church records have been made and are cited in Richard W. Hale, Jr., ed., *Guide to Photocopied Historical Materials in the United States and Canada* ([Ithaca, N. Y., 1961], 114-123).

The Manuscript Committee of the Connecticut Society of Colonial Dames was also instrumental in centralizing Connecticut church records. Under the supervision of Mary Kingsbury Talcott, church records of 106 parishes from 1639 to 1910 were carefully copied by hand and bound between 1935 and 1956. The collection was then given to The Connecticut Historical Society where it must be used in person.

Some church vital records have been printed and others have been abstracted for publication in genealogical periodicals. Of the printed church vital records, one of the most useful sources is Frederick W. Bailey's *Early Connecticut Marriages as Found in Ancient Church Records prior to 1800* (New Haven, 1896-1906). Copied from the books of churches established before 1800, this indexed compilation of marriages was one of the first attempts to publish vital records unavailable in town records.

Cemetery Records

Many Connecticut graveyards were adjacent to churches, others were laid out in a convenient place determined by the town inhabitants, and still others were simple plots located in a corner of the family property. In some cemeteries, perhaps as few as one tenth of the graves were marked by stones, or so it appears today. Those tombstones which were erected may have been inscribed years after the death and contain errors.[8] Although cemetery inscriptions are helpful to the genealogist to some extent,

8. Frank Farnsworth Starr, "Mark Cemeteries for Tercentenary," Middletown Genealogical Manuscript Collection, The Connecticut Historical Society, Hartford, Connecticut. In comparing Middletown death records with the number of gravestones in the earliest Middletown cemetery, Wm. Starr found that less than one tenth of the burials were marked by stones.

these factors should be considered in determining their reliability. Besides the name of the deceased and date of death, the inscription might tell the place and date of birth, relationships to other family members, military service, fraternal affiliations, and the cause of death.

As cited above, deaths were recorded by the town clerk, if they were reported, and by the minister in the church books. Early contemporary grave records are scarce. A few sexton's notebooks have survived and give a daily account of the graves he dug, causes of death, ages of the deceased, and the name of the next of kin whom the sexton billed for his labors.[9]

The practice of copying graveyard inscriptions began in the nineteenth century and increased in the 1900s. This coincided with the formation of hereditary and patriotic societies which not only collected data on soldiers but made every effort to mark their graves. A major project was conducted in the 1930s by State Librarian Charles Hale. Under his direction at least a million cemetery inscriptions were copied from more than two thousand Connecticut graveyards. These inscription abstracts, at the Connecticut State Library, are in bound volumes for each town and are indexed on slips in a single alphabetical file. The slips contain names and dates, but the bound volumes give more complete information on relationships. The library staff will check the Hale Collection for a specific name, and a microfilm made of the collection by the Church of Jesus Christ of Latter-Day Saints is also available. The Connecticut Historical Society, New Haven Colony Historical Society, and local historical societies and libraries have miscellaneous epitaphs which should be consulted as well.

Death certificates for this century will give the place of burial. In addition, most Connecticut town halls have kept chronological books of local burials and/or sexton's returns for the past one hundred years. Cemetery associations are now connected with the larger cemeteries and keep good records showing locations of family plots and burials there. Also, from the newspaper obituary, a researcher can often discover the funeral home which conducted the relative's funeral. Such establishments may have books dating back to the 1900s with the names of relatives who attended the funeral entered, along with the name of the cemetery where the person was buried.

Research can lead a genealogist to the cemetery in Connecticut where the ancestor is buried and where a photograph or rubbing of the inscription may be made. Finding the graveyard is facilitated by topographical maps at the State Library which show the location of the two thousand cemeteries in the Hale Collection.

Court Records

With perseverance, one's chances are fairly good of locating a male Connecticut ancestor in the state's court files as a juror, plaintiff, or de-

9. The Connecticut Historical Society (1 Elizabeth St., Hartford, Conn. 06105) houses a few sexton's records which must be researched in person.

124   *Connecticut Genealogical Research*

fendant, especially if he was a prominent lawyer, merchant, or tradesman. Many individuals besides criminals also left a record. Debts, trespass, slander, and other misdemeanors could warrant arrest and trial. Considering how many merchants, tradesmen, and farmers kept detailed account books, it would seem that a good number of townspeople would at some time in their lives be delinquent in pay and accountable for a "book-debt." Even if the issue was settled without being contested, the writs that were served the defendants may still survive along with the records of judgment.

During most of the seventeenth, eighteenth, and early nineteenth centuries, minor crimes were brought before justices of the peace, who were upstanding local men appointed to the position by the General Assembly. They handled such criminal matters as drunkenness, swearing, sabbath breaking, threats, and breach of peace, and they determined the punishment: whipping, setting in stocks, or imprisonment. Civil cases abounded with matters of debt, trespass, and damages for which the justice of the peace could pass judgment. He was responsible for keeping records of all transactions as well as the judgment made. The records were the justice's personal property, and although many have been lost or destroyed, a number of remaining records are in the state's archives.[10]

Although some civil and criminal offenses could not be appealed, appeals to higher courts were common in the Connecticut court system. Sometimes the judgment is finally located in the highest court. County courts, presided over by a judge and justices of the quorum, heard appeals from the justice courts. Prior to the division of Connecticut into counties, town appeals were heard by the Particular Court. The records of the Particular Courts, whose functions were absorbed by the county courts and Court of Assistants in 1665, are in print: "Records of the Particular Court of Connecticut 1639-1663," Vol. 22 in *Collections of The Connecticut Historical Society* (Hartford, 1928). The county courts tried civil disputes, minor criminal cases, probate matters (up to 1698), and provided for neglected children. Most of the records for the county courts and their successors are housed in the archives at the Connecticut State Library.[11]

From 1665 to 1711 the major appellate and trial court for Connecticut was the Court of Assistants, the predecessor of today's Superior Court. This court consisted of a chief judge and four judges whose jurisdiction extended to "all crimes, the punishment of which relate to life, limb or

10. The system of justice courts evolved over three centuries into town and municipal courts which continued until 1961. At that time a circuit court began operation where towns were grouped into various circuits and presided over by rotating judges who handled minor crimes. The circuit court was part of a reorganization of Connecticut's judicial system in 1976. The state now has a two-tier court system consisting of a supreme and superior court.

11. Connecticut counties continue today only as a geographic subdivision. The judicial power was divided among the Probate Courts, the Court of Common Pleas, and the Superior Court by 1855, and in 1959 the legislature determined that the county form of government was obsolete.

banishment, and to other high crimes, misdemeanors ... to adultery ... robbery, forgery, counterfeiting and horsestealing."[12] The Court of Assistants, or Superior Court, handled all appeals from the inferior courts, especially concerning land titles, debts over a certain amount, equity, and divorce. In most cases the judgment of the Court of Assistants, or Superior Court was final. Records of the Superior Court in Connecticut through the early nineteenth century are housed in the archives of the Connecticut State Library, and some are in print.[13]

The General Court or General Assembly was a combination of all phases of government—executive, judicial, and legislative—in Connecticut's early days. By 1638 it had become the highest court in the land. Gradually the General Assembly's judicial power was delegated to other courts.[14] The Supreme Court became the highest court, made up of the governor, lieutenant governor, and the council. As today, the decision of the Supreme Court was the final, binding decision. Records of the Supreme Court through the nineteenth century are housed in the archives at the Connecticut State Library, and some Supreme Court proceedings have been published.[15]

In the courts listed above in order from lowest to highest, cases which would interest the genealogist involve debts, trespass, divorce, paternity, guardianship, and care of homeless children. There were some matters such as support of the poor, indentures, apprenticeships, and expulsions of nonlegal inhabitants which were the responsibilities of the town selectmen, and an examination of town records is also advised.

The probate court records are probably the most useful to a genealogist since they contain information about family relationships, property holdings, land values, and estates. Connecticut's probate courts were established in 1698. Prior to that, records of wills and estates were kept by the General Court or Secretary of the Colony, then the Particular and county courts. Until 1719 the probate courts were not separated from the county courts and their geographic limits were the same. In that year a division of the four original probate districts occurred and this process of division continued until, now, there are about 130 probate districts. Probate estate papers (wills, inventories, bonds, accounts, and other documents to varying dates), are housed in the State Library archives along with microfilm copies of court record books. *A Checklist of Probate Records in the Connecticut State Library* may be obtained from there.

12. Zephaniah Swift, *A System of Laws of the State of Connecticut* (Boston, 1895), 95.

13. Ephraim Kirby, *Reports of Cases Adjudged in the Superior Court of the State of Connecticut from the Year 1785 to May 1788* ... (Litchfield, Conn., 1789); Jesse Root, *Reports of Cases Adjudged in the Superior Court and Supreme Court of Errors, from July A.D. 1789 ... to January A.D. 1798*, 2 vols. (Hartford, 1798-1802).

14. The General Assembly's judicial power was shared by the Particular Court in 1638 and the Superior Court in 1711, and finally taken over completely by the Supreme Court of Errors in 1784.

15. Thomas Day, *Digest of the Reported Cases, Decided by the Supreme Court of Errors, of the State of Connecticut from 1786-1838* ... (Hartford, 1840).

The records after 1900 and the original court record books remain with the probate courts.

For the most part, Connecticut's court records are centralized at the State Library, and *A Guide to the Records of the Judicial Department, Court Records in the Connecticut State Library* is available upon request. A list of the locations for all state court records not housed at the Connecticut State Library has been made and may be consulted there as well. The State Library staff will check the decedent index to the probate court records for a specific name. While other court records are available for research, there is no general index and the library staff cannot undertake a search of them for a correspondent.

Federal district court records are useful to the genealogist for immigration and naturalization papers. An immigrant could be naturalized in virtually any Connecticut court prior to the twentieth century. Some naturalization records and declarations of intention are still in the county courthouses, in the court files at the Connecticut State Library, or at the Federal Archives Records Center—Region One in Waltham, Massachusetts. Starting in 1906, Connecticut naturalization records were centralized and filed at the federal district courts in Hartford, New Haven, ɔr Bridgeport. If the researcher has no idea where to go or what district court may contain his ancestor's naturalization papers, he should seek assistance from his nearest office of immigration and naturalization.

Land Records

The English crown claimed title to all of New England, yet legal rights to settlement in Connecticut remained unclear until a charter was granted by King Charles II in 1662. The Warwick patent was perhaps the first legal title to the area, although the early settlers also recognized the Indians' rights of possession and purchased the land from them.[16] While few remain in the towns, some original Indian deeds are in the Connecticut State Library and The Connecticut Historical Society.

Land grants were given by the Connecticut General Assembly to proprietors with the understanding that they would build a home, till the soil, and establish the community. The proprietors, who were the original grantees, in turn were authorized to grant portions of the town lands to "late comers" who showed sound character and industriousness. Very few records of the proprietors' meetings and their decisions on grants and boundaries were kept. Once the proprietors were organized as a town, however, records of land transactions were usually written down.

By order of the General Assembly in 1639 each town was to provide an indexed ledger book of land deeds.[17] A property owner was required to register the extent of his property and transfers of holdings with the town clerk or suffer a fine. The transactions (deeds, mortgages, releases,

16. Charles Hoadly, *The Warwick Patent* (Hartford, 1902), 7; Trumbull, *Connecticut Public Records,* 1:Appendix 4.

17. Trumbull, *Connecticut Public Records,* 1:37, 38.

and related records) in the ledgers may reveal an ancestor's wealth, means of livelihood, previous residence, length of settlement, military service, and names of neighbors. The records are sometimes essential in determining relationships. For over a century land was transferred by inheritance and family relationships were often specified in the deed. Because land was transferred at times of marriage and after a death, those dates may also be confirmed by the land records.

Connecticut towns retain their land records and deed books, most with grantor-grantee indexes, and they may be consulted in the town clerk's office. The Church of Jesus Christ of Latter-Day Saints tried to microfilm all of Connecticut's proprietors' and land records in the 1930s. As a result, positive microfilms of Connecticut land deeds up to 1850 were deposited at the State Library and are cited in Robert Hale's *Guide to Photocopied Historical Materials.* For each town there is a grantor-grantee index where one exists; however, there is no general index to all of Connecticut's land deeds and the library staff will search for a correspondent only if the volume and page number of the microfilm are supplied. Other repositories in the state, as well as private individuals, have original land deeds in their possession. The public record was made in the town clerk's ledger and he was then obligated to give a copy to the individual(s) involved in the transaction. Many of these copies have been held in safekeeping since the seventeenth century and some may not appear in the public record books at all. Deeds and other land records after 1850 must be consulted in the town where the land is located.

Only some Hartford land record sources have been printed. "The Original Distribution of the Lands in Hartford among the Settlers in 1639" was issued as volume 14 of *Collections of The Connecticut Historical Society* (Hartford, 1912). This volume is indexed and covers the land transactions from 1639 to the 1680s. Along with these are Hartford's vital records of that time which were recorded in the same volume and first printed in the *Register* (12 [1858]: 173-175 and 13 [1859]: 141-148). Another excellent printed source is the *General Index of the Land Records of the Town of Hartford 1639-1879,* 4 vols. (Hartford, 1873-1883). The volumes are chronological, each with an alphabetical grantor and grantee index.

Tax Records

Although tax records are among the most important primary sources for genealogists and historians, this group is the least centralized of all such records in Connecticut, and the researcher often overlooks tax lists which might provide important data. The responsibility of each household head to support the civil and ecclesiastical affairs of the colony through taxation was clearly established in the Connecticut "Code of Laws."[18] At different times in Connecticut's history a town assessor was either appointed by the state or elected by the townspeople at the town meeting.

18. *Ibid.,* 509-563.

It was his responsibility to assess the land and personal property value of the town, from which the General Assembly would determine the town "rate." It was then the town constable or collector's duty to collect the tax according to the rate from each inhabitant.

From the genealogist's viewpoint, the Connecticut town tax records, consisting of the assessor's lists or "rate books," are the most interesting tax source. They were usually kept by year and give the names of household heads, the extent of their land and property, and the money or goods they owed as tax. Many of these record books were assumed to be the personal possession of the assessor or constable and have been lost. Others were submitted to the State Treasurer and eventually housed in the archives at the State Library. The records are not microfilmed and the researcher must consult them himself. The archives department of the State Library also has a list of tax records still in the various town halls. One should check The Connecticut Historical Society, local historical societies, and libraries in Connecticut with genealogical collections for Connecticut tax lists as well.

An extremely important federal tax is the 1798 Connecticut direct tax which is the first federal tax giving the names of town inhabitants/ taxpayers. An act was passed by Congress in 1798 to provide for the valuation of lands and dwelling houses, the enumeration of slaves, and the collection of a direct tax within the United States. A state board of commissioners was appointed who in turn appointed assessors and assistants to cover each of Connecticut's sixty-seven assessment districts. The records give the name of the home occupant, owner, valuation of the house, number of slaves, and those slaves who were disabled (in number only). The 1798 Direct Tax for Connecticut and similar federal tax lists for 1814, 1815, and 1816 for many towns are housed at The Connecticut Historical Society where they may be used. The later direct taxes list dwellings and personal property as specific as gold and silver watches.

School Records

As early as 1642 schools were set up in Hartford and New Haven colonies. By 1650 each town, depending upon its size, was required to build a primary school and "grammar" school or "academy."[19] Within each "school society," which roughly followed the boundaries of the ecclesiastical societies, were more than one schoolhouse, and each formed a "school district," headed by its own committee. Parents of school children had to contribute wood to the schoolhouse and pay a tuition fee according to the attendance figures.

Not every Connecticut family owned land or was brought before a court, but few were without school-aged children. School records are particularly important in pinpointing exactly when a family with children lived in a town, especially if they were transients or moved between the time federal

19. Charles L. Ames, "History of Education in Connecticut," Vol. 5 in Norris G. Osburn, ed., *History of Connecticut in Monographic Form* (New York, 1925), 178, 179.

censuses were taken. The records fall into three main categories: (1) the books, diaries, rules and regulations used in the course of instruction, (2) the minutes and account books of the school societies and school district committees and, perhaps most important, (3) the school registers.

Nearly every school kept an annual register. It gave the name of the instructor, lists of scholars (males separately from females), their ages, the days they attended school, visitors to the school, and the names of parents or guardians responsible for the tuition. Although some children in the town did not attend school and the registers for some schools have been lost, both the Connecticut State Library and The Connecticut Historical Society have school registers dating from the eighteenth century. They have not been microfilmed and the library staffs cannot undertake a search of them for correspondents. In addition, some town halls and local repositories still have the early school registers for their region.

Bible and Unofficial Records

Unofficial accounts of births, marriages, and deaths were kept by doctors, merchants, and farmers, and by people who wrote in personal diaries or family Bibles. Midwives' and doctors' personal records of the births, illnesses, or deaths they attended to are rare but the few that survive can be helpful in determining a date. Account books were frequently kept by businessmen, traders, and farmers. Not only are they a source for business transactions among townspeople, but sometimes they served as a convenient place to write down family events—much as the blank pages in an almanac. Those who kept memoirs and diaries sometimes recorded daily occurrences, weather conditions, or travel, and they often wrote about a friend's or relative's marriage, or the death or birth of a child; but searching in these records can be time-consuming. The genealogist must narrow his research to a specific town in Connecticut and a certain span of years before he can expect to best utilize such unofficial records as these in the state's archives and repositories.

Most Connecticut families owned Bibles in which pages were allotted for recording significant family occasions. Such records are accurate if they were entered at the time of the event. Other entries may have been drawn from recollections, in which case errors are frequent. If the publication date of the Bible is prior to the date of the earliest record, events were probably recorded as they occurred and the source is reliable. Too often, however, the title page of the Bible has been lost or worn out and all that remains are the record pages, making such a comparison of dates almost impossible.

Bible records are unique in that they contain the history of one family, and its connected lines, for a number of generations. No other primary source provides as much information on a specific group of related people. Bible records generally give names, dates, places, relationships, and establish allied surnames. The Connecticut State Library has collected and copied over twenty-five thousand Bible records for private individuals, hereditary societies, and through purchase. The originals have been copied and are bound in twenty-six indexed volumes and on slips of paper alphabetically by surname. The State Library staff will check the Family Bible Records Collection slip index for a specific name or two, and the collection has also been microfilmed by the Church of Jesus Christ of Latter-Day Saints. While The Connecticut Historical Society and other repositories in the state possess substantial files of copied and original Bible records, many still remain in private hands.

Very few Bible records have been printed, but the Connecticut chapter of the National Society Daughters of Founders and Patriots of America, Incorporated, did publish *Family Records* (New Haven, 1935), which is a compilation of previously unpublished Connecticut family papers, including Bible records with the Bible's imprint and owner.

Manuscript Genealogies

Genealogists who have used the resources of the state's libraries and archives for their research frequently donate their compilations on Connecticut families to those libraries. The Connecticut State Library and The Connecticut Historical Society in Hartford, the Godfrey Memorial Library in Middletown, the Ferguson Library in Stamford, the Otis Library in Norwich, the Greenwich Library, and the county historical societies house substantial collections of manuscript genealogies. Some of Connecticut's most notable genealogists have deposited their life's work in these repositories, including manuscripts from which genealogies were published. Other collections consist of working papers, data sheets, correspondence, family notes and copies of vital records, wills, deeds, taxes, school records, and cemetery inscriptions. The papers are usually filed by family and, although catalogued, they may not be indexed by individuals. The researcher then must do his own research, and such collections have rarely been microfilmed.

The genealogist whose family had a fairly long history of settlement in Connecticut will find these manuscript genealogies useful. It is possible that a predecessor working on the same family has already sifted pertinent data from the public records and other sources. At best, these manuscript genealogies may contain important references to records which no longer exist, or are in private hands; they also serve to direct the genealogist to further research.

Attracted by reports of a navigable river, fertile valley, dense forests, trade, and the opportunity for religious freedom, settlers began to migrate to Connecticut as early as 1630. A number of the original settlers and their descendants then moved on in all directions to settle other parts of the country. It is not surprising that so many genealogists today trace some of their lines back to this state. State hereditary societies and the two genealogical societies in Connecticut can boast ever-increasing membership rolls and widening circulation of their publications. Its genealogical societies are: the Connecticut Society of Genealogists, Incorporated

(P.O.B. 435, Glastonbury, Conn. 06033), which publishes *The Connecticut Nutmegger,* and the Stamford Genealogical Society, Incorporated (P.O.B. 249, Stamford, Conn. 06904), which publishes *Connecticut Ancestry.*

Connecticut has had a long history of record keeping and an early regard for the importance of family history. In fact, the first American genealogy was printed in Hartford in 1771: *The Genealogy of the Family of Mr. Samuel Stebbins and Mrs. Hannah Stebbins his wife from the year 1707 to the year 1771 . . .* , by Luke Stebbins. The various town halls, local libraries, historical societies, and the Connecticut State Library are vast storehouses of information for the researcher. The staffs of these institutions can generally be expected to check their special indexes for a correspondent. In addition, The Connecticut Historical Society has a loan collection of their duplicate genealogies and local histories, making it possible for out-of-state members to have access to printed Connecticut sources. Many finding their interest piqued, hire a genealogist to search the various primary records, or plan a trip to Connecticut themselves. Greater satisfaction is sometimes gained by personally consulting the records and making one's own discoveries. Genealogists are encouraged to visit the state and are invited to donate the results of their research to a library in Connecticut where it can be consulted by others now and in the future working on the same family. For it can be said that respect for one's heritage and concern for the safekeeping and accessibility of records which document family, town, and state history are values that continue to be held in Connecticut.

A SELECTED LIST OF CONNECTICUT VITAL STATISTICS IN PRINT:
TOWN, CHURCH, AND EPITAPHS

BETHANY

W. C. Sharpe, *Bethany, Sketches and Records Part I.* Seymour, Conn., 1908, 49-98.

BOLTON-VERNON

Vital Records of Bolton to 1854 and Vernon to 1852. Hartford, Conn., 1909.

CHESHIRE

Joseph Perkins Beach, *History of Cheshire, Connecticut from 1694 to 1840.* Cheshire, Conn., 1912, 446-521.

COLCHESTER

Epitaphs from Colchester, Connecticut. New York, N. Y., 1886.

COVENTRY

Susan Whitney Dimock, *Coventry Records.* New York, N. Y., 1897.

EAST GRANBY

Albert Carlos Bates, *Sundry Vital Records, East Granby, Connecticut 1737-1886.* Hartford, Conn., 1947.

EAST HAVEN

Stephen Dodd, *East Haven Register*. New Haven, Conn., 1910.

ENFIELD

Francis Olcott Allen, *The History of Enfield, Connecticut*. Lancaster, Penn., 1900. Vol. 2: 1585-1904.

HARTFORD

Scaeva's Hartford in the Olden Time. W. M. B. Hartley, ed., Hartford, Conn., 1853, 285-305.

MIDDLEFIELD

Thomas Atkins, *History of Middlefield & Long Hill*. Hartford, Conn., 1883, 95-118.

MILFORD

Morris W. Abbott, *Milford Tombstone Inscriptions*. Milford, Conn., 1967.

Nathan G. Pond, *Inscriptions on Tombstones in Milford, Connecticut*. New Haven, Conn., 1889.

————, *Ye Story of Ye Memorial*. 1889.

NEW HAVEN

Revolutionary Characters of New Haven. New Haven, Conn., 1911, 97-117.

Vital Records of New Haven 1649-1850. Hartford, Conn., 1917-1924.

NEW LONDON

Ye Antient Burial Place of New London, Connecticut. New London, Conn., 1899, 213-232.

NEW MILFORD

Samuel Orcutt, *History of the Towns of New Milford and Bridgewater, Connecticut*. Hartford, Conn., 1882, 312-414.

NORWALK

David H. VanHoosear, *A Complete Copy of the Inscriptions Found on the Monuments, Headstones, & C*. Bridgeport, Conn., 1895.

Charles M. Selleck, *Norwalk*. Norwalk, Conn., 1896. *28th Anniversary Roster of Buckingham Post No. 12*. Norwalk, Conn., 1908.

NORWICH

Vital Records of Norwich 1659-1848. 2 vols. Hartford, Conn., 1913.

OXFORD

W. C. Sharpe, *History of Oxford*. Seymour, Conn., 1885.

PORTLAND

The Portland Burying Ground Association and Its Cemetery. Portland, Conn., 1897.

PRESTON

George S. Porter, *Inscriptions from the Long Society Burying Ground, Preston, Connecticut*. Boston, Mass., 1906.

RIDGEFIELD

George L. Rockwell, *The History of Ridgefield, Connecticut*. Ridgefield, Conn., 1927, 451-517.

SALISBURY

Historical Collections Relating to the Town of Salisbury. New Haven, Conn., 1913-1916, 1:29-123; 2:39-166.

Malcolm Day Rudd, *Inscriptions at Salisbury Center, Lime Rock, etc*. Boston, Mass., 1898.

SAYBROOK

Vital Records of Saybrook 1647-1834. Hartford, Conn., 1952.

SEYMOUR

W. C. Sharpe, *Vital Statistics of Seymour, Connecticut*. Seymour, Conn., 1883.

SHARON

Born, Married and Died in Sharon, Conn. Sharon, Conn., 1897.

Burying Grounds of Sharon, Conn., Amenia and North East, New York. Amenia, N. Y., 1903.

SIMSBURY

Albert C. Bates, *Births, Marriages and Deaths*. Hartford, Conn., 1898.

STAMFORD

E. B. Huntington, *Soldiers' Memorial*. Stamford, Conn., 1869, 120-155.

————, *Stamford Registration of Births, Marriages and Deaths*. Stamford, Conn., 1874.

WATERTOWN

A Chronological List of Persons Interred in the Old Cemetery at Watertown, Connecticut. Woodbury, Conn., 1884.

The Old Burying Ground of Ancient Westbury and Present Watertown. Watertown, Conn., 1938.

WETHERSFIELD

Ronna L. Reynolds, *1775: Wethersfield Enters the Revolution*. Canton, Conn., 1975, 37-39.

Edward Sweetser Tillotson, *Wethersfield Inscriptions*. Hartford, Conn., 1899.

WINDSOR

Cemetery Inscriptions in Windsor, Connecticut. Windsor, Conn., 1929.

Matthew Grant Records. Hartford, Conn., 1930.

WOLCOTT

Wolcott Facts and Legends. Wolcott, Conn., n.d.

WOODBURY

Leon M. Barnes, *Mortality Record of the Town of Woodbury*. Woodbury, Conn., 1898.

William Cothren, *History of Ancient Woodbury, Vol. 3.* Waterbury, Conn., 1879.

WOODSTOCK
Vital Records of Woodstock 1686-1854. Hartford, Conn., 1914.

GENEALOGIES CONTAINED IN CONNECTICUT TOWN HISTORIES

BERLIN
Catharin M. North, *History of Berlin, Connecticut.* New Haven, Conn., 1916. Gen.: 26-149.

BETHANY
Eliza J. Lines, *Bethany and Its Hills.* New Haven, Conn., 1905.

BROOKFIELD
Emily C. Hawley, *Annals of Brookfield.* Brookfield, Conn., 1929. Gen.: 259-646.

CANTON
Abiel Brown, *Genealogical History with Short Sketches and Family Records of the Early Settlers of West Simsbury, now Canton, Connecticut.* Hartford, Conn., 1856. Passim.

CROMWELL
Charles Collard Adams, *Middletown Upper Houses.* New York, N. Y., 1908. Gen.: 509-772.

ELLINGTON
Darius Crane, *Biographical Sketches of Ellington Families.* Hartford, Conn., 1889.

FAIRFIELD
Donald Lines Jacobus, *History and Genealogy of the Families of Old Fairfield.* 3 vols. Fairfield, Conn., 1930. Passim.

GOSHEN
A. G. Hibbard, *History of the Town of Goshen, Connecticut.* Hartford, Conn.. 1897. Gen.: 407-572.

GREENWICH
Spencer P. Mead, *Ye Historie of Ye Town of Greenwich.* New York, N. Y., 1911. Gen.: 489-687.

HAMDEN
Hamden Men in the World War. New Haven, Conn., n.d.

HARTFORD
L. B. Barbour, *Families of Early Hartford, Connecticut.* Baltimore, Md., 1977. Passim.

William S. Porter, *Historical Notices of Connecticut.* Hartford, Conn., 1842. See chapter entitled: "Genealogy and Biography of the First Settlers of Hartford."

LEBANON

Robert G. Armstrong, *Historic Lebanon.* Lebanon, Conn., 1950.

LEDYARD

John Avery, *History of the Town of Ledyard 1650-1900.* Norwich, Conn., 1901. Gen.: 88-242.

LITCHFIELD

Payne Kenyon Kilbourne, *A Biographical History of the County of Litchfield, Connecticut.* New York, N. Y., 1851.

George C. Woodruff, *A Genealogical Register.* Hartford, Conn., 1900.

LISBON

Henry F. Bishop, *Historical Sketch of Lisbon, Connecticut.* New York, N. Y., 1903. Gen.: 45-63.

MERIDEN

C. Bancroft Gillespie, *A Century of Meriden.* Meriden, Conn., 1906. Gen.: 244-608.

MIDDLEFIELD

Thomas Atkins, *History of Middlefield and Long Hill.* Hartford, Conn., 1883. Gen.: Middlefield: 31-94; Long Hill: 126-170.

MILFORD

Susan Woodruff Abbott, *Families of Early Milford, Connecticut.* Baltimore, 1979.

MONTVILLE

Henry A. Baker, *History of Montville, Connecticut.* Hartford, Conn., 1896.

NEW BRITAIN

David N. Camp, *History of New Britain.* New Britain, Conn., 1889. Gen.: 379-508.

NEW HAVEN

Donald Lines Jacobus, *Families of Ancient New Haven.* 3 vols. Baltimore, 1974. Originally published as the *New Haven Genealogical Magazine,* vols. 1-8, 1922-1932.

NEW MILFORD

Samuel Orcutt, *History of the Towns of New Milford and Bridgewater, Connecticut, 1703-1882.* Hartford, Conn., 1882. Gen.: 639-813.

NORFOLK

Theron Wilmot Crissey, *History of Norfolk.* Everett, Mass., 1900. Gen.: 392-494.

NORTH HAVEN

Sheldon B. Thorpe, *North Haven Annals.* New Haven, Conn., 1892. Gen.: 5-253.

NORWALK

Edwin Hall, *The Ancient Historical Records of Norwalk, Connecticut.* Norwalk, Conn., 1847. Gen.: 181-320.

NORWICH

F. M. Caulkins, *History of Norwich, Connecticut.* Norwich, Conn., 1845. Gen.: 84-260.

William G. Gilman, *The Celebration of the 250th Anniversary of the Settlement of the Town of Norwich.* Norwich, Conn., 1912. Gen.: 204-236.

Mary E. Perkins, *Old Families of Norwich, Connecticut.* New London, Conn., 1900. Vol. 1, Part 1.

————, *Old Houses of the Antient Town of Norwich,* Norwich, Conn., 1895. Gen.: 407-600.

PLYMOUTH

Francis Atwater, *History of the Town of Plymouth, Connecticut.* Meriden, Conn., 1895. Gen.: 219-419.

REDDING

Charles Burr Todd, *The History of Redding, Connecticut.* Newburgh, N. Y., 1906. Gen.: 222-281.

SEYMOUR

Hollis A. Campbell, William C. Sharpe & Frank G. Bassett, *Seymour, Past and Present.* Seymour, Conn., 1902. Gen.: 364-606.

W. C. Sharpe, *History of Seymour, Connecticut, with Biographies and Genealogies.* Seymour, Conn., 1869. Gen.: 154-226.

SHARON

Charles F. Sedgwick, *A History of the Town of Sharon, Litchfield County, Connecticut.* Hartford, Conn., 1842. Gen.: 61-119.

SOUTH BRITAIN

W. C. Sharpe, *South Britain, Sketches and Records.* Seymour, Conn., 1898.

SOUTHINGTON

Heman R. Timlow, *Ecclesiastical and Other Sketches of Southington, Connecticut.* Hartford, Conn., 1875. Gen.: i-cclxxv.

STAMFORD

E. B. Huntington, *History of Stamford, Connecticut.* Stamford, Conn., 1868.

STONINGTON

Richard Anson Wheeler, *History of the Town of Stonington.* New London, Conn., 1900. Gen.: 199-703.

STRATFORD

Samuel Orcutt, *History of Stratford & Bridgeport.* 3 vols. Fairfield, Conn., 1884-1886.

TOLLAND

Loren P. Waldo, *The Early History of Tolland*. Hartford, Conn., 1861.

TORRINGTON

Samuel Orcutt, *History of Torrington, Connecticut*. Albany, N. Y., 1878.

TRUMBULL

E. Merrill Beach, *They Face the Rising Sun*. Chester, Conn., 1971. Gen.: 21-56.

UNION

Harvey M. Lawson, *The History of Union, Connecticut*. New Haven, Conn., 1893.

WALLINGFORD

Charles Henry Stanley Davis, *History of Wallingford, Connecticut*. Meriden, Conn., 1870. Gen.: 508-941.

WATERBURY

Joseph Anderson, *The Town and City of Waterbury, Connecticut*. New Haven, Conn., 1896. Gen.: Appendix, vol. 1.

Henry Bronson, *The History of Waterbury, Connecticut*. Waterbury, Conn., 1858. Gen.: 370-552.

Waterbury and the Naugatuck Valley. Chicago, Ill.; New York, N. Y., 1918. Gen.: vols. 2 & 3.

WETHERSFIELD

Henry R. Stiles, *The History of Ancient Wethersfield*. New Hampshire Pub. Co., 1975. Gen.: vol. 2.

WINDHAM

William L. Weaver, *History of Ancient Windham, Connecticut*. Willimantic, Conn., 1864. Gen.: Part I.

WINDSOR

Henry R. Stiles, *The History of Ancient Windsor*. New York, N. Y., 1859. Gen.: 515-842.

————, *The History of Ancient Windsor*. 2 vols. Hartford, Conn., 1891-1892: reprint edition, N. H. Pub. Co., 1976.

————, *A Supplement to the History of Ancient Windsor*. Albany, N. Y., 1863.

WOLCOTT

Samuel Orcutt, *History of the Town of Wolcott*. Waterbury, Conn., 1874. Gen.: 425-608.

WOODBURY

William Cothren, *History of Ancient Woodbury, Connecticut*. 2 vols. Waterbury, Conn., 1854. Passim.

WOODSTOCK
Clarence Winthrop Bowen, *The History of Woodstock, Connecticut.* 8 vols. Norwood, Mass., 1926. Passim.

Elizabeth Abbe is the librarian at The Connecticut Historical Society.

ADDITIONS AND CORRECTIONS

Page 115, footnote 1
Additional material on Connecticut genealogical repositories and resources includes: Elizabeth Abbe, "The Connecticut Historical Society," *The Connecticut Nutmegger,* 9 (1976):323-334; James R. Benn, ed., *Genealogical and Local History Resources in New London County Libraries* (New London, Conn., 1982); Robert Claus, *Guide to Archives in the Connecticut State Library,* 3rd ed. (Hartford, Conn., 1981); Thomas Jay Kemp, *Connecticut Researcher's Handbook* (Detroit, 1981); David Palmquist, ed., *Directory of Historical and Genealogical Resources of Fairfield County, Connecticut* (in progress); Kip Sperry, *Connecticut Sources for Family Historians and Genealogists* (Logan, Utah, 1980). Researchers are also advised to consult *Connecticut Ancestry,* published by the Stamford Genealogical Society, and *The Connecticut Nutmegger,* published by the Connecticut Society of Genealogists, for articles on Connecticut genealogical research.

Page 126
Only Hartford's probate records have appeared in print in Charles William Manwaring, *A Digest of the Early Connecticut Probate Records: Hartford District, 1635-1750.* 3 vols. (Hartford, Conn., 1904-1906).

Page 128
An explanation of Connecticut's tax system and a checklist of Connecticut tax records can be found in Diana McCain, "'As True As Taxes': An Historian's Guide to Direct Taxation and Tax Records in Connecticut, 1637-1820" (Master's thesis, Wesleyan University, 1981), available at the Connecticut Historical Society.

Page 132
Inadvertently dropped from the list of Connecticut Vital Statistics in print:

HARTFORD
William Harrison Taylor, *Souvenir of the Capitol.* Putnam, Conn., 1897.
Edwin Stanley Welles, *Births, Marriages and Deaths Returned from Hartford, Windsor and Fairfield.* Hartford, Conn., 1898.
Ruth Wyllys Chapter, DAR, *Restoration of the Ancient Burying-Ground of Hartford and the Widening of Gold Street.* Hartford, Conn., 1904.

LEBANON
Rev. Orlo D. Hine, *Early Lebanon.* Hartford, Conn., 1880, 143-176.

LITCHFIELD
Joyce MacKenzie Cropsey, *Register of Revolutionary Soldiers and Patriots Buried in Litchfield County.* Canaan, N.H., 1976.
Charles Thomas Payne, *Litchfield and Morris Inscriptions.* Litchfield, Conn., 1905.

LYME
Vital Records of Lyme, Conn., 1665-1850. Lyme, Conn., 1976.

MADISON
Glenn E. Griswold, *New Haven County, Conn., Inscriptions — Madison, North Madison.* Branford, Conn., 1936.

MANSFIELD
Susan W. Dimock, *Births, Baptisms, Marriages and Deaths, 1703-1850.* New York, 1898.

GENEALOGICAL RESEARCH IN RHODE ISLAND

Jane Fletcher Fiske

Rhode Island presents to the genealogist a challenge quite out of proportion to the diminutive size of this smallest of all the New England colonies. In the seventeenth and eighteenth centuries, Quakers rubbed shoulders with Congregationalists, Anglicans, and several varieties of Baptists, and it was not unusual for ministers to preach in pulpits of denominations other than their own. The worldly, bustling, slave-trading society of Newport bore little resemblance to the stony, hilly communities in the western part of the colony, and yet another contrast was provided by the gracious plantation life of the Narragansett country. In the nineteenth century, a developing industrialized society brought immigrant waves of Irish and French Canadians and introduced two very distinct Catholic cultures. Since a search for Rhode Island ancestry may lead in one or more quite different directions, determining where to begin may seem a formidable problem.

Some historical background is always of use in genealogy, but for Rhode Island a working knowledge of the colony's history is essential to understand what records were kept and in what manner. The purpose of this article is to show how present-day Rhode Island evolved from a few tiny settlements; to describe what material is available to the genealogist for various periods and groups; and to explain how best to approach it. To supplement the necessarily simplistic treatment here of the history, readers should consult further background material. There are several standard multi-volume works worth noting.[1] However, for the genealogical researcher who prefers a shorter account, volume two of Charles M. Andrews's *The Colonial Period of American History* (New Haven, 1938), provides a genealogically oriented overview. A lengthier, but equally readable, picture is presented in *Colonial Rhode Island — A History*, by Sydney James (New York, 1976), which contains an excellent bibliography. People with ancestry on early Aquidneck should certainly look at *Fat Mutton and Liberty of Conscience: Society in Rhode Island, 1636-1690* by Carl Bridenbaugh (Providence, 1974), a short and lively social history offering an unequalled view of the seventeenth century on the island that was the original "Rhode Island." In order to gain understanding of the early Narragansett settlements with their gracious, aristocratic society under the spiritual leadership of the Episcopal Reverend Dr. James McSparran, one might read *Plantation in*

---

1. These include Samuel Greene Arnold, *History of the State of Rhode Island and Providence Plantations,* 2 vols. (New York, 1859-1860); Edward Field, *State of Rhode Island and Providence Plantations at the End of the Century: A History,* 3 vols. (Boston, 1902); Thomas Bicknell, *History of the State of Rhode Island and Providence Plantations,* 5 vols. (New York, 1920); Charles Carroll, *Rhode Island, Three Centuries of Democracy,* 4 vols. (New York, 1932); and Irving B. Richman, *Rhode Island, Its Making and Meaning,* 2 vols. (New York, 1902).

Yankeeland by Carl Woodward (Chester, Conn., 1971).[2] While none of these books requires any great background of historical knowledge, all help to provide a context within which the genealogist may more surely work.

Because of its size, Rhode Island presents in its history a personal element for the genealogist that is missing in the other colonies. In 1708 the entire population numbered only 7,181 people. Most of the original settlers founded families there, and most at one time or another were actively involved in government, religious, or commercial affairs. Behind many a yeoman farmer who migrated to New York State following the Revolution are ancestral lines reaching back to colonial governors, the tempestuous Samuel Gorton, Quaker martyr Mary Dyer, or even Roger Williams. In reading about the history of Rhode Island, many of us are reading specifically about our own ancestors.

In 1636 the whole body of the lands now forming the State of Rhode Island was owned by the Indians then dwelling upon them.[3] The Massachusetts Bay Colony, on the other hand, was already sufficiently established to persecute those who did not subscribe to its own variety of religious freedom. The first white settlement in Rhode Island was begun that year by Roger Williams, who did it not so much out of conscious intent to establish a haven of religious liberty as from necessity, a decree of banishment having been issued against him in Boston. Warned by Governor John Winthrop of impending deportation, and forced to flee his Salem home in midwinter, he was only the first of many men and women who left to take refuge in the nearest place where they felt safe to follow their own consciences in peace and the hope of future prosperity.

It has been said that Rhode Island owed her very existence to the intolerance of Massachusetts and Connecticut, but it is equally true that the new colony was in part the product of Narragansett Indian policy[4]. Roger Williams had little choice available to him, for to the southeast was Plymouth Colony, where Governor Winslow, largely out of fear of Massachusetts Bay, issued a warning against trespassing, and to the southwest stood Connecticut, another Puritan theocracy. Between these two civilized yet ideologically hostile areas lay country owned and occupied by the Narragansetts, who very well understood the advantages of having a friendly buffer zone between themselves and their enemies to the east, the Wampanoags. That Roger Williams earned their respect by dealing fairly and intelligently with them from the beginning set a fortunate course for the future of the Rhode Island colony.

Accompanied by the eighteen-year-old Thomas Angell, Williams made his way south to Sowams, now Barrington, where they stayed with the

---

2. This book is not unbiased in its presentation of the first families of Narragansett, glossing over the associations with Connecticut rather lightly.

3. Sidney S. Rider, *The Lands of Rhode Island as They Were Known to Cannounicus and Miantunnomu (1636)* (Providence, 1904), 61.

4. Sydney James, *Colonial Rhode Island, 8.*

Indians for the remainder of that winter. A first settlement was begun at Seekonk, but when he learned that this was claimed by Plymouth, Williams left crops already planted and moved across the Great Salt River to begin a new settlement at the junction of two smaller rivers, the Moshassuc and the Wanasquatucket. There he obtained land from the Indians and distributed it to others who joined him, naming the place Providence Plantations in appreciation of God's mercy. William Harris, Francis Wicks and John Smith, a miller from Dorchester, who had also been banished from Boston, were among the first to arrive, followed by Joshua Verin and William Arnold.

A second settlement was made in the spring of 1638 on the northern end of Aquidneck Island, at a place the Indians called Pocasset, renamed Portsmouth by the English. It was founded by a group of people who had been exiled from Boston because of their association with Anne (Marbury) Hutchinson, labelled "Antinomian" for holding mystical religious beliefs which did not conform to Puritan doctrine in that they emphasized the importance of continued inspiration by the Holy Spirit. These families included the households of William Coddington, Dr. John Clarke, John Coggeshall, William Dyer, Randall Holden, John Sanford, Henry Bull, and others whose names have come down in Rhode Island history and genealogy. With the help of Roger Williams, Coddington bought the Island from the Indians and renamed it "Rhode" Island. Although the name is mentioned in Richard Hakluyt's account of the 1524 voyage of Giovanni di Verrazano, a more precise explanation of its origin is found in a letter written in 1666 by Roger Williams, in which he states that "Rode Island (in the Greeke language) is an Ile of Roses," referring probably to Aquidneck's native rhododendrons.[5] Until a bridge was built in the nineteenth century, it was known as the "Island," as opposed to the "Main," and many a Rhode Island Revolutionary pensioner later described his war service using those terms.

The Island had its own internal problems almost immediately. Samuel Gorton, a man of strong opinions who managed to stir up trouble wherever he went, precipitated a minor revolt in Portsmouth; Coddington and others withdrew to the southern end of Aquidneck, where they founded the third settlement, Newport. For one winter the two towns functioned separately, but then united with Coddington as governor and did not again separate until 1648. In the meantime more families, attracted by opportunity as much as necessity, arrived from Taunton and other Massachusetts and Plymouth towns.

A fourth settlement was made in 1642 at Shawomet by Samuel Gorton, who had earlier been expelled from Plymouth, refused freeman status by Providence, and finally forced to leave Portsmouth. He first attempted to settle at Pawtuxet, but finding that place already claimed by the Arnolds, who were scheming to have it annexed to Massachusetts, he and Dr. John Greene bought land from the Indians at Shawomet, just to the south. This was renamed Warwick in 1644 in honor of the Earl of Warwick, who was instrumental in helping to obtain its first royal charter.

By this time it had become clear to her neighbors that the new settlements represented, if not a danger, at least a threat to their peace of mind. The New England Confederation, formed in 1643, left out Rhode Island, on the grounds that she had no stable government and held anarchistic principles shocking to the other colonies. Roger Williams went to England to obtain a charter, returning in September 1644 with a patent authorizing the union of Providence, Portsmouth and Newport under "The Incorporation of Providence Plantations." After a bitter dispute with Massachusetts over ownership of the Shawomet land, during which Gorton, Randall Holden and others were dragged off to jail in Boston, Warwick obtained its own charter and joined the government of the others. The charter declared the colony's subjection to King Charles, but guaranteed the right of religious liberty for all.

One historian has observed that the four original towns in Rhode Island were all founded so that their inhabitants would not have to live with other people[6]; it might also be said that they had agreed to disagree. The Compact signed by the first inhabitants of Providence in 1636 clearly stated that the government was to have jurisdiction "only in civil things," and the Portsmouth Compact of 1638 stipulated that none was to be held accountable for his religious beliefs.

Many of the earliest surviving records for the four original towns are available in print: *Early Records of the Town of Portsmouth,* edited by Clarence S. Brigham (Providence, 1901), *Early Records of the Town of Warwick,* edited by Howard M. Chapin (Providence, 1926), and the *Early Records of the Town of Providence* in twenty-one volumes, edited by Horatio Rogers (Providence, 1892-1915) with an index published in 1949 by Richard LeBaron Bowen. The records of Newport are included in the first volume of *Records of the Colony of Rhode Island and Providence Plantations in New England,* edited by John Russell Bartlett (Providence, 1856-1862; reprint ed., New York, 1968). Volumes I through VII of this work contain the records of the Court of Commissioners and then the General Assembly, from 1636 to 1776, along with numerous other documents. A second set of volumes, *Records of the State of Rhode Island and Providence Plantations,* continues to 1792.[7] This work is often called "Colonial Records of Rhode Island" or simply, "Bartlett." It contains, scattered among records of legislation and foreign affairs of the colony, many references to ordinary inhabitants. The General

6. James, *Colonial Rhode Island,* 13.

7. Much of the original material is in the R.I. Archives, but some of it was copied from the British Public Record Office and other British sources, a transcript of which is at John Carter Brown Library of Brown University.

Assembly was made up of six representatives from each town, and during its earliest years especially, it dealt with many matters of individual cóncern which are of genealogical interest.

Commercial opportunities of the Narragansett Bay area had been early recognized by Roger Williams, and it was with the development of a trading post at Cocumscussoc, near present day Wickford, that settlement on the west side of the Bay began. Richard Smith, a wealthy planter with interests also in New York and Boston, built there a home which became known as "Smith's Castle." His daughter Catherine married Gysbert op Dyck, a Hempstead, New York, physician, and they became the progenitors of the prominent Updike family of Rhode Island. Making their fortunes in trade with New York, Boston, and the West Indies, these families maintained social and business relationships with both Roger Williams and Connecticut Governor John Winthrop, Jr. They laid the groundwork for a slavery-based plantation life which flourished in Narragansett from the late seventeenth century until sent into decline by the Revolution.

The unifying factor in Rhode Island's diversity became trade, which for many years depended upon the sea. Unable to produce great quantities of anything to export, Rhode Islanders learned to make a profit carrying goods produced by other people. "A surprising number of the first settlers became traders at least part time, and many more dabbled in small ventures; others tied their lives to commerce by fitting out or commanding vessels that carried the goods."[8] With a natural position as a seaport, Newport grew rapidly, developing a rather mobile population; by 1729 Antiguan planters were using it as a summer resort. It is characteristic of genealogical research in colonial Newport that one turns up names of many people who appear not to have settled there for any length of time, but are shown in probate or court files as merchants, mariners, or craftsmen, then pass out of written records without a trace. Until the Revolution, Newport easily maintained its economic and cultural prominence over the stodgier town of Providence.

In the latter half of the seventeenth century, hunger for land broke loose in the colony as men in the settled towns joined together to purchase large areas of land from the Indians. The Conanicut Purchase agreement of 1657, led by William Coddington and Benedict Arnold, was signed by a great number of men, mostly from Portsmouth and Newport, some in for only 1/900th of a share. In 1657 the Pettaquamscutt Purchasers, heáded by Samuel Wilbore, Thomas Mumford, John Porter, Samuel Wilson and John Hull, bought rights to the southeast quarter of the area since known popularly as "South County." At the same time the powerful William Harris was intriguing to get control of much of what became Providence County by obtaining "confirmatory deeds" from the Indians, siding with Connecticut in land disputes when it suited his purpose.

8. James, *Colonial Rhode Island*, 50.

Connecticut claimed all the territory south of Warwick east to Narragansett Bay, and in an attempt to make good the claim it established the town of Wickford; Rhode Island immediately countered by establishing the area as King's Province in 1666. Except for the trading post at Cocumscussoc, however, settlement on the west side of the Bay remained limited to a few dwellings like the garrison house of Jireh Bull, not far from the shore, and all were swept away in 1675 and 1676 by King Philip's War.

Both Rhode Island and the Narragansett Indians had tried to maintain their neutrality in that conflict, which originated with the Wampanoag Indians in Plymouth Colony. Indians in Connecticut and central Massachusetts were quickly involved, prompting those colonies to join forces with Plymouth, and Rhode Island was called upon to give naval support by transporting soldiers. The Battle of the Great Swamp Fight, which took place in December 1675 near Wickford, destroyed most of the Narragansetts who had been drawn into the conflict by the Wampanoags. Metacomet, or King Philip, the Wampanoag leader, was hunted down near Mount Hope by Benjamin Church, who, though his origins were in Plymouth Colony, became the ancestor of many Rhode Islanders. Captured Indians were sold into slavery. A few Narragansetts who, with their leader, Ninegret, had managed to remain neutral, continued to live in South County, and there are today many people who can trace some ancestry back to these Indians. The Rhode Island Archives contains manuscript material on the Narragansetts. *A Report of the Commissioners on the Affairs of the Narragansett Indians* (Providence, 1858) lists 122 persons claiming Indian descent and 75 who were occupying Indian land; a similar report of 1881 includes valuable genealogical material on descendants living at that date. The Westerly Public Library has several of these reports in one bound volume.

George M. Bodge's *Soldiers of King Philip's War* (Boston, 1906; reprint ed., Baltimore, 1976) describes that war and the period leading up to it and includes in the text numerous muster rolls and lists. Many men who fought from Massachusetts later settled in Rhode Island, particularly in East Greenwich, incorporated in 1677, where land was put up for sale by the colony. The end of the war made safe settlement possible throughout King's County, although the dispute with Connecticut was not settled until 1703, when the boundary was fixed at the Pawcatuck River, and some problems persisted another forty years.

As early as 1660, some Portsmouth people, including branches of the Wilcox, Slocum and Cornell families, had moved across the Sakonnet River into neighboring Plymouth Colony. After 1686, when Plymouth became part of the Massachusetts Bay Colony, Rhode Island men joined in the Pocasset Purchase to open up and develop the area which became Tiverton, some buying land also in Little Compton, which had earlier been laid out in lots for Plymouth people. Although part of present day Rhode Island, these towns remained in Massachusetts Bay until 1746/7.

While both Bartlett and Bodge may contain information about ancestors, genealogists will find that for actually tracing families in the Rhode Island of the seventeenth and early eighteenth centuries, there are two basic printed sources, both published a century ago. John O. Austin in 1887 (Albany, N.Y.) published his *Genealogical Dictionary of Rhode Island,* stating confidently on the title page that "any intelligent person is capable of becoming interested in family history." This cumbersome book, often relegated to back shelves of libraries because of its size, represents years of the compiler's life spent digging information out of ancient probate, land, town council and court records. It was reprinted (Baltimore, 1969) with additions and corrections by Mr. Austin himself and an appendix containing material written by G. Andrews Moriarty, a more recent authority on Rhode Island genealogy, which was published originally in *The American Genealogist* from 1943 to 1963.[9] This remains the most comprehensive and useful record of early Rhode Island people, covering 485 families in the first three or four generations. The greatest drawback of this work is its lack of references, for Mr. Austin never recorded where he found any particular bit of data. He did give place of residence for each family, however, and from the concisely stated information it is usually possible to deduce the likely source, enabling a check of the original document.

Mr. Austin also published *The Ancestry of Thirty-Three Rhode Islanders* (Albany, 1889; reprint ed., Rutland, Vt., 1970) and *One Hundred and Sixty Allied Families* (Providence, 1893).[10] The Rhode Island Historical Society owns one large notebook in which he was collecting material for a projected second volume of his *Dictionary*; this includes information on later generations of some families treated in the earlier volume, as well as some data on families omitted from the first.

The other basic reference work in print for earlier Rhode Island genealogy, covering the period up to 1850, was compiled by James N. Arnold during the same years that Austin was working. Arnold began his work as editor of *The Narragansett Historical Register,* a quarterly devoted to genealogy and history of southern Rhode Island, published from 1883 until 1891. Included in that journal are vital records of various Rhode Island towns, and when it ceased publication he brought these out in book form. The complete series totals twenty-one volumes, although only the first six are actually vital records, entitled *The Vital Record of Rhode Island* (Providence, 1891-1912)[11]. Its title is singular, subtitled by Mr. Arnold "A Family Register for the People," but over the years it has

9. Additions and corrections to Austin by Robert S. Wakefield and others have continued to appear in *The American Genealogist*; see Appendix B.
10. These and other books by Austin were reprinted in their original form, without corrections, and should therefore be used with some caution.
11. Photocopy reprints of the various individual volumes of Arnold have been available from University Microfilms, Ann Arbor, Michigan since 1973.

come to be known in the plural as Arnold's "Vital Records" or more simply just by the name of its compiler, as "Arnold."

The first six volumes contain the vital records of Rhode Island towns from the earliest recorded event up to 1850. These are arranged by county and town, with first marriages and then births and deaths listed alphabetically by surname. For most towns, each entry is preceded by a hyphenated number, i.e. "2-39," which refers to the volume and page of the town record from which the entry was taken.[12] With marriages, it is advisable to check the entry under the groom's name, since more complete information is often given there than under the name of the bride.

Unfortunately, Arnold did not abstract most of the information himself. It is legend in Rhode Island that he would visit with local officials while clerks copied off material for him. Many of the copyists were unfamiliar with early handwriting as well as with some of the names, resulting in numerous errors, worse for some towns than for others. Jamestown records in particular are badly done. If no corroborating evidence for an entry in Arnold exists elsewhere, or if there is the slightest doubt as to its accuracy, the original record should be sought out and checked.

Within the past few years a series of books entitled *The New Vital Record of Rhode Island* (Princeton, Mass., 1975-   ), compiled and edited by Alden G. Beaman, has begun publication and at the time of writing totals nine volumes. To date only Washington and Kent counties have been covered. Beaman has extracted from probate and gravestone records information about many births and marriages never actually recorded and therefore not included in Arnold. These are arranged alphabetically and because they incorporate records of several towns are helpful in locating families within the areas covered. The method of presentation, however, prevents the reader from evaluating the references without examining the actual documents cited.

There are many excellent printed genealogies of Rhode Island families and both the Society and the Rhode Island Historical Society have collections of manuscript material of varying degrees of completeness. More difficult to locate are the articles buried in various periodicals, past and present, which contain genealogical material. Specifically Rhode Island journals are *The Newport Historical Magazine* (1880-1884) and its successor, *The Rhode Island Historical Magazine* (1884-1887); *The Narragansett Historical Register* (1882-1891); *Rhode Island Historical Tracts* (1877-1896) edited by Sidney S. Rider; and the publications of the Rhode Island Historical Society, which include *The Rhode Island Historical Society Collections* (1827-1941), *Rhode Island Historical Society Proceedings* (1872-1914), and *Rhode Island Historical Society Publications* (1893-1900). Current publications are *Rhode Island History,* the quarterly of the Rhode Island Historical Society, which is now printing articles

---

12. North Kingstown entries are not thus cited.

of chiefly historical interest; *Rhode Island Roots,* the journal of the Rhode Island Genealogical Society, which began publication in 1975; and *Rhode Island Genealogical Register,* edited by Alden G. Beaman, which has been issued quarterly since July 1978. Many articles on Rhode Island families have appeared in the *Register* and *The American Genealogist,* some in the *New York Genealogical & Biographical Record* and *National Genealogical Society Quarterly,* and a few in the *Magazine of the Detroit Society for Genealogical Research.*

In an appendix to his *Index of the Early Records of the Town of Providence,* Richard LeBaron Bowen includes a list of articles of Rhode Island relevance appearing in the *Register, The American Genealogist,* and *Rhode Island Historical Society Collections* through 1949. Articles appearing in the first two journals from 1950 to 1975 were listed by Robert S. Wakefield in *Rhode Island Roots,* 1 (1975-1976): 1, 3-5, and those in *Rhode Island History* from 1950 to 1960 were indexed by Henry L. P. Beckwith, Jr., in *Rhode Island Roots,* 2 (1976): 6. *Index to Genealogical Periodicals* by Donald Lines Jacobus is an excellent finding aid for further material, and should be supplemented by the various annual indexes to genealogical periodicals which have appeared since 1953.

In making the transition from printed material on the early colonial period in Rhode Island to primary source material for that time, the genealogist is inescapably headed for something known as the town council book. In colonial times, as even today, almost all matters were handled by and in the towns. Counties in Rhode Island serve as geographical definitions within which the towns exist and as judicial districts, but nothing other than court records have ever been kept on a county-wide level. The freemen of each town met in town meeting to choose from among their own number various officers who included deputies to the General Assembly, constables, surveyors of highways, pound keeper, fence viewers, jurymen, councillors and a town clerk.

The town council took care of the probating of wills, licensing of public houses, welfare matters, and all manner of other business. It was the job of the town clerk to keep the records and to enter births and marriages which were brought to him, as well as to record deeds. He also kept track of ear marks, used by each man in town to distinguish his own livestock. Since paper was not plentiful, all these things are likely to be found jumbled together in the earliest town council book of any town. Sometimes books were begun from both front and back, perhaps for different kinds of business but not necessarily so, and many have been rebound over the years with pages from something else inserted somewhere in the middle. Blank spaces were filled as need arose, usually with records of births or marriages, which are unlikely to appear chronologically. To expect any order in these early records is to invite frustration, yet they contain much of genealogical importance that has never been extracted and published.

James writes, "the towns without penalty disregarded laws on many subjects, from collecting taxes to recording land titles and vital statistics. In fact, town government proceeded largely on its own, conducting public business of many kinds, while the colony feebly tried to manage what was left to it."[13] Given that situation, it is perhaps understandable that the researcher is faced with systems of record keeping that vary from town to town. In 1647 the General Assembly passed an act requiring that marriage intentions be published, but with no penalty for not doing so, many ignored the rule. It is not unusual to find a marriage recorded years after the event by means of a deposition from someone who had been witness to it. When births were recorded, the usual method was for a parent to carry to the town clerk a Bible record or piece of paper on which was written the names of all children in the family born up to that date, in which case later children born in the same family might never be recorded. Sometimes it is stated in the record book that the information was written "as told me by the mother," a lengthy list with many scratch overs indicating that mother's memory was not infallible. One occasionally finds children born to a woman by more than one marriage recorded on the same page, providing a juxtaposition that is lost in the alphabetized record given by Arnold.

Most genealogical searches proceed from vital records to probate and land records, and in Rhode Island both of these are also found in the town hall. The town council admitted wills to probate and appointed administrators to distribute the estates of those who died intestate. It ordered the taking of inventories, and in some Rhode Island towns the date of death of the decedent was noted on the inventory when it was presented, often providing the only exact record of that event. In the late seventeenth century are found a few cases where a man died without a will but leaving a large family; one of the heirs might request the town council to "make a will," which amounted to ordering a lawful distribution of the estate.[14] Such was the case with Captain Thomas Cooke who died in Portsmouth in 1670 and with John Spencer of East Greenwich who died in 1684. Some towns, like Charlestown, were more careful than others about recording receipts from heirs; when found, these provide helpful information about relationships and places of residence.

Most towns did keep town meeting books separate from town council books from the beginning; the former usually contain records of officers chosen for various responsibilities and such matters as laying out of highways, but sometimes one does find in them the kind of business usually reserved for town council books. It is wise to consult both. Few

---

13. James, *Colonial Rhode Island,* 71.
14. The misleading statement in the recent edition of *Genealogical Research: Methods and Sources,* Vol. 1, revised, that in Rhode Island a man's neighbors sometimes made his will, is traceable to a statement in the earlier edition by Edward H. West which was taken out of context. Mr. West was making the point that because early Rhode Island towns were small, the town council members who performed this function were undoubtedly neighbors or friends of the deceased.

towns kept their "Will Books" separate from town council books from the first, and it is common to find the earliest books labelled "Town Council & Probate." Intestate proceedings are almost always found in the town council book. In East Greenwich and Portsmouth a few probates are found in the earliest deed books. New Shoreham at first combined everything in one book. It was standard procedure in Rhode Island to give original wills back to the family, but Portsmouth has a large book, long known as "The Scrapbook," in which are pasted some original wills and inventories found in 1903 in the basement of the town hall. Many of these date from the seventeenth century and were unknown to Austin when he compiled his *Dictionary*.

It cannot be emphasized strongly enough that there is no hard and fast rule for early Rhode Island town records. When visiting a town hall, it is wise to take time enough to look around and become acquainted with the arrangement of records before plunging into a search. If something is not found in the logical book, look somewhere else. Clarence S. Brigham's compiled "Report on the Archives of Rhode Island" was published in the *Annual Report of the American Historical Association for The Year 1903* (Washington, 1904). It is to be hoped that this will be reprinted in a more readily available form, for it remains the most complete and accurate inventory and description of all records in each town hall and every other public repository in the state, including everything up to the date of its publication. Except for court records, most of the records are now where they were then, although many town halls have moved to more modern quarters.[15] By recent legislation, town clerks are forbidden to dispose of any old records without first notifying the Division of Community Affairs, but no measures have yet been taken to enforce the ruling.

While considering the original records kept in the towns, it must be pointed out that these are in the care of each town clerk, who may or may not be kindly disposed towards genealogical inquiry. Most are occupied with the daily business of registering deeds and issuing beach permits and have little interest in or knowledge about the earliest records in their custody. A few tend to be overprotective, while a few others may seem rather careless to those who realize the value of the old books. When going on a field trip to a town hall, it is a good idea to take along photocopies of references from Arnold or other sources, for it may otherwise be difficult to locate a particular entry. Some towns have good indexes, others do not. A few have copies of Arnold's volume pertaining to their own records and a few have copies of Beaman's books but do not usually know how to interpret the references. It is best not to expect the staff to know how to read handwriting of the seventeenth and eighteenth

15. Two exceptions are the early town council records of Smithfield, which in 1903 were in a basement vault in the Central Falls City Hall and cannot now be located, and the early vital records of Warren, which have disappeared within the past few years.

centuries, though occasionally they can recommend a local historian who may be able to help.

Those genealogists able and willing to take the time to browse through town council records of the early years may find there more obscure references to families who seem to have dropped out of sight. Each colonial Rhode Island town was a tiny welfare state which took care of its own people, and the town council was in charge of all welfare matters.[16] Individuals wishing to settle in town were required to present to the council some proof of ownership of land or other means of support, lest they become "chargeable" to the town, that is, dependent upon public support. Strangers staying in the homes of town residents were suspect, as were all transients. Gregory Cooke, desirous of settling in South Kingstown in December 1767, informed the council that he was born in Philadelphia and was given until the following June to obtain a certificate from that city or leave town.[17] In some cases bonds were given by relatives to enable people to stay; these may provide clues to otherwise unknown relationships. If suitable means of support could not be proven, the persons concerned were "warned out," or ordered to return to the communities to which they belonged; if necessary the town constable was ordered to remove them to the last place of residence. Litigation between towns sometimes arose over such matters as which held responsibility for support of an illegitimate child.

On the other hand, legal inhabitants of a town who wished to move elsewhere might request from the town council a certificate identifying themselves. Those people who belonged there but fell on hard times were taken care of out of the town treasury. In cases of need, a family member might apply to the council for aid, and would be given food, clothing, or lodging, as called for in any particular situation. Death records sometimes are found in references to a few shillings granted someone for making a coffin or digging a grave. With a parent's permission, children might be bound out, or apprenticed, to suitable people. Andrew Pitcher of East Greenwich, whose father deserted the family in 1698, was bound out to a Potowomut weaver named Greene at the age of three.[18] When a person or family known to have lived in a particular town disappears without explanation from other records, the town council books should always be searched.

Although deeds are recorded on the town level in Rhode Island, some land evidence for the earliest years may also be found in the State Archives. Certain deeds for one reason or another ended up among the Colony records, and these have been collected into four volumes called "Rhode Island Land Evidence"; an abstract of the first volume is in print

---

16. See also Bruce C. Daniels, "Poor Relief, Local Finance, and Town Government in Eighteenth-Century Rhode Island," *Rhode Island History*, 40 (1981): 75-87.
17. South Kingstown Town Clerk's Office, Town Council & Probate Book, 5:194.
18. East Greenwich Town Clerk's Office, Town Council, 1:52.

as *Rhode Island Land Evidence, Volume 1* (Providence, 1921; reprint ed., Baltimore, 1970).[19] Further volumes at the Archives include also notarial papers, such as powers of attorney, protests by ship captains, and even an occasional apprenticeship indenture. There is a typed abstract, inaccurately termed an index, to each volume, made by the late Archivist, Miss Mary T. Quinn.

Early Proprietors' records in some cases have survived in town halls like East Greenwich and Jamestown, but in other instances are part of private collections like the Harris Papers at Rhode Island Historical Society. James in the bibliography of his *Colonial Rhode Island* provides a thorough list and description.

Most towns have overall indexes to their deeds, though some, like Coventry, use a difficult, archaic system said to have been marketed to town clerks at one time. Others, such as Glocester, index only by the first letter of surname and, since entries are not chronologically arranged, it is necessary to continue to the end of the letter in order to pick up even all early entries for any particular name. Some old books have individual indexes in the front of each book, and where these have survived wear and tear and rebinding, they may provide unexpected genealogical help. In Glocester a deed was recently found indexed as "Obadiah Inman's deed from his father," and in Charlestown one to "James Ladd from his father John,"[20] although the deeds themselves make no mention of any relationship. Since the index in each of these cases was in the handwriting of the clerk who recorded the deed, it may safely be assumed to be contemporary evidence.

Until 1747, the Colony consisted of only the island of Aquidneck, tiny Block Island, Providence, and the area south of the Blackstone River; the territory to the east was part of Massachusetts. In that year, by royal decree, the towns of Tiverton, Little Compton, Bristol, Warren and Cumberland became part of Rhode Island, increasing its population by 5,000. It is important to remember that earliest records for these towns do not conform to the pattern set in other Rhode Island communities before that date, but rather to the rule in Massachusetts, where probate and land records are kept in the county. At the time of the separation Taunton replaced Bristol as county seat of Bristol County, Massachusetts, and there both deeds and probates up to 1747 are preserved, along with some of the early court records. The Fall River District Deeds Registry has handwritten copies of deeds relating to the Tiverton area before the separation.

Other early records for these towns will be found in the Massachusetts Archives and among the court records kept by Suffolk County Superior

19. The index to the one volume in print includes only grantees and grantors, omitting witnesses and other names. Newport Historical Society has manuscript abstracts of the first three volumes of land evidence.

20. Glocester Town Clerk's Office, Deeds, 9:501; Charlestown Town Clerk's Office, Deeds, 3:79.

Court on the fourteenth floor of the court house in Boston. From 1686 to 1688, a short-lived attempt was made by King James II to unite all of New England, New Jersey, and Pennsylvania as one colony under Governor Edmund Andros, and during this time all estates over £50 were required to be probated in Boston. Rhode Island wills and administrations falling into this category were those of Philip Jones, Richard Barns, Bartholomew Hunt, Sr., John Peabody, Mary Sisson, John Williams and Joshua Coggeshall.[21] At that time it was also necessary to obtain marriage bonds in Boston; two good Quakers, Christopher Allen of Newport and Elizabeth Leyouge of Little Compton were in 1687 married "in Boston according to the cannons and constitutions of the Church of England."[22] The original bonds are among Suffolk County court papers.

Record books of the Superior Court of Judicature held in Bristol County, from 1693 to 1782, are among the court records kept by the clerk of the Supreme Court of Suffolk County. These include many land cases involving Tiverton and Little Compton people, and the files often contain informative depositions. Reports of inquests are also found in these court papers, which are kept in large bound scrapbooks. There are surname and case indexes. The books themselves are kept in locked glass-doored cupboards reaching from floor to ceiling, and any one search may involve several volumes.

The Massachusetts Archives also contain interesting material on Rhode Island families, such as the documents which tell a swashbuckling tale of how Christopher Almy, Jr., with accomplice Nathaniel Warren, both of Tiverton, in 1696 attempted to defraud privateer George Mountjoy of Boston out of an impressive amount of plate and pieces of eight by staging a fake robbery in that town. Depositions were made by several neighbors from which it appears that Mountjoy got back his treasure, and in typical Rhode Island style no one was really any the worse for the incident.[23]

Moving into the eighteenth century, the genealogist gradually leaves the period covered by Austin, but Arnold remains a basic printed resource until 1850. The town records, as time progresses, become better organized and easier to read with deeds and probates in properly separated books, although vital records are still likely to be found mixed in with town council matters. As the populations of the older towns increased, new towns were set off.[24] If a family lived for several

21. See Winifred Lovering Holman and Mary Lovering Holman, "Suffolk County Probate (1686-1692)," *The American Genealogist*, 12 (1935-1936): 175-177, 13 (1936-1937): 98-106, and 14 (1937-1938): 34-45, and also G. A. Taylor, "Stray Wills at Suffolk County, (Mass.) Probate Registry," *The American Genealogist*, 13 (1936-1937): 55-56.
22. South Kingstown Town Clerk's Office, transcript of North Kingstown Town Council, Book 1, p. 32b (from back of the book).
23. Massachusetts Archives, 40:592-604.
24. In 1723 Kings Towne was divided into North and South Kingstown, in 1731 Smithfield, Glocester and Scituate were set off from Providence and incorporated as towns, in 1741 Coventry was taken from Warwick and West Greenwich from East Greenwich, in 1738

generations in a town that was taken from an older one, its records would be found in the parent town up to the date of separation. For instance, to properly document the history of a family who lived in Foster in 1800, one would have to search not only the Foster records, but those of Scituate and of Providence for the appropriate periods of time, taking into consideration also that deeds may have been recorded some time after the actual date of transaction and may therefore be somewhere other than the logical place.

Although almost all records are kept in the office of each town clerk, there are a few exceptions. Early Smithfield records, along with those of Lincoln, are kept at the city hall in Central Falls. Early North Providence records are kept at Pawtucket City Hall. The early probate, town council, and town meeting records of Johnston, which was set off from Providence in 1759, are in the probate office at Providence City Hall; Johnston's deeds are in its own town hall. In a few cases there are some transcriptions of records in other town offices; these will be noted in Appendix A.

Newport is a special situation. The British occupied the entire island for three years during the Revolution, and when they retreated to New York in 1779, the Tory sheriff, Walter Chaloner, took with him the town records. The ship carrying them sank in New York Harbor. Through the efforts of General Washington, alerted to the loss by General Nathaniel Greene, the records were salvaged after a few days in the water, but they were left in a storehouse for three years before being returned to Newport. Researchers were then permitted to use them, reducing many papers to fragments; eventually what survived was preserved by the then popular Emery process, in which documents were placed between layers of fine silk. They were then bound into scrapbooks. The Newport Historical Society has two sets of these volumes, one for deeds and one for town council records, along with a card index to each; but because of fragmentation and fading, the original papers are very difficult to read.

Newport records for the period after the Revolution to the present day are at the city hall, where there is a separate office for probate. Deeds are in the office of the city clerk, and quite well indexed although a few appear to have been missed.[25] The city clerk also has a card index to births, marriages and deaths.

If searches through Austin, Arnold, and the records available in town offices prove negative or incomplete, there are other resources to consider. The kind of church records which exist in Massachusetts or Connecticut are simply not available for Rhode Island, where, except for

---

Charlestown from Westerly, in 1743 Exeter from North Kingstown, in 1747 Richmond from Charlestown, in 1757 Hopkinton from Westerly, in 1770 Barrington from Warren, and in 1781 Foster from Scituate.

25. In a recent effort to film deeds for microfiche, pages were cut from some deed books; when discovered, it was found that margins were not sufficient for rebinding, but some restoration is reportedly planned.

New Shoreham, people from the beginning "thought otherwise." There are a few Congregational church records at the town halls in Bristol and Little Compton, dating from the years when those towns were part of the Massachusetts Bay Colony, and among the Suffolk court records are a couple of lists censuring some Bristol residents for not attending meetings of public worship. The Massachusetts Archives has a petition from the inhabitants of Tiverton in 1709 protesting a tax levied on them for support of a minister. As the early fervor for individuality of beliefs faded, it left behind a diversity of creeds with widely varied systems of record keeping.

The first Quaker missionaries arrived from England in 1657 and found waiting for them a large number of Rhode Islanders who already believed in the inspiration of the Holy Spirit but who badly needed some kind of religious structure. Quakerism thus gained a quick foothold, providing yet another bone of contention with Massachusetts. Many Aquidneck families like the Eastons and Coggeshalls became Friends, and Mary Dyer, wife of William Dyer of Newport, was hanged on Boston Common for her repeated insistence on preaching her beliefs there.

Quakers are traditionally known for the fine records they keep. Their marriage records often state names of parents and places of residence, and include a list of witnesses which can usually be counted on to contain the names of some relatives. The minutes of their monthly meetings record such matters as dismissals of members for having taken part in military endeavors or for marrying out of meeting, censures to parents who permitted their children to marry out, and certificates given members to travel to or settle in other parts of the country or brought by members from other meetings. Few Friends lived so quietly that they were not noted in the records at one time or another.

Volume 7 of Arnold's *Vital Record* contains births, marriages and deaths for Rhode Island Friends and Narragansett Friends, arranged alphabetically. It is unfortunate that he did not include the names of witnesses to marriages, which add so much to the value of the Shrewsbury, New Jersey, Friends records as published by John E. Stillwell in Volume 1 of his *Historical and Genealogical Miscellany* (New York, 1903). These New Jersey records will be of interest to many with early Rhode Island ancestry, for there was a close sea link between Newport and New Jersey in the late seventeenth century, and one of the earliest migrations out of Rhode Island was that of a number of Quaker families from Newport and Portsmouth who settled in Monmouth County. Records of the Allens, Parkers, Cooks, Bordens, Tallmans and Greenes are but a few found in both places.

The original Friends records for Rhode Island, which included Newport, Portsmouth, and some Jamestown records, are at the Newport Historical Society. Those for the rest of the colony are in the manuscripts department of the Rhode Island Historical Society, where a special curator who is a member of the Society of Friends is available one day a week for researchers who want to consult with her or to use the records. There are microfilm copies of these in the main reading room of the library, along with microfilm of Friends records from all over New England.

Quakers tended to travel a good deal. Early Rhode Island was closely linked by trade with Barbados, and some Quaker families like the Rodmans lived there before coming to New England; others moved back and forth. For records on these families, see G. Andrews Moriarty's "Barbadian Notes" in the *Register*, 67 (1913): 360-371. Many Quakers migrated out of Rhode Island, not only to New Jersey but to Dutchess County, New York; a few, like Ephraim Bull and William Borden, joined Nantucket Quakers in a small migration to North Carolina about 1750. Even before the Revolution, many moved into New York State and may be followed in records of Friends meetings there, presently kept at the Haviland Records Room of the Society of Friends in New York City.

Two Anglican churches were established in Rhode Island in the last decade of the seventeenth century. Trinity Church had a congregation at Newport for some time before an actual church was built, as did St. Paul's at Narragansett. With the home government in England lending an encouraging hand, both soon gained members from among the wealthy merchant families, some of whom were already Quakers. Gabriel Bernon, a prominent Huguenot merchant, was instrumental in founding a third Anglican Church, St. John's, in Providence in 1727. The earliest surviving baptismal record of Trinity Church is 1709; baptisms and marriages have been printed in Arnold's volume 10, but like his other abstracts have lost the value to be found in chronological order. The original Trinity records have recently been deposited at Newport Historical Society. *Annals of Trinity Church, Newport, R.I., 1698-1821*, ed. George C. Mason (Newport, 1890) provides a history of that church with references to members, but of more value to genealogists is the three-volume *History of the Narragansett Church* by Wilkins Updike (Boston, 1907), which includes a literal transcript of the parish register from 1718 to 1774 and fairly complete genealogical notes on the various families mentioned. Records of this church, which was physically moved in 1800 to the town of Wickford from its original location, are included in Arnold's volume 10 and cover the period 1718 to 1875.

Those Rhode Islanders who fell heir to Roger Williams's "Biblicist" approach to religion, as opposed to the mysticism of Anne Hutchinson and her followers, soon divided into several varieties of Baptists who differed from one another on certain and often rather fine points of doctrine. The Seventh Day, or Sabbatarian, Baptists, who observed the Sabbath on Saturday, the "seventh day," established a church in Newport about 1661 under the leadership of Samuel Hubbard. Families who joined this group included the Maxsons, Burdicks and Crandalls, and a second Sabbatarian Church was soon founded at Westerly, which for a long time had no other church. The records of both churches are now at Newport Historical Society and may be of interest to genealogists although, like other Baptists, they did not practice infant baptism and considered spiritual events in the life of an individual of more interest than the physical events which genealogy strives to reconstruct.

Baptist ministers traditionally considered records of marriages performed by them to be personal property which they retained if they moved to other churches. Many such records were included by Arnold in volumes 7, 8, 10 through 13, and 21 of his *Vital Record,* under the names of the ministers concerned, such as "Michael Eddy's Marriages" or "Gardner Thurston's Marriages." The originals of many of these are in the Newport Historical Society, as are early records of Newport's Congregational churches, the First Baptist Church, and a Moravian church founded there in 1749. The Rhode Island Historical Society has some original church records, and some records are still with the churches, as is the case with the Stone Church (Six Principle Baptist) in Tiverton and the Second Baptist Church of Newport. The Westerly Library, which had held the records of some churches in that area, returned them a few years ago to the churches concerned.

There have been several attempts to inventory the church records of Rhode Island,[26] but the most up-to-date list of such records and their whereabouts is held by the State Archives and was made when the Church of Latter Day Saints was microfilming in Rhode Island. It includes all churches up to about 1970, indicating what records were located for each and where the originals were kept, some of them in private hands. Information may be obtained by contacting the Archivist.

Colonial Newport had a substantial Jewish congregation, most of its members of Portuguese or Spanish origin who arrived by way of New Amsterdam, Holland or Curaçao. The General Assembly in 1684 accorded them the same protection extended to other strangers, and many later became freemen of the colony. An early group who had arrived in Newport about 1656 had dispersed by 1700, and a new influx took place in the 1750s. The Touro Synagogue, designed by Peter Harrison of Newport, an Anglican, and built with the help of contributions from Jews throughout the British Empire, was dedicated in 1763 at Hannukkah. Families like those of Aaron Lopez, the Riveras and Naphtali Hart played a vital role in Newport's commercial life until the Revolution. The Newport Historical Society has a large collection of Lopez's correspondence and papers. For an account of the Jews in Newport, see

26. Earlier inventories of church records include: Rhode Island State Record Commissioner, Annual Report (1906): "Church Records, Abstract from Returns of Custodians of Records on File in State Record Commissioner's Office"; original questionnaires now at R.I. Archives; Historical Records Survey, *Directory of Churches and Religious Organizations of Rhode Island,* (Providence, 1939); Historical Records Survey, Division of Community Service Projects, Works Project Administration, *Inventory of the Church Archives of Rhode Island,* (Providence, 1941).

"The Israelites in Rhode Island" by Reverend Frederic Denison, in *Narragansett Historical Register,* 4 (1885-1886): 301-317. *A Biographical Dictionary of Early American Jews, Colonial Times through 1800* by Joseph R. Rosenbloom (Lexington, Ky., 1960) includes much specific genealogical information about the early Newport Jewish families.

A French Huguenot settlement was attempted at East Greenwich in the 1680s, but rival land claims soon forced these people to leave that area. A few, like their leader, Daniel Ayrault, remained in Rhode Island, where they were assimilated into the population; some names became anglicized, i.e. Lemoine to Mooney or Mawney, Ganeaux to Gano, Targé to Tourgee. "Records of the French Church at Narragansett, 1686-1691," translated by Effingham de Forest, were printed in the *New York Genealogical and Biographical Record,* 70 (1939): 236-241, 359-365, and 71 (1940): 51-61. See also Elisha Potter Reynolds, "Memoirs Concerning the French Settlements in Colonial Rhode Island," in Rider, *Historical Tracts,* first series, no. 5 (1879); reprint ed., Baltimore, 1968.

Diaries are often useful in genealogical research, and Rhode Island is fortunate to have had a number of people who left journals of value to the genealogist as well as the historian. John Comer, pastor of the First and then of the Second Baptist Church of Newport until 1732, kept a diary which was published as volume 8 (1893), *Collections of the Rhode Island Historical Society.* Better known is *The Literary Diary of Ezra Stiles* (ed. Franklin B. Dexter; 3 vols., New York, 1901), minister of the Second Congregational Church of Newport who later went on to become president of Yale. Dr. Stiles kept records of his pastoral visits, and his wide interests brought him into contact with many from other congregations.

Peleg Burroughs, a Baptist minister who was born in Newport but lived and worked in Tiverton and Little Compton from 1774 until his death in 1800, kept a remarkably frank and open diary of most of those years which has been published by the Rhode Island Genealogical Society as *Peleg Burroughs's Journal, 1778-1798: The Tiverton, R.I., Years of the Humbly Bold Baptist Minister,* edited by Ruth Wilder Sherman (Warwick, R.I., 1981). Because he lived among the ordinary people of that rural area, his comments and observations about his neighbors both add to our historical knowledge of the times and provide much genealogical information not available elsewhere.

Jeffrey Watson, a South Kingstown Friend, kept a diary from 1740 to 1784; manuscript copies by Caroline E. Robinson are in several libraries and genealogical abstracts were printed in the *Rhode Island Genealogical Register,* 3 (1980-1981): 1-17. Thomas Benjamin Hazard, also a Friend, kept *Nailor Tom's Diary* from 1778 to 1840 (Boston, 1930), including thousands of references to births, marriages and deaths of people he knew. It lacks an index, but the Rhode Island Historical Society has several handwritten notebooks of abstracted genealogical items from it. Redwood Library at Newport has most of the original diary, except for a small portion which is at the Newport Historical Society. The almanacs of Harris Smith covered much of the nineteenth century in South Kingstown and nearby areas; the Rhode Island Historical Society has a typed index of genealogical items from these.

One of the foremost difficulties in Rhode Island genealogical research is to determine an ancestor's specific home town. The most direct way to attack this problem is through use of census records. Although the first Rhode Island colony census was ordered in 1706 by the General Assembly, the earliest known to be extant today is the 1730 census for the town of Portsmouth and for part of South Kingstown. These list the number of inhabitants, both black and white, in each household. The Portsmouth schedule, discovered in the Portsmouth Scrapbook, was published in *Rhode Island Roots,* 7 (1981): 16, 17, and it is hoped that the 1730 lists for some other towns may yet be found. Many towns have tax lists dating from before the Revolution, either in the town offices, in the State Archives, or at the Rhode Island Historical Society.

The first actual census that has survived almost in its entirety is that of 1774, which has been printed with an index (Baltimore, 1969); the original is in the Archives. Returns for the town of New Shoreham (Block Island) are missing. Listed are heads of households, with other members of the family enumerated by sex and whether under or over sixteen years of age. The number of Blacks and Indians in each household is included. This census is particularly valuable in that it caught at home many people who had moved elsewhere by the time the next full census was taken in 1782. The population of Rhode Island, which had increased almost 50 percent from 1755 to a high of 59,678 in 1774, declined to 55,011 by 1776 and still further to 51,869 by 1782.[27] Some Loyalists left during this period, but much of the decline reflects the waning economy which drove Newport merchants and tradesmen to seek opportunity elsewhere and farmers to migrate into newly opened western lands.

Although earlier censuses appear not to have survived, it is possible to locate individuals within the colony by means of an index of freemen that is kept at the State Archives. This card index includes every man who appears on the various lists turned in by the towns over the years. A freemen normally was a man at least twenty-one years of age who owned some real estate in town and was thus both privileged to vote in town meetings and obligated to hold town office if chosen to do so.[28]

In 1746 the General Assembly passed an act requiring that all freemen take an oath against bribery and corruption, which meant that all freemen in the colony at that time had to take the oath and be readmitted

27. Coleman, Peter J., *The Transformation of Rhode Island, 1790-1860* (Providence, 1969), p. 21.

28. Occasional exceptions to this formula are seen. Sometimes a young man who had inherited land from a deceased father would be admitted freeman before he was 21, and one also finds cases where the son of a prosperous landowning father was allowed freeman status even though no deed for land appeared in his own name.

in 1747, thus creating what amounts to a census of men entitled to vote at that date. For a list of those men admitted from 1747 through 1755, along with a careful explanation of the evolution of qualifications for freeman status from 1638 to 1760, see Bruce C. MacGunnigle, *Rhode Island Freemen, 1747-1755* (Baltimore, 1977). The original lists for the entire colonial period are at the Archives, arranged chronologically by each town; many are included in Bartlett.

Another extremely valuable resource for locating people in Rhode Island and discovering what matters they were involved in are the petitions to the General Assembly, also kept at the Archives. These were placed in bound volumes many years ago and a thorough card index made to the whole set. Each volume also has a typed index bound in the front, as well as an abstract showing the date and nature of each petition. These cover a variety of concerns both public and private; most are petitions by inhabitants of a particular town, like those of Glocester who in 1750 requested that the bridge across the river at Chepachet be mended.[29] As the population of the towns increased, members of their trained bands petitioned that new bands be established so that some men would not have so far to travel in bad weather. Townsmen petitioned to have counterfeiting neighbors released from jail, or to ask that a new grist mill be permitted in town, and petitions for new banks and issues of paper money were commonplace. From these lists of signatures one learns who lived where and with whom, as well as what their immediate concerns were, all items of interest to the genealogist.

In 1777, by order of the General Assembly, a military census was taken to determine the number of men in the colony able to bear arms. Within each town, all men are listed in age groupings: from 16 to 50, able or unable, from 50 to 60, able or unable, and from 60 up. If for some reason a man considered it against his conscience to serve, as was the case with Quakers, he might take an affirmation of loyalty to the government or present a certificate from his Friends Meeting, and that fact was duly noted. The census included Negroes, Indians, and Mustees, the name in common use for those who were half Indian and half Negro. Residences of men belonging to towns other than that in which they were enumerated were listed; many Aquidneck men went from the Island during the British occupation to serve from nearby towns on the mainland. There are no returns for the occupied towns, Portsmouth, Middletown and Newport, and none appears to have survived for Exeter, Little Compton and New Shoreham. This census is currently being published for the first time in *Rhode Island Roots,* 7 (1981): 43-51 and ongoing, transcribed by Mildred Mosher Chamberlain from the original manuscript in the Rhode Island Archives. At present the only index to it is the card file on revolutionary soldiers and sailors, kept at the Archives, which will be discussed along with other military records.

29. Petitions to the General Assembly, Rhode Island Archives, 7:165.

The next census was taken in 1782 and listed within each town the heads of households, numbers of males and females under 16, from 16 to 22, from 22 to 50, and over 50, as well as numbers of Indians, mulattoes, and blacks. The original manuscript is at Rhode Island Historical Society along with a microfilm copy and a typewritten copy, containing some errors[30], which was transcribed by Katherine V. Waterman and printed in the *Register,* 127 (1973): 3-17, 138-150, 216-229, 302-312; 128 (1974): 49-63, 124-135, 214-224, 293-304; and 129 (1975): 53-67, 270-277, 379-387. The entire census is now in print alphabetically in book form, edited by Jay Holbrook (Oxford, Mass., 1979), incorporating data from tax lists to supply information for the towns of Smithfield and North Providence, which were missing from the original schedules.

The first federal census of Rhode Island, made in 1790, has long been in print with an index. Recent indexes for succeeding federal censuses up through 1850 have been published by Accelerated Index Systems of Provo, Utah, and are available at the Rhode Island Historical Society, the Society, and many other libraries with genealogical collections.[31] In 1865 the state began taking decennial censuses, which will be described in connection with other records available for research in the nineteenth century.

There are for Rhode Island numerous collections of cemetery records, more properly called gravestone inscriptions, but these are scattered; for a definitive guide, see David Dumas, "Rhode Island Grave Records," *Rhode Island Roots,* 3 (1977): 1-6. One of the largest collections is that made by James Arnold, working in the last decades of the nineteenth century; this is divided between the Rhode Island Historical Society and Knight Memorial Library (also known as the Elmwood Library) in Providence. Toward the end of his life Arnold had a disagreement with one of the officers of the Rhode Island Historical Society and left his remaining records to the Knight Library with the provision that they remain there, where a small room has been set aside for them; it contains also some other genealogical material, mostly printed books. There is a complete card index to the gravestone records, which are typed and fill several loose-leaf notebooks, arranged by town; they include complete inscriptions and often descriptions of the stones, many of which have long since disappeared. The Rhode Island Historical Society has a five-volume handwritten set of Scituate gravestones copied by Arnold from 1891 to 1904, and also sets of inscriptions for Warwick, Cranston, Lincoln, and Coventry, all with indexes prepared by John H. Wells.

Another important collection of gravestone inscriptions, by Charles and Martha Benns, is in typescript at the East Greenwich Public Library.

---

30. In the 1782 census as printed in the *Register,* all residents of Jamestown are listed in Tiverton, all residents of Portsmouth in Middletown, and some residents of Scituate in Foster.

31. It should perhaps be noted that these computerized indexes contain a fairly high number of errors and omissions.

The index is divided into several sections, each of which should be examined. The Rhode Island Historical Society has a copy of the index and a microfilm copy of the records; there is a copy also in the Library of the Daughters of the American Revolution in Washington. This collection covers stones from all over Rhode Island and also neighboring towns in Massachusetts and Connecticut. The Rhode Island Historical Society has three volumes of handwritten records made many years ago by George J. Harris, entitled "A Visitation to the Cemeteries of Ancient Kingstowne." These are not indexed, and although scanning through them is a time-consuming business, it is well worth the effort for someone working on a family that lived in King's (now Washington) County.

The Newport Historical Society has an extensive collection of records of gravestones on the island of Aquidneck, most in manuscript. These include copies made by Dr. Henry Turner of stones in the Newport Common Burial Ground, the large and very old cemetery sprawled over the hill in the heart of the city. Many attempts have been made to record the inscriptions in this historic burial ground but no one list appears to be complete. Typescript versions at the Society do not include all the stones recorded in other compilations, and still others are described in *Newport Historical Society Bulletin,* no. 10 (Dec. 1913): 3-46. Newport Historical Society has a huge map of the cemetery, made in 1903, divided into grids, with an attempt to map the stones then standing; a recent index to the grid map made by Edwin Connally provides the best chance of locating specific stones in that interesting and ancient cemetery.

An alphabetized list of inscriptions from Newport, Middletown and Portsmouth appeared in a Newport paper many years ago, and a copy of these clippings, without date, is included in one of Arnold's notebooks, labelled "Newport," in the Knight Library. Some of the finer examples of early gravestone art in Newport are included in the photograph collection of Daniel Farber at the American Antiquarian Society in Worcester, and although this is not designed for genealogical purposes, the searcher may well find pictured there the stone of an ancestor.

The Historic Graves Commission for Rhode Island in 1970 listed all cemeteries and family burying grounds designated "historical," alphabetized the names by which they are known, and correlated the names with the numbers which appear on the square white signs placed years ago in historical cemeteries. The Archives and Rhode Island Historical Society have copies of the master list. Unfortunately, some small old grounds, among them the plot off Glen Road in Portsmouth where John Cook (1630-1691) and his wife Mary Borden are buried, were never designated historical and have thus been omitted. Each town clerk has a map of historical cemeteries within the town. A unique problem exists for Tiverton and Little Compton, however, in that stones in these two towns were copied some years ago by three very capable genealogists, Grace (Stafford) Durfee, Waldo C. Sprague and Benjamin F. Wilbour, who assigned to them numbers of their own which do not correspond to numbers given to them as historical cemeteries. These transcripts were printed in the *Register,* 1961-1964 (see Appendix A), with typescript copies deposited at the Society and the Rhode Island Historical Society. In order to locate any of the burial grounds concerned, it is best to consult the directions given in the transcript by Durfee, Sprague and Wilbour before examining the map at the town hall.

Providence has two large cemeteries, North Burial Ground and Swan Point, to which were made removals from small family burying grounds. The Rhode Island Historical Society has some inscriptions from North Burial Ground, made about 1925 by Dr. Frank T. Calef, who also copied stones in the smaller Locust Grove Cemetery. Actual records of interments in North Burial Ground are kept at the cemetery office, but these are chronological and unindexed; to find a particular entry one must have an approximate date. Providence City Archives has the business records of that cemetery, which contain information on owners of lots; some of these records are somewhat incongruously included in volumes 18 and 19 of the printed *Early Records of the Town of Providence.* The more modern Swan Point Cemetery has excellent records, useful to genealogists, and these are on microfilm at Rhode Island Historical Society.

Military records for Rhode Island men are available both in print and in manuscript. A listing of men who served in both military and civil capacities is provided by Joseph J. Smith, *Civil and Military List of Rhode Island, 1647-1850,* 3 volumes (Providence, 1900-1907); for the Revolutionary War, however, this names only officers of state units. The original index, which included only surnames, was replaced by a full name index published in 1907. In addition to Bodge's *History of King Philip's War,* another source for the period up to 1700 is Ebenezer W. Pierce's *Colonial Lists: Civil, Military and Professional Lists of Plymouth and Rhode Island Colonies* (Boston, 1881; reprint ed., Baltimore, 1968).

Because of her commercial dependence upon the sea, Rhode Island was actively drawn into the struggles between England and other European countries known broadly as the colonial wars. A great number of men served on privateering ships. Many a Rhode Island ancestor marched off to Canada or Crown Point, sometimes at a more advanced age than seems reasonable today, and many more lent their horses for shorter journeys. There are in the State Archives a series of volumes containing original documents such as muster rolls, pay receipts, and disbursements for services and goods supplied for the troops; the only index for these is in each volume. Of interest to those seeking information about this period are three books by Howard M. Chapin, *Rhode Island in the Colonial Wars: A List of Rhode Island Soldiers & Sailors in King George's War, 1740-1748* (Providence, 1920), *Rhode Island Privateers in King George's War, 1739-1748* (Providence, 1926), and *A List of Rhode*

Island Soldiers and Sailors in the Old French and Indian War, 1755-1762 (Providence, 1918). See also Society of Colonial Wars, Rhode Island, *Nine Muster Rolls of Rhode Island Troops Enlisted During the Old French War* (Providence, 1915), and Clarkson A. Collins, *A Muster Roll of Newport County Troops Sent Toward Albany in 1757* (Providence, 1961). "Muster Rolls of New York Provincial Troops, 1755-1764," *New York Historical Society Collections,* vol. 24 (1891), includes names and physical descriptions of many men who gave Rhode Island as birthplace when enlisting in New York regiments during that period.

For Revolutionary service records, the best printed source is Benjamin Cowell's *Spirit of '76 in Rhode Island* (Providence, 1850; reprint ed., with index Baltimore, 1973), originally indexed in Arnold's Volume 12. There is in the State Archives a card index to Revolutionary soldiers made by the late Miss Mary T. Quinn. This may contain more than one card or slip of paper for the same man, since information was drawn from a variety of sources which are noted on each card. These include the military census of 1777, the Cowell Collection, the Shepley Collection, now at the Rhode Island Historical Society, the Pardon Gray Seabury Papers at New Bedford Public Library, and a number of small private collections not easily accessible today. Also used in compiling the index were federal pension records, more readily available now by means of the National Genealogical Society's *Index to Revolutionary War Pensions* (Washington, 1976). The Rhode Island Historical Society has a growing collection of microfilm reels of pension records, initiated by Rhode Island Society of Mayflower Descendants, to which further contributions may be made by interested persons or groups. The Benjamin Cowell Collection at John Hay Library, Brown University (catalogued under the Rider Collection) contains original correspondence having to do with pension applications; you may find there two versions of a deposition, the one that was done "off the cuff," containing some interesting side lights on the pensioners and their families, and the official version which was edited and sent off to Washington. There are eight volumes, each with an index of sorts.

Throughout the history of Rhode Island a relationship with the sea was the one thing shared by almost everyone. The sea was the mainstay of the colony's economic life; directly or indirectly everyone was to some extent dependent upon it. Much of the travel within the colony was by water, the predominant routes being east and west across Narragansett Bay and the Sakonnet River by ferries rather than north and south. *A History of Rhode Island Ferries 1640-1923* by Anna Augusta and Charles V. Chapin (Providence, 1925) reveals that many Rhode Island families were directly involved at some time, either as ferry keepers, or as proprietors of one of the licensed public houses which stood near the wharves for the comfort and entertainment of travelers who waited for the next boat.

Privateering was everybody's business in early Rhode Island, with prize shares distributed to each member of the crew down to cabin boy; many young men shipped on such vessels before settling down, just as later men might sign on trading ships for a couple of voyages in order to make enough money to buy a good farm. Ships often were owned by several men in shares, the master included, in order to divide the risk. The genealogist should remember that there may be maritime records which contain information relevant to any Rhode Island family. The State Archives has manuscript material on maritime affairs and some for masters of vessels. The Works Progress Administration produced a series of volumes, fully indexed, describing ships built and fitted out at various ports, including Newport, Providence, Bristol and Warren. Volume 2 of Field's *State of Rhode Island and Providence Plantations at the Turn of the Century* contains a list of Rhode Island ships with names of their masters. Howard W. Preston, *Rhode Island and the Sea* (Providence, 1932) also lists privateer ships active during the colonial wars. Information on crews of privateering vessels is included in some of the sources given above for military records.

After the Revolution, impressment into the British Navy became a problem and the Seaman's Protection Registration was instituted to provide mariners with identification papers. These certificates, issued through the customs houses in various ports, are of genealogical value, often including place and date of birth. There are collections of these in both the Newport Historical Society and Rhode Island Historical Society. The New Bedford Public Library also has an immensely valuable index to crews of whaling ships from that port, by means of which it is possible to find a physical description of a sailor ancestor and to follow his career on different ships up to the Civil War period. Men came from all over Rhode Island and from areas as far away as New Jersey and western New York State to ship on the whalers, and in these lists may occasionally be found clues to the whereabouts of families who had left Rhode Island a generation or so earlier.

Newport's wealth depended upon the sea, and when her trade was cut off by the British occupation during the Revolution, her position slipped rapidly and never recovered. Merchants moved elsewhere, many settling in southern seaport cities, others in New Bedford or Providence, both of which continued to grow. Rhode Island's population declined as western lands opened up and people began migrating out in large numbers, some to western Massachusetts and Vermont and even Pennsylvania and Ohio, but especially to New York State. For many genealogists this period presents the greatest difficulty, for once a family left Rhode Island the name of the town from which they came was likely to be obscured, with later records of them stating birthplace as simply "Rhode Island," or sometimes even "Providence," the two being almost synonymous to people who were unfamiliar with both.

Although in such cases a search must begin with the records of the place to which the family migrated, there are sources in Rhode Island that may help to locate the town of origin. One of the better aids in tracing both merchants who moved to other cities and yeomen farmers who went westward are newspaper records. Several papers in Providence and Newport regularly printed brief death and marriage notices which included items from all over the country having to do with people formerly of Rhode Island. Arnold, in his volumes 12 through 21, published abstracts of such notices, arranged by newspaper and time period, then alphabetically. The newspapers themselves may be consulted on microfilm at Rhode Island Historical Society, but often give no more information than that included by Arnold.

The Newport Historical Society maintains a large card index arranged alphabetically by surname which includes, among many other things, references to such notices which appeared in the *Newport Mercury*. The Society has some original copies of early newspapers, as well as photostats and microfilm of others. The *New Bedford Morning Mercury* also noted marriages and deaths, 1807-1874, covering nearby Tiverton and Little Compton areas, and there is in the New Bedford Public Library a typed index to these.[32] Occasionally events were noted in Boston newspapers as well, so that it may be worthwhile to consult the widely available indexes to the *Columbian Centinel* and the *Boston Weekly News-Letter.*

Another aid to locating emigrant Rhode Islanders may be found in a new quarterly, *The Rhode Island Genealogical Register,* in a continuing series of articles entitled "They Left Rhode Island," consisting of references found in deeds and probates of various Rhode Island towns to people then living in other places. This is valuable for clues, but the original document cited must be checked to learn the full content. Town deed books contain many such references, usually in cases where the grantors were already living elsewhere when they sold their land back home. Probate records sometimes include receipts for legacies which show where the heirs were then living. The same series includes names of people listed in the 1850 census of other states as born in Rhode Island.

One old tactic helpful in solving this kind of genealogical problem is to examine the names of neighbors and friends with whom the ancestor associated in his new place of settlement. People did not usually migrate alone, and hopefully there will be among the population of the new home town a name which can be easily located on the 1774 census of Rhode Island. Its small size, combined with the fact that certain names tend to be concentrated in particular towns, makes this approach unusually valid for Rhode Island research.

Records of the sizable migration of Rhode Island people to Canada which occurred about 1758 were printed in an article by Ray Greene Huling in "The Rhode Island Emigration to Nova Scotia" in *Narragansett*

32. The Society and Rhode Island Historical Society each have copies of death index 1807-1845.

Historical Register, 7 (1889): 89-136. This involved families from Portsmouth, Newport, and the Narragansett Country who moved into Nova Scotia, which had been recently recovered from the French, and had nothing to do with political sympathies; some men returned to fight in the Revolution. A more recent article by Thaire H. Adamson in *Rhode Island Genealogical Register,* 3 (1980-1981): 145-148, discusses the Nova Scotia settlers and material available on them. This and other early migrations are briefly covered by G. Andrews Moriarty in "Migrations from Rhode Island in the Seventeenth and Eighteenth Centuries," *National Genealogical Society Quarterly,* 47 (1959): 70, 71, 197.

The nineteenth century brought industrialization to Rhode Island, with a shift of capital from maritime operations into manufacturing that began before the War of 1812.[33] Along the Blackstone River northwest of Providence and also in Fall River, which soon overshadowed Tiverton on the east side of the Sakonnet, good water power encouraged the development of the textile mills which became the primary source of wealth in Rhode Island. As the mills grew, so did the population of Irish and Canadian French who came to work in them. When Central Falls was incorporated in 1895, nearly half its population was foreign born, from French Canada, England and Ireland.[34] By the end of the century, Rhode Island had the highest proportion of foreign-born of any state in the Union, one in every three inhabitants, and it had become a predominantly Catholic state.[35] Italians, Portuguese and other nationalities added to its diversity.

It is suggested that genealogists interested in Catholic records and history look at *Catholicism in Rhode Island: The Formative Era* by Patrick T. Conley and Matthew J. Smith (Providence, 1976). As this work notes, at first there were two distinct Catholic groups, the Irish and the French Canadians, and they did not voluntarily mix. Printed accounts of the Irish in Rhode Island have emphasized the early colonists who were of Irish origin rather than the working Irish who came to help in building projects like that of Fort Adams in Newport about 1820. Unlike their predecessors, the Irish of the nineteenth century were Catholic and required the services of a circuit priest who came from Boston once a month. The records of these earliest baptisms and marriages are now in the Chancery Archives of the Archdiocese of Boston. It was 1844 before the Irish in Rhode Island had a church of their own.

A French settlement was begun at Woonsocket as early as 1815, and although these people tended to hold themselves aloof, thus preserving their own culture, illiteracy in the early years resulted in the Anglicization of many French names, i.e. Balcon to Balcom, a name more familiar to Rhode Island ears, or Morin to Mowry. After the Civil War, when they

33. Coleman, *Transformation of Rhode Island,* 71.
34. Rhode Island Historic Preservation Commission, *Central Falls* (Providence, 1978), 40.
35. Coleman, *Transformation of Rhode Island,* 301.

had priests and churches of their own, the French founded schools and institutions which have survived until the present day. There is an active American French Genealogical Society in Pawtucket, and the Mallet Library in Woonsocket may be used by anyone interested in tracing French Canadian ancestry. French church records from Woonsocket and Central Falls are being steadily published by Quintin Publications in Pawtucket; copies are on the shelves of the Rhode Island Historical Society.

Records of individual Catholic churches remain in the parishes, with permission to make genealogical searches depending upon the priest in charge. The Archives of the Diocese of Providence holds microfilm copies of all parish registers within its jurisdiction and will make searches on request; the records are considered sacramental and are not open to the public. The Diocesan Cemetery Office has records for all Catholic cemeteries in the Diocese and will respond to specific requests for information.

The National Archives has a "Soundex" index which includes Federal District Court naturalizations at Providence, 1842-1904, and a few from county courts as early as 1789. The clerk of the United States District Court in Providence has a master index to naturalizations in federal courts, which may be used also as a guide to several books of naturalization petitions and declarations, 1842 to 1945, held by the Federal Records Center at Waltham, Massachusetts. Locating naturalizations in state records may be more difficult. There is an index to the naturalizations and petitions of the Supreme Court records, 1842-1854, but many people were naturalized through the various Courts of Common Pleas, which have no indexes. A card index for later Supreme Court records is estimated to contain only about one tenth of all original entries; common practice at one time was for clerks to hand over to inquirers the card from the file; many were lost in that way. Most of the existing records are now at Providence College Archives along with other Rhode Island court records. These are presently being organized and catalogued.

Census records for the nineteenth century and later include not only federal censuses through 1900 (except for the burned 1890 census), but also state schedules which were made every ten years from 1865 through 1935, with the exception of 1895, which is missing. The Rhode Island Historical Society has a microfilm copy of the 1865 census for the entire state, with a card index that includes every name; the original is at the Archives. The City Archives of Providence has a copy of the books for Providence, and some town offices have copies of their own schedules. The State Archives has the 1875 census and is preparing an index to it. The censuses of 1885 and 1905 through 1935 are at the State Records Center in Providence.

Arnold's coverage of vital records ends in 1850, and there was a three-year gap before registration of births, marriages and deaths became statewide in 1853. Vital records from 1850 to 1853 will be found only in the towns. From 1853 to 1921, each town sent a copy of its records to the Department of Health, but more recently the originals have been sent, the copies kept in the towns. Until a few years ago all the state records were kept at the Health Department, whose director is staunchly opposed to opening them for genealogical inquiry despite a state law permitting it. Marriage and death records have now been moved to the Records Center, where they may be used in what amounts to a warehouse setting but with a friendly staff. Indexes cover 1853-1900 for marriages and births, but the birth records are still at the Health Department, which also, inexplicably, retains the index to deaths. These indexes are arranged by surname for each year; a search may be rather time consuming unless one already has some specific dates in mind. Indexes for records 1901-1920 are easier to use. The Records Center does not have complete indexes after 1920, and it is unable to provide certified copies, which must be obtained either from the Health Department or the clerk of the town in which the event occurred. If the town is known, it may still be the easiest place to search for a late record.

An index to the vital records of the City of Providence from 1850 to 1945 is available in print in several volumes. The Westerly Public Library has a set of scrapbooks labelled "Westerly Vital Statistics" which in fact contain indexed death and marriage notices from local newspapers arranged by year to 1908; these include references from as far away as Dartmouth, Massachusetts. The Rhode Island Historical Society has several indexed collections of newspaper obituaries.

The 1865 census lists as soldiers many men who were in Civil War service at that time. To learn more, one may consult *Rhode Island Adjutant General's Office, Annual Report . . . for the Year 1865 (Official Register, Rhode Island Officers and Enlisted Men, U.S. Army & Navy, 1861-1865),* 2 vols. (1893-1895). The State Records Center also has Civil War material.

Court records in Rhode Island present a special problem. Since 1729, there have been Inferior Courts of Common Pleas and a Superior Court in each county, in addition to the Supreme Court. Divorces were processed through any of the courts and are thoroughly mixed in with other business. Many cases were simple actions of debts due "by book," i.e. for goods sold or services rendered, or on promissory notes, which rarely provide genealogical information. There were also a fair number of trespass cases involving suits over land; these often produced informative depositions along with evidence of ownership or relationship of several generations.

There are some court record books and indexes at the Law Library in the Providence County Court House, in an attic room without much light or any working space. These include a fine set of King's County (now Washington County) record books, early Bristol County record books, and an index to some Providence County books. The Newport

County Court Clerk has a card index to plaintiffs and defendants, which includes the date and nature of each case.

Until recently each county had custody of its own court records; Brigham in his 1903 report listed what was then extant. The files of Washington County have since suffered water damage and those of Newport were thoroughly scrambled. Many were collected at the Records Center, and eventually the entire state collection was transferred to the archives of Providence College, where a staff of several people spent a year putting them in boxes in some order. One archivist is now attempting to further organize and catalogue them, beginning with Providence County, working backwards from later to earlier records. These are open to serious researchers, but it must be emphasized that they will not be in any condition to be useful for genealogical research for a long time. The College cannot now handle any but the most straightforward inquiries.

Those interested in Black or Indian genealogy will find varied resources in Rhode Island. Many Indians were enslaved following King Philip's War, and many Negroes were imported during the colony's long history of slave trading. Probate records contain many specific references to slaves or indentured servants, both Indian and Black, and it is sometimes possible to trace such families through documents left by their white owners. Deed books record the sale of slaves and also manumissions, indexed under the owner's name. When freeing a slave, the former owner often was required to post a bond to protect the town should the slave prove unable to maintain himself, and sometimes free Negroes brought legal action to preserve their rights. Court records show that many free Blacks and Indians were involved in trade, crafts and commerce. Blacks and Indians appear in vital, church, and cemetery records. Since many assumed their owner's surname, it is wise to first search records of white families. The Rhode Island Black Heritage Society, organized in 1975 under the auspices of the Rhode Island Historical Society, has as its goal the research and preservation of the history of Blacks in Rhode Island.

Genealogical research in Rhode Island, as elsewhere, requires some attention to geography. In 1936 the State Planning Board issued a series of maps showing territorial bounds at various time periods from 1659; these have been widely reprinted and are helpful in understanding territorial disputes and changes which occurred over the years. A valuable map prepared by Richard LeBaron Bowen and printed in Volume 1 of his *Early Rehoboth,* 4 vols. (Concord, N.H., 1945-1950) sets Rhode Island towns within the context of surrounding towns in Massachusetts and Connecticut.

The 1746/7 boundary change added five towns to Rhode Island; a later adjustment in 1862 returned to Massachusetts the northern part of old Tiverton, Fall River, along with some land in eastern Tiverton which became part of Westport, Massachusetts. At the same time part of

Seekonk, Massachusetts, was ceded to Rhode Island and incorporated as East Providence. Fall River, a growing mill town, attracted many Rhode Islanders, and its records should not be overlooked. Its Oak Grove and North cemeteries have records that help in tracing some Rhode Island families. An index to the unpublished Fall River vital records to 1844 is in the Fall River Public Library.

New Bedford, also late to develop, was not set off from Dartmouth until 1787; it gained momentum as Newport declined. Like Fall River, much of its population was drawn from nearby Rhode Island. When the *Vital Records of New Bedford,* 3 vols. (Boston, 1932-1941) were published, gravestone inscriptions were used to supplement the few surviving birth records; thus one finds in *New Bedford Births* many people who happen to have died in that town but who were born elsewhere. Good cemetery records kept at New Bedford's Rural Cemetery office may be of help. Collections such as the Leonard Papers at the New Bedford Public Library contain much material on Rhode Island families.

Other border areas with neighboring states should not be neglected. Westerly people often appear in records of Stonington, Connecticut, and people from northern towns like Burrillville moved in and out of the nearby Worcester County, Massachusetts, mill towns.

This article has emphasized the use of available records, but something must be added about the various libraries in Rhode Island. The Rhode Island Historical Society in Providence has by far the largest collection of printed books and manuscript material on Rhode Island families and towns. It is important to be aware of an unusual distinction that library makes between manuscripts and genealogical manuscripts. The Friends Records, Providence Town Records, and many other collections useful to the genealogist are found in the second floor manuscripts department, but they are catalogued only there and are not considered genealogical manuscripts. The orientation in this department is historical and may confuse any researcher who does not have a clear objective. Genealogical manuscripts, on the other hand, are classified as such in the main catalogue downstairs, and must be accessed by call slips at the main desk. These include Austin's notebook and the several books and boxes of genealogy on the descendants of Randall Holden. The open shelves contain many typed or handwritten works in bindings, while some rare printed books are stored upstairs, blurring the distinction between manuscript and other genealogical material.

The Rhode Island Historical Society has copies of the annual reports of the Genealogical Records Committee of Rhode Island Daughters of the American Revolution, with a card index. These contain Bible and cemetery records, abstracts of probates from various towns, copies of census and mortality schedules, and other miscellany. Several collections left by individual genealogists over the years include the Louise Prosser Bates papers, now available only on microfilm because of their fragility, and a Sweet card index with hundreds of references to that family. Of interest to those with ancestry in Kent County is a copy of Arnold's *Vital Record,* Volume 1, annotated in pencil by the late Amanda Spencer Briggs, who knew personally many of the people listed.

The Rhode Island Historical Society also has microfilm of important collections like the Barbour Records for Connecticut, the Nova Scotia Archives, New Bedford Library manuscripts, probate and town records for some Rhode Island towns, and the collection of Revolutionary Pension records. The indexed Pierce Collection covers North Kingstown land records.

The Newport Historical Society has a fair collection of printed material for Rhode Island, but its strength is in its manuscripts for Newport and the rest of the Island of Aquidneck. These include the Rhode Island Friends Records, the surviving early town records of Newport, and innumerable church, cemetery and family records. Material left by Dr. Henry Turner includes information on many early Newport families; the story goes that when called to visit a home, he would ask to see the Bible before he saw the patient. The manuscripts curator, Mrs. Peter Bolhouse, has held that position since 1946; both her knowledge of the collections and interest in Newport's past are extraordinary.

The Newport Historical Society has a card index to names which covers notices in newspapers, Customs House oaths, references to the many scrapbooks of the late G.H. Richardson, and other sources. It has a growing collection of microfilm material for other parts of Rhode Island, and a good selection of early Newport newspapers. The late Gilbert H. Doane, F.A.S.G., for many years editor of the *Register,* lived most of his retirement years in Newport and was active in the Society.

The Providence Public Library has the principal printed works on Rhode Island newspapers, microfilm of the early Providence town records, and the index to the *Providence Journal* known as the Rhode Island index. Two smaller libraries in Rhode Island have better genealogical collections. The East Greenwich Public Library has the original Benns cemetery records as well as a good selection of printed material on Rhode Island. The Westerly Library has a manuscript genealogy of the Jeffrey Champlin family, manuscript material on the Bliven and York families, and a copy of the typescript Saunders genealogy by N. B. Vars, compiled 1880-1902. Other resources here include a few notebooks kept by Ray Greene Huling, a vertical file on Rhode Island families, the collection of death and marriage notices called "Westerly Vital Statistics," and a very good collection of printed material not only for Rhode Island but for neighboring areas and places to which Rhode Islanders migrated as well.

In 1975 the Rhode Island Genealogical Society was formed. This active group is working to collect and distribute genealogical data, and to promote sound techniques through workshops held twice a year at varying locations throughout the state. In 1981 it brought out its first published book, *Peleg Burroughs's Journal.* The society's quarterly publication, *Rhode Island Roots,* prints articles of genealogical interest and source material, many of which have been cited in this article.

Town histories, so important in other New England states, are not of much use to Rhode Island genealogy. Most of those in print are relatively superficial and do not include sections on local families. Genealogies given in the printed histories of the various counties tend to be unreliable, although they do contain items of nineteenth-century interest.

The only book of town scope in Rhode Island, *Little Compton Families* by Benjamin Franklin Wilbour (Little Compton, R.I., 1967; revised 1974), thoroughly covers the genealogies of people who lived there, though it is not a town history. R. L. Bowen's *Early Rehoboth* is an important work to Rhode Island genealogists. Parts of Rehoboth were incorporated into Rhode Island in the boundary changes, under other names, and the early history of that town and of Rhode Island can hardly be separated.[36] Elisha Potter's *The Early History of Narragansett,* first published in 1835, includes genealogies of some of the families of that region. Wilkins Updike's treatment of Episcopal families in his *History of the Narragansett Church* is also noteworthy. *Débuts de la Colonie Franco-Américaine de Woonsocket,* by Marie-Louise Bonier (Framingham, Mass., 1920), presents, in French, histories of some of the early families of that town. One book of distinctly limited scope is R. L. Bowen's *Rhode Island Colonial Money and its Counterfeiting, 1647-1726* (Providence, 1942), which contains good genealogical material on the families who engaged in that old-fashioned Rhode Island pastime.

There are of course many other sources for and ways of approaching genealogy in Rhode Island. It should be evident that, although working there does present some problems, no serious genealogist need feel intimidated. If Rhode Island research is approached without expectation of finding the order which prevailed in the Puritan colonies, one soon learns to appreciate and enjoy the diversity of materials available. Though tiny, this state has excellent historical societies and libraries which provide endless opportunities for exploring material gathered by other genealogists over the years. Primary resources in town offices hold a wealth of information above and beyond what has been transcribed; working with them provides practice in reading the handwriting of past centuries, a skill so important to a realistic comprehension of those times. The effort required to reach for an understanding of the colorful and varied background of the people who settled here and kept these records is a small price to pay for the reward of bringing one's ancestors into close perspective.

36. Robert S. Trim of Rehoboth has made extensive transcriptions of Rehoboth and Swansea cemeteries, some of which are at Rhode Island Historical Society; more are in progress.

Jane Fletcher Fiske resides in Boxford, Massachusetts, and is currently vice-president of the Rhode Island Genealogical Society.

APPENDIX A:
Towns and Cities in Rhode Island

CR = Church Records   TC = Town Council
VR = Vital Records   TM = Town Meeting
RIHS = Rhode Island Historical Society

Vital records, deeds and probates for each of the following towns or cities will be found in the town house or city hall, unless otherwise noted. *The Rhode Island Genealogical Register* (*RIGR*), published quarterly July 1978 to date, contains abstracts of early wills for most towns and deeds for some; these should be used with care. Brigham's 1903 report, already cited, defines existing records for each town, and may be supplemented by the several volumes of *Inventory of the Town and City Archives of Rhode Island* prepared by the Rhode Island Historical Records Survey Division of Community Service Projects, Work Projects Administration (Providence, 1942). The relevant volumes of Arnold's *Vital Record of Rhode Island* are listed below for each town, along with pertinent material which has been printed in other journals. Records of the Society of Friends, in Arnold, volume 7, may contain vital records not found in town records.

Barrington, inc. from Warren 1770. Probate and land records before 1747 are in Taunton, from 1747 to 1770 at Warren. Town clerk has TM 1718-1744 and other town records from 1718; proprietors' records, 1652-1797, and some Congregational Church records. Two volumes of TM records, 1770-1776 and 1808-1814, listed in Brigham's 1903 report, are now missing. VR Arnold vol. 6; CR vols. 8 and 10.

Bristol, annexed 1747 from Massachusetts; originally inc. by Plymouth Colony 1681; part annexed to Warren 1873. Records after 1746 are in the town hall, also some private records of marriages, burials, and gravestones. RIHS has militia and tax lists for Bristol, 1819-1827, and a transcript of VR 1683-1817. Deeds and probates before 1747 are in Taunton, but town clerk has abstracts of early deeds. VR Arnold vol. 6; CR vol. 8.

Burrillville, inc. 1806 from Glocester; town house at Harrisville. Arnold vol. 3.

Central Falls, inc. 1895 as city, from Lincoln. Exception in that city clerk has records of parent towns of Lincoln and Smithfield, q.v. Records accessible but in deteriorating condition. Early records listed by Brigham in 1903 as in basement vault have disappeared.

Charlestown, inc. 22 Aug. 1738 from Westerly. Richmond taken off 1747. Town hall on country road; some early books have been photocopied. VR Arnold vol. 5.

Coventry, inc. 21 Aug. 1741 from Warwick. Town house at Anthony; VR Arnold vol. 1; CR vol. 10.

Cranston, inc. 14 June 1754 from Providence; part reannexed to Providence 1868 and 1873. City Clerk's office has good indexes, including TC records. Providence Deeds Registry has photocopy of Cranston deed indexes. Arnold vol. 2.

Cumberland, annexed 17 Feb. 1746/7 from Mass.; known before that date as Attleboro Gore. Woonsocket set off 1867. Records from 1747 are at the town house in Valley Falls. Records before 1747 at Taunton; some may be found in Suffolk Co., Mass. Arnold vol. 3.

East Greenwich, inc. 31 Oct. 1677; divided 1741 to form West Greenwich. Records at town house include some proprietors' records. Some records for period 1762-1823 at RIHS, including 1778 tax list. VR Arnold vol. 1; CR vols. 10, 11; see also annotated vol. 1 at RIHS.

East Providence, annexed 1 March 1862 from Massachusetts. Land and probate before 1862 at Taunton; TM and VR to 1812 are at Rehoboth, 1812-1876 at Seekonk. VR

1841-1862 also at Massachusetts Registry of Vital Statistics, Boston. Arnold vol. 10. Recent compilation cemetery records (unpublished) by Robert S. Trim, Rehoboth.

Exeter, inc. 8 March 1742/3 from North Kingstown. Some records 1740-1870 are at RIHS, including tax lists, militia, poor records, bonds, etc., described in *Rhode Island Historical Society Proceedings,* 4:35, 6:43. Cemetery records, *RIGR;* good abstracts of wills and transcription of VR and Friends Records in R.G. Huling notebooks, Westerly Library. VR Arnold vol. 5; CR vol. 10.

Foster, inc. 24 Aug. 1781 from Scituate. VR Arnold vol. 3.

Glocester, inc. 20 Feb. 1730/1 from Providence. Burrillville taken off 1806. Town house at Chepachet has 1778 tax list. Arnold vol. 3.

Hopkinton, inc. 19 March 1757 from Westerly. Cemetery records currently in *R.I. Roots.* VR Arnold vol. 5; CR vols. 10, 11.

Jamestown, inc. 4 Nov. 1678. Records at town house include some proprietors' records. Cemetery records and VR transcript at the Society; Arnold vol. 4.

Johnston, inc. 6 March 1759 from Providence; in 1898 most was reannexed to Providence. Deeds at town clerk's office, but early TC, TM, and probate records are at Providence City Hall. Early tax and school records in Providence City Archives. Arnold vols. 2 and 3.

Lincoln, inc. 8 March 1871 from Smithfield; Central Falls set off 1895. Records before 1895 are at Central Falls. Town clerk has copy of deeds from 1871-1898.

Little Compton, annexed 27 Jan. 1746/7 from Massachusetts; originally inc. by Plymouth Colony in 1682. Settled by Plymouth people; some Congregational Church records in office of town clerk. Records at town hall have good indexes, but some additions were made by early town clerk, so they should be used with care; copy of Proprietors' Records 1673-1755. VR Arnold vol. 4; CR vol. 8. See Benjamin F. Wilbour, *Little Compton Families;* "Cemetery Inscriptions in Little Compton," *Register,* 15 (1961): 169-180, 257-268; 116 (1962): 45-56, 121-126, 213-220.

Middletown, inc. 16 June 1743 as the "Middle Town" on Aquidneck, from Newport. Records at town hall include Newport Proprietors' records 1701-1756. Abstracts of first 4 vols. of wills, by Mrs. Oliver W. Cushman, "Abstracts of Wills: Probate Records of the Town of Middletown, R.I.," *Register,* 122 (1968): 100-107, 211-215, 295-301. Arnold vol. 4.

Narragansett, inc. 22 March 1888 from South Kingstown as a district, 1901 as town.

New Shoreham, purchased and occupied April 1661; admitted to the colony as Block Island 4 May 1664; name changed and inc. 6 Nov. 1672. Part of Newport County until Sept. 1963 when joined to Washington County. Records at town offices on the island. RIHS has transcript of first two TC books. Arnold vol. 4. "Block Island Cemetery Records," *Rhode Island History,* 12 (1953): 90-97, 122-128; 13 (1954): 25-33, 56-65, 88-97, 125-129; 14 (1955): 25-33, 59-65, 94-97. G. Andrews Moriarty, "Notes on Block Island Families," see Appendix B.

Newport, settled 1639, boundary with Portsmouth est. 14 Sept. 1640; Middletown set off 1743; records after 1783 are at City Hall, well indexed, including VR. Pre-Revolutionary records which survived the salt water in 1779 are in the care of the Newport Historical Society. Abstracts of early town records (probates) by Edith M. Tilley in *The Grafton Magazine,* 2 (1909-1910): 216-223. Birth and mortality list 1760-1764, *Register,* 62 (1908): 283-291, 63 (1909): 51-58; "Sons and Daughters of Newport," *Register,* 125 (1971): 171-183, 236-245; 126 (1972): 20-25. VR Arnold vol. 4; CR vols. 7, 8, 10, 11, 12.

North Kingstown, inc. 28 Oct. 1674 as Kings Towne; name changed to Rochester in 1686 but renamed Kings Towne 1689; divided into North and South Kingstown in Feb. 1722/3; Exeter set off 1743. Town house at Wickford; a fire in 1870 damaged all the town books, which have been repaired using Emery process. Some tax lists, militia records, etc. 1784-1823 at RIHS; South Kingstown has copies of record books before the 1722/3 separation. 1687 tax list *Register,* 35 (1881): 124-127. VR Arnold vol. 5; CR vols. 7, 8, 10, 11.

North Providence, inc. 13 June 1765 from Providence; small portion returned to Providence 29 June 1767 and more 28 March 1873; divided 27 March 1874, when part annexed to Providence and part to Pawtucket. Records for 1765-1874 are at Pawtucket City Hall. Arnold vol. 2.

North Smithfield, inc. 8 March 1871 from Smithfield. Town clerk's office is in Slatersville.

Pawtucket, inc. as city 27 March 1885; comprises (1) Massachusetts town of Pawtucket, separated from Seekonk 1828, ceded to Rhode Island 1862, inc. as RI town 1 March 1862, and (2) village of Pawtucket in North Providence, which was annexed to town of Pawtucket 1 May 1874. Vital records at City Hall are well indexed and include North Providence. VR 1841-1862 also at Massachusetts Registry of Vital Statistics in Boston. Deeds and probate records before 1862 at Taunton, Mass. VR Arnold vols. 9, 10, 11; CR vols. 9, 10.

Portsmouth, settled 1638. Good indexes. Portsmouth Scrapbook contains records found in basement in 1903, including original wills, inventories, census of 1730 and miscellaneous papers. Town records 1638-1639 in Bartlett 1:45-69. First book of records 1639-1697 printed 1901 as *Early Records of the Town of Portsmouth,* indexed. See also Bartlett 1:70-85, made from transcript in town clerk's office, for records 1639-1647. "Diary of Elisha Fish 1785-1804," *Register,* 56 (1902): 121-132; VR Arnold vol. 4.

Providence, original town, settled 1636, inc. as city 5 Nov. 1831; originally comprised whole of present Providence County; Glocester, Scituate and Smithfield set off 1731, Cranston 1754, Johnston 1759, North Providence 1765; inc. as city 5 Nov. 1831. Portions of North Providence annexed 1767, 1873, and 1874, portions of Cranston in 1868, 1873 and 1892, and part of Johnston 1898. Early records in print in 21 volumes as *Early Records of the Town of Providence.* Wills and probate records are in the Probate Registry in City Hall, which also has Johnston probates. Land evidence is in the Deed Registry in the same building; indexes are in main room, but older deed books are in a back room, not in good order and with no working space available. VR are at Registry of Vital Statistics on the main floor of City Hall, but are not open to genealogists, a situation which may be circumvented by using the printed indexes to the Providence records, available at the City Archives and other libraries, and the records at the Records Center. Providence has recently established a City Archives in the City Hall with facilities for research; earlier records here include tax lists from 1778, Poor Records, and state censuses (for the city only). Copies of relevant books and printed material available; staff will assist researchers who have problems with other departments. VR Arnold 2; CR vol. 10.

Richmond, inc. 18 Aug. 1747 from Charlestown. Two books were lost in 1812 (see *RIHSP* 1:161), but many deeds were re-recorded afterwards. Early books photocopied. Town clerk has some local genealogical materials, old Bibles, etc. Some records at RIHS, including tax lists 1798, 1823, militia list 1810. VR Arnold vol. 5; CR vols. 10, 11.

Scituate, inc. 20 Feb. 1730/1 from Providence; Foster set off 1781. Town house at North Scituate. Cyrus Walker, "The History of Scituate, R.I. from the Acquisition of the Territory in 1659, to the Close of the Nineteenth Century" (manuscript, microfilm RIHS); Charles W. Farnham, "Scituate, R.I. Removals 1784-1811 and Where They Went," *The American Genealogist,* 44 (1968): 40, 41. "Scituate, R.I. Census, 1779" (actually a tax list), *National Genealogical Society Quarterly,* 14 (1925): 30-31. Arnold vol. 3.

Smithfield, inc. 20 Feb. 1730/1 from Providence; divided 1871 into Smithfield, North Smithfield and Lincoln, with small part annexed to Woonsocket. Records to 1871 are in Central Falls City Clerk's office, but the earliest TC records, described by Brigham in 1903 as unbound in a basement vault, have disappeared; RIHS has early abstract of some of these. An index kept in the office has recently vanished, but there are in Drawer E three small books of abstracts of early records which provide some indexing (included RI DAR 1938-1939). Later records are at the town hall in Greenville. VR Arnold vol. 3; CR vols. 7, 10.

South Kingstown, settled Jan. 1657/8; inc. 22 Feb. 1723 in division of Kings Towne. Records at town house in Wakefield include transcript of North Kingstown records before the separation; good collection of early tax lists. Copies of Arnold and Beaman available. VR Arnold vol. 5; CR vol. 7, 8, 10, 11.

Tiverton, annexed 17 Jan. 1746/7 from Massachusetts; originally inc. 1694 by Massachusetts; as annexed to R.I. it included small parts of Dartmouth and Freetown. Northern part inc. as Fall River, R.I. 1856, transferred to Massachusetts 1 March 1862. Deeds and probate records before 1747 in Taunton, Mass. "Cemetery Inscriptions in Tiverton, R.I.," *Register,* 117 (1963): 18-27, 133-139, 208-221, 283-295; 118 (1964): 64-67, 147-153. "Inscriptions from the Pleasant View Cemetery, Tiverton, R.I.," *Register,* 118 (1964): 308-311. "Deaths from the Records of Constant Hart, of Tiverton, R.I.," *Register,* 105 (1951): 213-217. VR Arnold vol. 4; CR vol. 8.

178   *Rhode Island Genealogy*

Warren, inc. 27 Jan. 1746/7 when annexed from Massachusetts; Barrington set off 1770. Deeds and probates before 1747 at Taunton. Original VR before 1850 now missing. VR Arnold vol. 6; CR vol. 8. "Inscriptions in Kickemuit Cemetery, Warren, R.I.," *Register,* 120 (1916): 24-33.

Warwick, est. 1642 as Shawomet, renamed Warwick 1644; Coventry set off 1741. Most records are at City Hall, Apponaug, but a couple of TC books are at RIHS, which also has a recently discovered 1798 property tax list describing each dwelling in town, listing both owner and occupant. Arnold vol. 1.

West Greenwich, inc. 1741 from East Greenwich. Records at new town hall on Route 102. VR Arnold vol. 1; CR vol. 10.

Westerly, inc. 14 May 1669; named Haversham during Andros period. Charlestown set off 1738; Richmond 1746; Hopkinton 1757. Records at town hall at Westerly; see Robert C. Anderson's detailed guide to record books, *Rhode Island Roots,* 7 (1981): 25-27. Cemetery records included in Rev. Frederick Denison, *Westerly and Its Witnesses* (Providence, 1878). VR Arnold vol. 5; CR vol. 11.

Woonsocket, inc. 31 Jan. 1867 from Cumberland; inc. as city 13 June 1888. Records at city hall include transcript of Smithfield and Cumberland deeds 1847-1867. CR, Quintin Publ. Co., Pawtucket, at RIHS. M. L. Bonier, *Débuts de la Colonie Franco-Américaine de Woonsocket* (Framingham, Mass. 1920).

APPENDIX B:
A Bibliography for 100 Colonial Rhode Island Families
Compiled by Gary Boyd Roberts

Listed below are the major printed sources for 100 colonial Rhode Island families—most of those for whom a major monograph, often a journal article, identifies an immigrant's English origin and immediate ancestry, and for whom in addition one or more book-length genealogies cover American progeny. The list is alphabetical by surname. Immigrants sharing the same family name are grouped together, whether related or not, listed towns are each immigrant's principal residence, and asterisks indicate known origins, in a few cases non-English. Many immigrants of unknown origin with sizable and at least fairly well covered Rhode Island progeny are included as well, as are a few immigrants to Massachusetts whose sons migrated to Rhode Island. Deliberately excluded, however, are those families with Rhode Island connections the bulk of whose descendants, at least until the mid-eighteenth century, are associated with Bristol County, Massachusetts—especially Taunton, Rehoboth, Dartmouth and New Bedford; Stonington, Connecticut; or Monmouth County, New Jersey. For various Rhode Island-connected Rehoboth and Monmouth County families see Richard LeBaron Bowen, *Early Rehoboth, Documented Historical Studies of Families and Events in this Plymouth Colony Township,* 4 vols. (Rehoboth, 1945-1950), and John Edwin Stillwell, *Historical and Genealogical Miscellany: Data Relating to the Settlement and Settlers of New York and New Jersey,* 5 vols. (New York, 1903-1932; reprint ed., Baltimore, 1970).

For any seventeenth-century Rhode Island family, researchers should first check Clarence Almon Torrey, *New England Marriages Prior to*

1700, microfilm (Boston, 1979) (see the *Register,* 135 [1981]: 57-61), Meredith B. Colket, Jr., *Founders of Early American Families: Emigrants from Europe, 1607-1657* (Cleveland, 1975), and the already cited *Genealogical Dictionary of Rhode Island* (especially the additions and corrections by G.A. Moriarty and R.S. Wakefield), *160 Allied Families,* and bibliographies of journal articles by R. LeB. Bowen, R.S. Wakefield, and H.L.P. Beckwith. G.A. Moriarty, the greatest Rhode Island genealogist after J.O. Austin, was the author not only of the major series to date of additions to the *Genealogical Dictionary,* and of many of the immigrant origin *Register* articles cited below. He also contributed a series of "Barbadian Notes," with outlines of many Rhode Island connections, to the *Register,* 67 (1913): 360-371 and 68 (1914): 177-181, a "Genealogical Section" and a set of "Portsmouth, Rhode Island Genealogical Gleanings," to *Rhode Island Historical Society Collections,* 11 (1918): 26-28, 62-63, 68, and 21 (1928): 126-132, and a survey of seventeenth- and eighteenth-century Block Island families to the *Register,* 105 (1951): 162-182, 249-272. This last includes extensive notes on the Ray, Rathbone, Dodge, Sands, Guthrie, Niles, Mott, Williams, Mitchell, Dickens, Rodman, Kenyon, and Card families of the seventeenth century, and the Champlin, Franklin, Gardiner, Hull, Littlefield, Sheffield, and Westcott families of the eighteenth. Earlier Mr. Moriarty had compiled genealogies of five Block Island families in his own ancestry, also published in the *Register*—those of Thomas Mitchell (82 [1928]: 456-464); John Payne and Richard Card (83 [1929]: 84-93); Ichabod[5] Clarke (85 [1931]: 417-423); and Caleb[3] Littlefield (86 [1932]: 71-77). In addition, moreover, to the Rehoboth volumes and bibliography of pre-1950 articles, R. LeB. Bowen also compiled *The Providence Oath of Allegiance and Its Signers, 1651-2* (Providence, 1943), which contains full biographical and genealogical accounts of its subjects.

The only Rhode Island town all of whose residents through 1850 or so are treated in a single work is Little Compton, many of whose early settlers belonged to families largely associated with Massachusetts. Benjamin Franklin Wilbour's *Little Compton Families* (Little Compton, R.I., 1967; rev. ed., 1974), contains four or more pages on residents with the following surnames: Almy, Bailey, Briggs, (Nicholas) Brown, Brownell, Burgess, Case, Chase, Church, Clapp, Coe, (Thomas) Cook, Davenport, Davol, Dyer, Gifford, Gray, Grinnell, Hart, Head, Hilliard, Howland, Hunt, Irish, Little, Manchester, Pabodie, Palmer, Pearce, Peckham, Richmond, Seabury, Shaw, Simmons, Sisson, Snell, Soule, Southworth, Stoddard, Tabor, Taylor, Tompkins, White, Wilbor, Wilcox, Wood, and Woodman. Among Rhode Islanders of royal descent, Jeremiah Clarke, Mrs. Anne (Marbury) Hutchinson, Mrs. Catherine (Marbury) Scott, and John Throckmorton, all listed below, are also treated in Frederick Lewis Weis and Walter Lee Sheppard, Jr., *Ancestral Roots of 60 Colonists Who Came to New England Between*

1623 and 1650, 5th ed. (Baltimore, 1976), lines 11, 14 (for the Marbury sisters) and 208 respectively; and Clarke, John Cranston, the Marbury sisters and Throckmorton are treated also in Weis, Arthur Adams, and Sheppard, *The Magna Charta Sureties, 1215,* 3rd ed. (Baltimore, 1979), lines 100, 41, 34 (for the Marbury sisters) and 117 respectively. The only other Rhode Island immigrants of proved royal descent are the three Dungans —Thomas Dungan of Newport, later of Bucks County, Pennsylvania, and his sisters, Mrs. Barbara (Dungan) Barker and Mrs. Frances (Dungan) Holden, both listed below.

The following bibliography is an attempt to consolidate many of the sources listed by Torrey, Colket, Bowen, Wakefield and Beckwith, to include as well the best journal articles and Rhode Island genealogies of the past ten years, and to designate major typescripts at the Society (all those whose location is not designated), the Rhode Island Historical Society (henceforth RIHS), and, to some extent, the Library of Congress. Manuscripts, more difficult to locate, examine, and evaluate, have been purposely excluded; those acquired before 1913 by the Rhode Island Historical Society, however, are listed in the *Register,* 67 (1913): 299-301. For the smallest New England state the materials cited below and the more general items listed above cover together a sizable portion of its entire colonial population.

1. GEORGE ALDRICH, Mendon, Mass. (father of Joseph Aldrich of Providence) —Alvin James Aldrich, *The George Aldrich Genealogy,* 2 vols. Decorah, Iowa, 1971.

*2. WILLIAM ALMY, Portsmouth—*Register,* 71 (1917): 310-324; 78 (1924): 391-395; Charles Kingsbury Miller, *Historic Families of America: William Almy of Portsmouth, 1630, Joris Janssen De Rapalje of Fort Orange (Albany), New Amsterdam, and Brooklyn, 1623.* Chicago, 1897; Elva Lawton, "The Descendants of William Almy of Portsmouth, Rhode Island." Seattle, Wash., 1977 (typescript at RIHS); *Almy Family Newsletter,* 1975-

3. THOMAS ANGELL, Providence—Avery F. Angell, *Genealogy of the Descendants of Thomas Angell Who Settled in Providence, 1636.* Providence, 1872.

4. JOHN ANTHONY, Portsmouth—Charles L. Anthony, *Genealogy of the Anthony Family from 1495 to 1904.* Sterling, Ill., 1904.

*5. THOMAS and WILLIAM ARNOLD, Providence—*Register,* 69 (1915): 64-69; *Rhode Island Historical Society Collections,* 14 (1921): 33-49, 68-86; *Rhode Island History,* 13 (1954): 111-123 (progeny of Thomas); Elisha Stephen Arnold, *The Arnold Memorial: William Arnold of Providence and Pawtucket, 1587-1675, and a Genealogy of His Descendants.* Rutland, Vt., 1935.

6. ROBERT AUSTIN, Kingstown—Edith (Austin) Moore, *A Genealogy of the Descendants of Robert Austin of Kingstown, Rhode Island.* St. Petersburg, Fla., 1951.

7. JAMES BABCOCK, Westerly—Stephen Babcock, *Babcock Genealogy,* New York, 1903; Cyrus H. Brown, *Genealogical Record of Nathaniel Babcock, Simeon Main, Isaac Miner, Ezekiel Main.* Boston, 1909.

8. WILLIAM BAILEY, Newport—Hannah Clarke (Bailey) Hopkins, *Records of the Bailey Family: Descendants of William Bailey of Newport, R.I., Chiefly in the Line of His Son, Hugh Bailey of East Greenwich, R.I.* Providence, 1895.

9. MATURIN BALLOU, Providence—Adin Ballou, *An Elaborate History and Genealogy of the Ballous in America.* Providence, 1888; Myrtle M. Jillson, *An Addendum to the Original History and Genealogy of the Ballous in America.* Woonsocket, R.I., 1942.

*10. JAMES BARKER, Newport, and Mrs. BARBARA (DUNGAN) BARKER, his wife—*New York Genealogical and Biographical Record,* 41 (1910): 59; Alfred Rudolph Justice, *Ancestry of Jeremy Clarke of Rhode Island and Dungan Genealogy.* Philadelphia, 1922; *Forebears,* 15 (1972): 103-106, and *The Colonial Genealogist,* 8 (1977): 200-212 (royal descent of Barbara Dungan); Elizabeth Frye Barker, *Barker Genealogy.* New York, 1927.

*11. RICHARD BORDEN, Portsmouth—*Register,* 75 (1921): 226-233; 84 (1930): 70-84, 225-229; Hattie (Borden) Weld, *Historical and Genealogical Record of the Descendants As Far As Known of Richard and Joan Borden Who Settled In Portsmouth, Rhode Island, May, 1638, With Historical and Biographical Sketches of Some of Their Descendants.* Los Angeles?, 1899?

12. FRANCIS BRAYTON, Portsmouth—Clifford Brayton, *Brayton Family History.* vol. 1, Albion, N.Y., 1978.

13. JOHN BRIGGS, Portsmouth—Bertha B. B. Aldridge, *The Briggs Genealogy, Including the Ancestors and Descendants of Ichabod White Briggs, 1609-1953.* Victor, N.Y., 1953; Lilla (Briggs) Sampson, "John Briggs of Newport and Portsmouth, Rhode Island." 3 vols. n.p., 1930? (typescript at the Library of Congress).

14. REV. CHAD BROWNE, Providence—*Register,* 80 (1926): 73-86, 170-185; 105 (1951): 234; 128 (1974): 152-153, 306-308; Abby Isabel (Brown) Bulkley, *The Chad Browne Memorial.* Brooklyn, N.Y., 1888; James B. Hedges, *The Browns of Providence Plantations: Colonial Years.* Cambridge, Mass., 1952, and *The Browns of Providence Plantations: The Nineteenth Century.* Providence, 1968.

*15. THOMAS BROWNELL, Portsmouth—*The American Genealogist,* 36 (1960): 126-127; George Grant Brownell, *Genealogical Record of the Descendants of Thomas Brownell.* Jamestown, N.Y., 1910.

16. NATHANIEL BROWNING, Portsmouth—Edward Franklin Browning, *Genealogy of the Brownings in America From 1621 to 1908.* Newburgh, N.Y., 1908?

17. ROBERT BURDICK, Westerly—Nellie (Willard) Johnson, *The Descendants of Robert Burdick of Rhode Island.* Syracuse, N.Y., 1937, and "Supplement to The Descendants of Robert Burdick of Rhode Island." Norwich, N.Y., 1952-1953 (typescript).

*18. ROGER BURLINGAME, Warwick—Nelson Burlingame, "Burlingham-Burlingame Family." 8 vols. n.p., 1971 (typescript at RIHS).

19. RICHARD CARD, Jamestown—*Rhode Island Genealogical Register,* 3 (1980-1981): 193-202, 303-313; 4 (1981-1982): 18-29, 112-122, 273-282, 347-354 (ongoing); Thomas A. Card, *The Descendants of Richard⁴ Card in Kings County now Hants County, Nova Scotia, Canada.* Riverside, Calif., 1973; Maxine (Phelps) Lines, "Descendants of Job Card of Charlestown and South Kingstown, R.I." Mesa, Ariz., 1976 (typescript).

20. RICHARD CARDER, Warwick—Robert Webster Carder, "Richard Carder of Warwick, Rhode Island, and Some of His Descendants." Stamford, Conn., 1965 (typescript).

21. CALEB and ROBERT CARR, Newport—*Register,* 102 (1948): 203-218; Edson I. Carr, *The Carr Family Records.* Rockton, Ill., 1894; Arthur A. Carr, *The Carr Book: Sketches of the Lives of Many of the Descendants of Robert and Caleb Carr.* Ticonderoga, N.Y., 1947.

22. JEFFREY CHAMPLIN, Westerly—*The American Genealogist,* 20 (1943-1944): 106-109; *New York Genealogical and Biographical Record,* 46 (1915): 324-330; David W. Dumas, "Samuel Champlin of Exeter, Rhode Island, and His Descendants." Providence, 1973 (typescript).

*23. JEREMIAH CLARKE, Newport, and JOSEPH CLARKE, Westerly (not related)—*Register,* 74 (1920): 68-76, 130-140 (Jeremiah); 75 (1921): 273-301; 91 (1937): 249-252; 92 (1938): 61-65 (Joseph); Alfred Rudolph Justice, *Ancestry of Jeremy Clarke of Rhode Island and Dungan Genealogy.* Philadelphia, 1922; George Austin Morrison, Jr., *Clarke Genealogies: The "Clarke" Families of Rhode Island.* New York, 1902.

182   *Rhode Island Genealogy*

*24. JOHN COGGESHALL, Newport—*Register,* 73 (1919): 19-32; 76 (1922): 278-295; 79 (1925): 84; 86 (1932): 257; 99 (1945): 315-322; 100 (1946): 14-24; 103 (1949): 182-183; Charles P. and Thellwell R. Coggeshall, *The Coggeshalls in America.* Boston, 1930.

25. JOHN COOKE, Warwick, and *THOMAS COOKE, Portsmouth (not related)— *The American Genealogist,* 52 (1976): 1-10 (John); 56 (1980): 93-94 (Thomas); *Rhode Island Historical Society Collections,* 26 (1933): 59-61 (Thomas), and forthcoming Thomas Cooke genealogy by Jane (Fletcher) Fiske.

*26. THOMAS CORNELL, Portsmouth—John Ross Delafield, *Delafield, The Family History,* vol. 2. New York, 1945, 647-650; *The American Genealogist,* 35 (1959): 107; 36 (1960): 16-18; 51 (1975): 115-116; 54 (1978): 25-30; John Cornell, *Genealogy of the Cornell Family, Being An Account of the Descendants of Thomas Cornell of Portsmouth, R.I.* New York, 1902; Prentiss Glazier, "Thomas Cornell (or Cornwell) (1594-1655/6) of Massachusetts, New York, and Rhode Island, His English Origin and His Family in America." Sarasota, Fla., 1975, (typescript).

27. JOHN CRANDALL, Newport—John Cortland Crandall, *Elder John Crandall of Rhode Island and His Descendants.* New Woodstock, N.Y., 1949.

*28. DR. JOHN CRANSTON, Newport—*Register,* 79 (1925): 57-66, 247-268, 344-358; 80 (1926): 30-54, 138-169, 232-265, 336-337, 447-449; 87 (1933): 74-80; 90 (1936): 296-297.

29. ROBERT DENNIS, Portsmouth—*Register,* 49 (1895): 441-444; Elaine (Dennis) Young, *Some Descendants of Robert Dennis of Portsmouth, Rhode Island.* Norwalk, Ohio, 1957.

*30. REV. GREGORY DEXTER, Providence—Bradford F. Swan, *Gregory Dexter of London and New England, 1610-1700.* Rochester, N.Y., 1949; *Rhode Island History,* 20 (1961): 125-126; Sylvanus Chace Newman, *Dexter Genealogy, Being A Record of the Families Descended from Rev. Gregory Dexter.* Providence, 1859; George Washington Dexter, *A Record of the Descendants of Col. Stephen Dexter.* Putnam, Conn., 1902?; Hannah Smith Hammond, "Dexter/Hammond" and "Dexter, Arnold, Simmons, and Hammond." East Killingly, Conn., 1960 (typescript at RIHS).

31. THOMAS DURFEE, Portsmouth—William F. Reed, *The Descendants of Thomas Durfee of Portsmouth, R.I.,* 2 vols. Washington, D.C., 1902-1905.

*32. WILLIAM DYER, Newport, and Mrs. MARY (BARRETT) DYER, his wife, the Quaker martyr—*Rhode Island Historical Society Collections,* 30 (1937): 9-26; *Register,* 104 (1950): 40-42; *Notable American Women, 1607-1950, A Biographical Dictionary,* vol. 1. Cambridge, Mass., 1971, 536, 537; Lelia (Morse) Wilson, *Ten Generations from William and Mary Dyer, Pioneer Settlers in Newport, Rhode Island.* Putnam, Conn., 1949.

*33. RALPH EARLE, Portsmouth—*New York Genealogical and Biographical Record,* 67 (1936): 390-393; *Register,* 93 (1939): 361-362; Pliny Earle, *Ralph Earle and His Descendants.* Worcester, 1883; Amos Earle Voorhees, *Supplement to Ralph Earle and His Descendants.* Grants Pass, Ore., 1932, and *The Amos S. Earle Branch of the Ralph Earle Family in America.* Grants Pass, 1940.

34. WILLIAM ELLERY, Gloucester, Mass. (father of Benjamin Ellery of Newport)— *Newport Historical Magazine,* 4 (1883): 180-196; Harrison Ellery, *Pedigree of Ellery, of the United States of America.* Boston, 1881; James Benjamin Ellery, *Records of Ellery-Dennison-Parsons Families.* West Newton, Mass., 1956.

*35. ARTHUR FENNER, Providence—*The American Genealogist,* 15 (1938-1939): 80-86; *Rhode Island Historical Magazine,* 7 (1886-1887): 19-37, 161-183.

*36. THOMAS FISH, Portsmouth—*New York Genealogical and Biographical Record,* 53 (1922): 53-68; Lester Warren Fish, *The Fish Family in England and America, Genealogical and Biographical Records and Sketches.* Rutland, Vt., 1948.

37. GEORGE GARDINER, Newport—*The American Genealogist,* 20 (1943-1944): 202-207; 21 (1944-1945): 191-200; *Rhode Island History,* 11 (1952): 84-92; Lillian M. and Charles M. Gardner, *Gardner History and Genealogy.* Erie, Pa., 1907; Caroline

E. Robinson, *The Gardiners of Narragansett, Being A Genealogy of the Descendants of George Gardiner, the Colonist, 1638.* Providence, 1919.

38. JAMES GIBBS, Newport—George Gibbs, *The Gibbs Family of Rhode Island and Some Related Families.* New York, 1933.

*39. SAMUEL GORTON, Warwick—*Register,* 51 (1899): 199-200; 70 (1916): 115-118, 282; 82 (1928): 185-193, 333-342; Adelos Gorton, *The Life and Times of Samuel Gorton . . . With A Genealogy of Samuel Gorton's Descendants to the Present Time.* Philadelphia, 1907.

*40. DR. JOHN GREENE, Warwick and JOHN GREENE, Newport and Quidnesset— *Rhode Island Historical Society Collections,* 11 (1918): 69-78, 117-121; 12 (1919): 15-26; 14 (1921): 5-6; 23 (1930): 70-71; *Register,* 103 (1949): 185-188; Principal F. L. Greene, *Descendants of Joseph Greene of Westerly, R.I.* Albany, 1894; George Sears Greene and Louise (Brownell) Clarke, *The Greenes of Rhode Island with Historical Records of English Ancestry, 1534-1902.* New York, 1903; Lora S. LaMance, *The Greene Family and Its Branches From A.D. 861 to A.D. 1904.* Floral Park, N.Y., 1904; Walter and Ella Greene, *The Greene Family of St. Albans, Vermont, Together With the Origin and the History of the Greene Family in England and Rhode Island.* Schenectady, N.Y., 1964; *Supplement to the Greene Family of St. Albans, Vermont.* Schenectady, N.Y., 1969, and *A Greene Family History: An Account of the Ancestors and Descendants of Nathan and Job Greene Who Pioneered the Settlement of St. Albans, Vermont.* Schenectady, 1981.

41. JOHN GREENMAN, Newport—Richard LeBaron Bowen, *Rhode Island Colonial Money and Its Counterfeiting, 1647-1726.* Providence, 1942, 93-101; Carroll W. Greenman, *The Greenman Family in America.* Delmar, N.Y., 1976-1979.

42. JOHN HALL, Newport and WILLIAM HALL, Portsmouth (not related)— *Register,* 87 (1933): 352-358 (John); David B. Hall, *The Halls of New England, Genealogical and Biographical.* Albany, 1883 (William).

43. STEPHEN HARDING, Providence—Mary (Lovering) Holman, "Harding Ancestry," n.p., 1924 (typescript); Wilber J. Harding, *The Hardings in America.* Keystone, Iowa, 1925; Clara (Gardner) Miller, *The Ancestry of President Harding and its Relation to the Hardings of Wyoming Valley and Clifford, Pennsylvania.* Wilkes Barre, Pa., 1928 (reprinted in *Proceedings and Collections of the Wyoming Historical and Genealogical Society,* 21 [1930]: 1-46.)

44. THOMAS HAZARD, Newport—Caroline E. Robinson, *The Hazard Family of Rhode Island, 1635-1894.* Boston, 1895; John Ross Delafield, *Delafield: The Family History,* vol. 2. New York, 1945, 491-496.

*45. CHRISTOPHER HELME, Warwick—*Register,* 98 (1944): 11-25; 127 (1973): 214-215; *New York Genealogical & Biographical Record,* 102 (1971): 193-202; 104 (1973): 249.

*46. RANDALL HOLDEN, Warwick, and Mrs. FRANCES (DUNGAN) HOLDEN, his wife, sister of Mrs. Barbara (Dungan) Barker—A. R. Justice, *Forebears,* and *The Colonial Genealogist,* as per Barker (royal descent of Frances Dungan); Eben Putnam, *The Holden Genealogy: Ancestry and Descendants of Richard and Justinian Holden and of Randall Holden,* vol. 1. Boston, 1923.

47. CHRISTOPHER HOLDER, Newport—Charles Frederick Holder, *The Holders of Holderness: A History and Genealogy of the Holder Family with Special Reference to Christopher Holder.* Pasadena, Calif.?, 1902.

*48. REV. OBADIAH HOLMES, Newport—*Register,* 64 (1910): 237-239; 67 (1913): 21-23; James Taylor Holmes, *The American Family of Rev. Obadiah Holmes.* Columbus, Ohio, 1915.

*49. THOMAS HOPKINS, Providence—Frank Roy Kepler, *Thomas Hopkins of Providence and Oyster Bay, and Many of His Descendants.* 2nd ed., Detroit, 1954, and *Supplement to Second Edition, 1954.* Detroit, 1957.

*50. WILLIAM HUTCHINSON, Newport, and Mrs. ANNE (MARBURY) HUTCHINSON, his wife, the noted religious liberal—*Register,* 19 (1865): 13-18; 20 (1866): 355-367; 79 (1925): 170-175; 123 (1969): 180-181; *New York Genealogical &*

Biographical Record, 45 (1914): 17-26, 164-169; Meredith B. Colket, Jr., *The English Ancestry of Anne Marbury Hutchinson and Katherine Marbury Scott.* Philadelphia, 1936; *Notable American Women, 1607-1950, A Biographical Dictionary,* vol. 2. Cambridge, Mass., 1971, 245-247.

51. WILLIAM JAMES, Westerly—*Register,* 126 (1972): 247-254; 127 (1973): 30-37, 86-91.

*52. JOSEPH JENKS, Lynn, Mass. (father of Joseph Jenks of Providence)—*Register,* 110 (1956): 9-20, 81-93, 161-172, 244-256 (reprinted as Meredith B. Colket, *The Jenks Family of England.* Boston, 1956); 122 (1968): 168-171; William B. Browne, *Genealogy of the Jenks Family of America.* Concord, N.H., 1952.

*53. JAMES and JOHN KENYON, Westerly—Howard N. Kenyon, *American Kenyons.* Rutland, Vt., 1935.

54. ANDREW and LAWRENCE LANGWORTHY, Newport—William Franklin Langworthy, *The Langworthy Family: Some Descendants of Andrew and Rachel (Hubbard) Langworthy, Who Were Married at Newport, Rhode Island November 3, 1658.* Hamilton, N.Y., 1940; *The American Genealogist,* 15 (1938-1939): 1-8 (Lawrence).

55. EDWARD LARKIN, Newport—William Harrison Larkin, Jr., "Chronicle of the Larkin Family in the Town of Westerlie and Colony of Rhoad Island in New England", number 3, Arlington, Mass., 1935 (typescript), and forthcoming genealogy by Elizabeth B. and Murl Larkin.

56. GEORGE and THOMAS LAWTON, Portsmouth—Elva Lawton, "The Descendants of Thomas Lawton of Portsmouth, Rhode Island." New York, 1949 (typescript); "Additions for the 1949 Genealogy of Thomas Lawton of Portsmouth, Rhode Island." Seattle, Washington, 1977 (typescript at RIHS); and "The Descendants of George Lawton of Portsmouth, Rhode Island." Seattle, 1977 (typescript at RIHS).

57. JOHN LIPPITT, Warwick—*Register,* 27 (1873): 70-73; Henry F. Lippitt II, *The Lippitt Family (A Collection of Notes and Items of Interest By One of Its Members).* Los Angeles, 1959.

58. THOMAS MANCHESTER, Portsmouth—*Register,* 101 (1947): 175, 308-313, 329-331; 102 (1948): 10-28, 314-315; 104 (1950): 167-168; 105 (1951): 75; 110 (1956): 236.

59. RICHARD MAXSON, Portsmouth—Walter LeRoy Brown, *The Maxson Family, Descendants of John Maxson and Wife Mary Mosher of Westerly, Rhode Island.* Albion, N.Y., 1954; John H. Wells, "Index of the Maxson Family." n.d., n.p. (typescript at RIHS).

60. HUGH MOSHER, Portsmouth—Mildred (Mosher) Chamberlain and Laura (McGaffey) Clarenbach, *Descendants of Hugh Mosher and Rebecca Maxson through Seven Generations.* n.p., 1980.

61. ROGER MOWRY, Providence—William A. Mowry, *The Descendants of Nathaniel Mowry of Rhode Island.* Providence, 1878; *Supplement to the Descendants of Nathaniel Mowry.* Boston, 1900; and *The Descendants of John Mowry of Rhode Island.* Providence, 1909.

62. THOMAS MUMFORD, Kingstown—James Gregory Mumford, *Mumford Memoirs, Being the Story of the New England Mumfords From the Year 1655 to the Present Time.* Boston, 1900.

*63. THOMAS OLNEY, Providence—*The American Genealogist,* 10 (1933-1934): 88-90; James H. Olney, *A Genealogy of the Descendants of Thomas Olney, An Original Proprietor of Providence, R.I., Who Came From England in 1635.* Providence, 1889.

*64. RICHARD PEARCE, Portsmouth—*Register,* 84 (1930): 427-433; Frederick Clifton Pierce, *Pearce Genealogy, Being the Record of the Posterity of Richard Pearce, An Early Inhabitant of Portsmouth in Rhode Island.* Rockford, Ill., 1888; Clifford George Hurlburt, *Pierce Genealogy, Being a Partial Record of the Posterity of Richard Pearse.* San Diego, Calif., 1927.

65. JOHN PECKHAM, Newport—*Register,* 57 (1903): 31-39, 154-163; Stephen Farnum Peckham, *Peckham Genealogy: The English Ancestry and American Descendants of John Peckham of Newport, Rhode Island, 1630.* New York, 1922; W. P. and J. E. Bentley, *Genealogy of One Branch of the Peckham Family of Newport and Westerly, R.I. and its Allied Families.* Dallas?, 1957?

66. GEORGE and NATHANIEL POTTER, Portsmouth, and ROBERT POTTER, Warwick—Charles Edward Potter, *Genealogies of the Potter Families and Their Descendants in America to the Present Generation with Historical and Biographical Sketches.* Boston, 1888, Parts 2, 8 and 10; *Rhode Island Genealogical Register,* 1 (1978-1979): 163-169; 3 (1980-1981): 208-217, 318-328; 4 (1981-1982): 181-184.

67. JOHN REMINGTON, Rowley and Roxbury, Mass. (father of John Remington of Warwick)—*The American Genealogist,* 47 (1971): 129-135; 57 (1981): 15-23; George Brainerd Blodgette and Amos Everett Jewett, *Early Settlers of Rowley, Massachusetts.* Rowley, 1933 (reprint ed., Somersworth, N.H., 1981), 319-321; Boyd Scott Remington, *Remington Descendants.* 3rd ed., Ames, Iowa, 1957.

68. JAMES REYNOLDS, Kingstown—*Rhode Island Genealogical Register,* 1 (1978-1979): 227-235; 2 (1979-1980): 36-42; 4 (1981-1982): 335-339; Thomas A. and William A. Reynolds, *Ancestors and Descendants of William and Elizabeth Reynolds of North Kingstown, R.I.* Philadelphia, 1903; *Reynolds Family Association of America, 1892-1922, Thirty-First Annual Report.* Brooklyn, N.Y., 1922, 49-120, *Thirty-Third and Thirty-Fourth Annual.* Brooklyn, 1925, 56-159; Stephen F. Tillman, *Christopher Reynolds and His Descendants.* Chevy Chase, Md., 1959 (the immigrant James is #4946).

*69. THOMAS RODMAN, Newport—*Register,* 67 (1913): 367-368; Charles Henry Jones, *Genealogy of the Rodman Family, 1620 to 1886.* Philadelphia, 1886.

70. JOHN SANFORD, Portsmouth—*Register,* 56 (1902): 294-297; 103 (1949): 208-216, 271-277; 104 (1950): 73-77, 304-307; 114 (1960): 83-95; 117 (1963): 146-147; Jack Minard Sanford, *President John Sanford of Boston, Massachusetts and Portsmouth, Rhode Island, 1605-1695 and His Descendants with Many Allied Families.* Rutland, Vt., 1966.

*71. RICHARD SCOTT, Providence, and Mrs. KATHERINE (MARBURY) SCOTT, his wife, sister of Mrs. Anne (Marbury) Hutchinson—*Register,* 19 and 123, *New York Genealogical & Biographical Record,* 45, and Colket, as per Hutchinson; *Register,* 60 (1906): 168-175; 96 (1942): 1-27, 192-194; Sir Anthony Richard Wagner, *English Genealogy.* 2nd ed., Oxford, 1972, 415-416, and *The American Genealogist,* 16 (1939-1940): 81-88; Katherine (Mosher) Holmes, "The Richard Scott Family of Providence, Rhode Island." n.p., 1973 (typescript at RIHS).

*72. ICHABOD SHEFFIELD, Portsmouth—*Register,* 77 (1923): 190-194; 104 (1950): 3-14; 105 (1951): 75.

*73. PHILIP SHERMAN, Portsmouth—Bertha L. Stratton, *Transatlantic Shermans.* Staten Island, N.Y., 1969; Roy V. Sherman, *Some of the Descendants of Philip Sherman, The First Secretary of Rhode Island.* Akron, Ohio?, 1968.

74. DAVID SHIPPEE, East Greenwich—Lenn Alan Bersten, *The David Shippee Family Genealogy.* rev., Topsfield, Mass., 1974; *Family Affiliation of Abraham Shippee.* Topsfield, 1977.

75. GILES SLOCUM, Portsmouth—*Register,* 70 (1916): 283-284; 78 (1924): 395-396; 110 (1956): 77-78; Charles Elihu Slocum, *A Short History of the Slocums, Slocumbs, and Slocombs of America,* 2 vols. Syracuse, N.Y. and Defiance, Ohio, 1882-1908; Bertha W. Clark, "Giles¹ Slocum, Peleg² Slocum, Anthony Slocum." Boston, 1955 (typescript).

76. JOHN SMITH, the Miller, Providence—*Rhode Island History,* 20 (1961): 109-118; 21 (1962): 16-29, 49-62, 95-105, 124-135; 22 (1963): 22-31, 51-58, 82-93, 124-129; 23 (1964): 23-32, 51-60, 90-97, 117-125; 24 (1965): 30-33, 55-61, 93-97 (reprinted as Charles William Farnham, "John Smith the Miller of Providence, Rhode Island: Some of his Descendants." 1966, typescript).

77. ROBERT SPINK, Kingstown—*Rhode Island Genealogical Register,* 2 (1979-1980): 121-122, 167-170, 234-239; 3 (1980-1981): 85-87, 258-260; 4 (1981-1982): 193-215, 289-307 (ongoing).

78. ROBERT STANTON, Newport—William Henry Stanton, *A Book Called Our Ancestors the Stantons*. Philadelphia, 1922.

79. JOHN STEERE, Providence—*The American Genealogist*, 37 (1961): 139-140; James Pierce Root, *Steere Genealogy: A Record of the Descendants of John Steere, Who Settled in Providence, Rhode Island, About the Year 1660*. Cambridge, Mass., 1890; Robert E. Steere, *John Steere Family Branches*. n.p., 1972.

80. PHILIP TABER, Tiverton—George L. Randall, *Taber Genealogy: Descendants of Thomas son of Philip Taber*. New Bedford, 1924; Anna A. and Albert H. Wright, *Taber-Tabor Genealogy, Descendants of Joseph and Philip, Sons of Philip Taber*, 2 vols. Ithaca, N.Y., 1957.

*81. PETER TALLMAN, Portsmouth—*Register*, 85 (1931): 69-74; William M. Emery, *Honorable Peter Tallman, 1764-1841, His Ancestors and Descendants*. Boston, 1935.

82. JOHN TEFFT, Portsmouth—*Rhode Island Genealogical Register*, 1 (1978-1979): 193-201; Maria E. (Maxon) Tifft, *A Partial Record of the Descendants of John Tefft of Portsmouth, Rhode Island, and the Nearly Complete Record of the Descendants of John Tifft of Nassau, New York*. Buffalo, N.Y., 1896; Charles H. W. Stocking, *The Tefft Ancestry, Comprising Many Hitherto Unpublished Records of Descendants of John Tefft of Portsmouth, Rhode Island*. Chicago, 1904.

*83. JOHN THROCKMORTON, Newport—*Register*, 98 (1944): 67-72, 111-123, 271-279; 101 (1947): 290-295; 109 (1955): 17-31, 236; 110 (1956): 122-127, 180-182; 117 (1963): 234; George Andrews Moriarty, Jr., "Ancestry of George Andrews Moriarty, Jr." 19 vols., mss. at the Society; Sara Frances (Grimes) Sitherwood, *Throckmorton Family History, Being the Record of the Throckmortons in the United States of America with Cognate Branches*. Bloomington, Ill., 1930; C. Wickliffe Throckmorton, *A Genealogical and Historical Account of the Throckmorton Family in England and the United States with Brief Notes on Some of the Allied Families*. Richmond, 1930.

84. EDWARD THURSTON, Newport—Brown Thurston, *Thurston Genealogies, 1635-1892*. 2nd ed., Portland, Me., 1892.

*85. PARDON TILLINGHAST, Providence—*The American Genealogist*, 37 (1961): 34-38; 15 (1938-1939): 84-85; Rose C. Tillinghast, *The Tillinghast Family, 1560-1971*. n.p., 1972; William Richmond Tillinghast, "Genealogy of the Tillinghast Family." n.p., 1942, and "Index to the Tillinghast Genealogy." n.p., 1942 (typescript at RIHS); *Pardon's Progeny* (a family journal). 1974 — (a *possible* royal descent is outlined in vol. 1, #2, Nov. 1974, 9-13).

86. JOHN TRIPP, Portsmouth—*Newport Historical Magazine*, 4 (1883): 50-57; Arthur D. Dean, *Genealogy of the Tripp Family Descended from Isaac Tripp of Warwick, R.I. and Wilkes Barre, Pa.* Scranton, Pa., 1903; George L. Randall, *Tripp Genealogy: Descendants of James son of John Tripp*. New Bedford, 1924; Valentine Research Studio, *Tripp Wills, Deeds, and Ways*. Washington, D.C., 1932.

87. NICHOLAS UTTER, Westerly—Katharine M. (Utter) Waterman, George B. Utter and Wilfred B. Utter, *Nicholas Utter of Westerly, Rhode Island, and A Few of His Descendants*. Westerly, 1941.

88. JOHN VAUGHAN, Newport—H. Vaughan Griffin, Jr., *John Vaughan Settled Newport, Rhode Island, 1638, A Genealogical Record of His Descendants Including Twelve Branches Started By Twelve Pioneers Who Left Rhode Island*. Rutland, Vt., 1976.

89. THOMAS WAIT, Portsmouth—*Register*, 73 (1919): 291-304; 107 (1953): 316-317; 116 (1962): 153; John Cassan Wait, *Family Records of the Descendants of Thomas Wait of Portsmouth, Rhode Island*. New York, 1904; Stuart G. Waite, *Bennington Waite, An Ohio Pioneer: His Antecedents and Descendants*. Springfield, Mass., n.d.; Edythe (Wilson) Thoeson, "Thomas Wait and Descendants of Portsmouth, Rhode Island." Boulder, Calif., 1964 (typescript at RIHS).

90. EDWARD WANTON, Scituate, Mass. (father of Joseph Wanton of Tiverton and William, John and Philip Wanton of Newport)—John Russell Bartlett, *History of the Wanton Family of Newport, Rhode Island*. Providence, 1878 (*Rhode Island Historical Tracts*, no. 3).

91. JOHN WARD, Newport—*Correspondence of Governor Samuel Ward, May 1775-March 1776, With A Biographical Introduction Based Chiefly on the Ward Papers Covering the Period 1726-1776* (Bernhard Knollenberg, ed.) and *Genealogy of the Ward Family: Thomas Ward, son of John, of Newport and Some of His Descendants* (Clifford P. Monahan, comp.). Providence, 1952.

92. RICHARD WATERMAN, Providence—Donald Lines Jacobus and Edgar Francis Waterman, *The Waterman Family, Volume III: Descendants of Richard Waterman of Providence, Rhode Island, Together with Many Other Family Groups of the Waterman Name.* Hartford, 1954.

93. CLEMENT WEAVER, Newport—Lucius E. Weaver, *History and Genealogy of A Branch of the Weaver Family.* Rochester, N.Y., 1928.

*94. JAMES WEEDEN, Portsmouth—*Register,* 76 (1922): 115-129; 78 (1924): 147-153; 106 (1952): 87-88; 108 (1954): 46-53, 202-204; Eleanor (Steltz) Kebler, *Weedon Genealogy.* Washington, D.C.?, 1960.

95. STUKELY WESTCOTT, Warwick—*The American Genealogist,* 45 (1969): 157; Roscoe L. Whitman, *History and Genealogy of the Ancestors and Some Descendants of Stukely Westcott.* 2 vols. n.p., 1932-1939.

96. JOHN WHIPPLE, Providence—Clair A. H. Newton, *Captain John Whipple, 1617-1685, and His Descendants.* Naperville, Ill., 1946; Clara (Hammond) McGuigan, *The Antecedents and Descendants of Noah Whipple of the Rogerene Community at Quakertown, Connecticut.* Tokyo, 1971.

*97. SAMUEL and WILLIAM WILBORE, Portsmouth—*Register,* 99 (1945): 175-176; 112 (1958): 108-118, 184-190, 250-257; 113 (1959): 55-58, 94-104; John Reid Wilbor and Benjamin Franklin Wilbour, *The Wildbores in America, A Family Tree.* 2nd ed., 5 vols., 1933-41, and "Consolidated Index." 2 vols., n.p., n.d. (typescript).

98. EDWARD WILCOX, Portsmouth—*Register,* 87 (1933): 73-74; *The American Genealogist,* 19 (1942-1943): 23-31; 24 (1948): 260; *Rhode Island Genealogical Register,* 2 (1979-1980): 91-100; *The Mayflower Quarterly,* 47 (1981): 69-70; 48 (1982): 18-19; Janet Barrett Fee, "A Portion of the Descendants of Edward Wilcox of Rhode Island." White Plains, N.Y., 1941 (typescript at the Library of Congress); Herbert A. Wilcox, *Daniel Wilcox of Puncatest and the Genealogy of Some of His Descendants.* South Pasadena, Calif., 1943.

99. LAWRENCE WILKINSON, Providence—*The American Genealogist,* 26 (1950): 28-29; Israel Wilkinson, *Memoirs of the Wilkinson Family in America.* Jacksonville, Ill., 1869; M.M. Wilkinson, *Genealogy of Wilkinson and Kindred Families.* Shelby, Miss., 1949. (Both of these last works should be used with caution.)

*100. ROGER WILLIAMS, Providence—*The American Genealogist,* 28 (1952): 197-209 and Winifred Lovering Holman, "Roger Williams· (Brief Notes)," Lexington, Mass., 1951 (typescript); *Register,* 43 (1889): 290-303, 427; 47 (1893): 498-499; 67 (1913): 90-91; 78 (1924): 272-276; 97 (1943): 173-181; 113 (1959): 189-192; *Rhode Island Historical Society Collections,* 16 (1923): 78-83; 29 (1936): 65-80, and *Rhode Island History,* 3 (1944): 23-30, 67-71, 91-102; Bertha (Williams) Anthony, *Roger Williams of Providence, R.I.,* 2 vols. Cranston, R.I., 1949-1966.

ADDITIONS AND CORRECTIONS

Page 147, footnote 11

Reprints of Arnold's *Vital Record* are being published by Hunterdon House, Lambertville, N.J. 08530; the original volumes have been broken down into towns, with one to three per new volume.

Page 170, first paragraph

The retirement of the Director of the Division of Vital Statistics in the Health Department may affect the genealogical use of records at the Records Center. At the time of writing, the new Director indicates a willingness to work with genealogists, but the situation is rather unclear. It must be stressed that Rhode Island is not an "open records" state. Under the current law one must either be a member of a properly incorporated genealogical society or demonstrate a tangiblé reason for a search. Concerned individuals are urged to work towards a better liason between genealogists and officials on the state level; the present situation makes this a critical time.

Additions to "Appendix B: A Bibliography for 100 Colonial Rhode Island Families," compiled by Gary Boyd Roberts

Genealogies of Rhode Island Families from Rhode Island Periodicals, a two-volume consolidation of all genealogical articles from six Rhode Island journals — the *Publications* and *Collections* series of the Rhode Island Historical Society, *Rhode Island History, The Newport Historical Magazine, The Narragansett Historical Register,* and *Rhode Island Historical Tracts* — was published in early 1983 by Genealogical Publishing Company of Baltimore. These volumes include many articles cited in the bibliography for 100 colonial families. Their indexes should be among the first sources checked, moreover, for virtually any genealogical problem in Rhode Island. A later volume will extract Rhode Island genealogies from the *Register,* and a forthcoming multi-volume series extracting immigrant origin data from the *Register* will cover many Rhode Island settlers as well.

Ancestral Lines Revised: 190 Families in England, Wales, Germany, New England, New York, New Jersey, and Pennsylvania. (Newhall, Calif., 1981), compiled by Carl Boyer, 3rd, contains sections on the Rhode Island Anthony (pp. 30-35), Babcock (38-58), Borden (73-76), Brownell (134-136), Carr (155-156), Coggeshall (166-171), Durfee (183-185), Fish (196-198), Hazard (224-226), Holmes (233-236), Jenks (254-258), George Lawton (277-279), Pearce (317-318), Nathaniel Potter (321-323), Remington (332-340), Reynolds (340-342), Sherman (352-359), Tallman (425-428), Tefft (432-433), Thurston (435-436), Tripp (448-451), and Wilbore (487-489) families, all among the 100, plus various Block Islanders also. Each article treats immigrant origins, often in detail, and although a few known sources were overlooked, new or difficult-of-access material is presented in this regard for both Remington and Tallman. Additionally the following articles or books were published or came to the compiler's attention in 1982; they are listed by immigrants, as numbered in the original bibliography.

1. George Aldrich — Alvin James Aldrich, *The George Aldrich Genealogy,* vols. 3-4. Cedar Rapids, Iowa, 1977-1979.

12. Francis Brayton — Clifford Ross Brayton, *Brayton Family History,* vol. 2., Albion, N.Y., 1982.

19. Richard Card — *Rhode Island Genealogical Register,* 5 (1982-1983): 50-57; *The American Genealogist,* 58 (1982): 40-41.

26. Thomas Cornell — *The American Genealogist,* 58 (1982): 77-83.

37. George Gardiner — Sheridan Ellsworth Gardiner, "Gardiner Genealogy," Lexington, Mass., 1962? (typescript).

39. Samuel Gorton — Thomas Gorton, *Samuel Gorton of Rhode Island and His Descendants*. Baltimore, 1982.

52. Joseph Jenks — *Genealogical Journal,* 11 (1982): 68-72.

77. Robert Spink — *Rhode Island Genealogical Register,* 5 (1982-1983): 20-24.

86. John Tripp — *The Genealogist* (New York), 4 (1983): 59-128.

Corrections

56. George and Thomas Lawton, lines 5 & 6: *Delete* "at RIHS" (the George Lawton typescript is also at NEHGS). Additionally, as their English origin is known, an asterisk (*) should precede their listing.

74. David Shippee, line 1: *For* Bersten *substitute* Bergsten.

89. Thomas Wait, line 6: *For* Calif. *substitute* Colo.